INCLUSIVE LEADERSHIP IN SOCIAL WORK AND SOCIAL CARE

Trish Hafford-Letchfield, Sharon Lambley, Gary Spolander
and Christine Cocker

With contributions from Niall Daly

First published in Great Britain in 2014 by

Policy Press
University of Bristol
6th Floor
Howard House
Queen's Avenue
Clifton
Bristol BS8 1SD
UK
t: +44 (0)117 331 5020
f: +44 (0)117 331 5369
pp-info@bristol.ac.uk
www.policypress.co.uk

North America office:
Policy Press
c/o The University of Chicago Press
1427 East 60th Street
Chicago, IL 60637, USA
t: +1 773 702 7700
f: +1 773 702 9756
sales@press.uchicago.edu
www.press.uchicago.edu

Every attempt has been made to trace the owner of photograph 2.1 (p 39). If you are the copyright owner please contact Policy Press.

British Library Cataloguing in Publication Data
A catalogue record for this book is available from the British Library

Library of Congress Cataloging-in-Publication Data
A catalog record for this book has been requested

ISBN 978 1 44730 025 0 paperback
ISBN 978 1 44730 026 7 hardcover

The right of Trish Hafford-Letchfield, Sharon Lambley, Gary Spolander, Christine Cocker and Niall Daly to be identified as authors of this work has been asserted by them in accordance with the Copyright, Designs and Patents Act 1988.

The statements and opinions contained within this publication are solely those of the authors and not of the University of Bristol or Policy Press. The University of Bristol and Policy Press disclaim responsibility for any injury to persons or property resulting from any material published in this publication.

Policy Press works to counter discrimination on grounds of gender, race, disability, age and sexuality.

Cover design by Policy Press
Front cover image: istock.com
Printed and bound in Great Britain by TJ International, Padstow
Policy Press uses environmentally responsible print partners

Dedicated to

Guardsman Michael Roland, 1st Battalion Grenadier Guards,

died 27 April 2012, Afghanistan, aged 22 years.

Brave and respected leader;

father, son, brother, nephew, cousin and friend

who will never be forgotten.

When I think of a leader I think of you.

And for Peter Hafford, beloved father.

Contents

List of tables, figures and photographs

Tables

Figures

Photographs

About the authors

Christine Cocker is a qualified social worker and senior lecturer in social work at the University of East Anglia, UK. She is also a trustee for the British Association of Adoption and Fostering, and an independent member of a local authority adoption panel. Christine completed her social work training in New Zealand in the 1980s. She moved to England in 1988 and worked as a social worker and a social work manager in the children and families department of an inner London local authority for 13 years (including a multi-agency service), before joining a national voluntary sector consultation service as a service development director. Christine began her academic career in 2003. Her research and publications are predominantly in the area of social work with looked-after children, child protection and lesbian and gay fostering and adoption. Among her many publications are *Social work with lesbians and gay men* with Helen Cosis Brown (2011, Sage Publications), and *Advanced social work with children and families* (2011) and the second edition of *Social work with looked after children* (2013), both with Lucille Allain, published by Learning Matters with Sage Publications.

Trish Hafford-Letchfield is reader in social work at Middlesex University, London, UK. Trish is a qualified nurse and social worker and has had a long career in social work including more than 10 years of managing social work and social care services for adult services in a statutory organisation. Trish has worked in supported housing to develop enhanced care for older people. She has a wide range of experience in leadership and professional development for managers in the field, where she has established interagency mentoring schemes and succession planning initiatives. Within higher education she has led and taught on interprofessional leadership programmes for a number of years and seeks to promote a high degree of experiential learning to enhance management confidence and competence at work. Trish is widely published with her key research interests in educational gerontology and social care, use of the arts in learning and teaching, widening participation in education, sexuality and intimacy in social work and social care, leadership and organisational development. She is an active trustee, mentor and coach within the voluntary sector and has developed a number of initiatives to promote user involvement. She is a member of the National Executive of the Association of Ageing and Education. Some of her publications include *Interprofessional social work: Collaborative approaches* (2012) with Anne Quinney; *Becoming a better manager in social work and social care* with Les Gallop (2012); *Social care management: Strategy and business planning* (2010), and *Sexuality and sexual identities in social work: Research and reflections from women in the field* (2011) with Priscilla Dunk-West. Trish is also the series editor for *Essential Skills in Managing Care* with Jessica Kingsley Publishers.

Sharon Lambley is a lecturer in social work at the University of Sussex, UK. She has worked in many roles prior to entering higher education, including social work roles and community management, and has retained a practice focus by taking up a secondment to work in a local authority while based in higher education. Sharon is an active researcher and has been engaged in consultancy and research projects since 1991, including community evaluations, organisational development and workforce planning projects, as well as evaluating change programmes. She has also worked with colleagues from other European educational institutions on developing and undertaking collaborative research. Her publications include a management text, *Proactive management in social work* by Learning Matters (2010), and she has responded to critics of social work management by adopting a critical review of social work management, for example, through her article 'Managers: are they really to blame?' published by the *Social Work and Social Sciences Review* (2010). Sharon adopts a critical approach to social work management and is keen to work with others in developing this field of study. She also completed research for the Social Care Institute for Excellence (SCIE) in *Best practice in supervision* published in 2012.

Gary Spolander is principal lecturer in social and health care management at Coventry University, UK. He has worked as a frontline social worker at an international level and has several years' experience of management in the private and public sectors across a range of services and organisations. He has been involved in a variety of human resource and workforce development initiatives, and has an active interest in health and social work service delivery, management and workforce development, international social work and public health. Gary has also undertaken training in public health, business management and human resource development. His research interests include critical perspectives on leadership and management, neoliberal economic perspectives, international leadership and professional practice, public health, professional identity and training, service design and how organisations in public services learn from errors. Gary is the principal investigator on a European Union Marie Currie IRSES (International Research Staff Exchange Scheme) project exploring the public health implications of neoliberal policy and management on professionals and vulnerable populations. The project involves researchers from Finland, India, Italy, Russia and South Africa. He is the co-author with Linda Martin of *Successful project management in social work and social care* (2012, Jessica Kingsley Publishers).

Contributor

Niall Daly is an experienced consultant social worker in an out-of-hours service in London and associate lecturer for Middlesex University, London, UK. He draws on a wide range of disciplines in his writing to enhance critical thinking, and is particularly interested in how other disciplines such as those in design and the arts can contribute to theorising about social work and organisational studies. Niall's teaching expertise is with developing expert practice, supporting students preparing for practice and working with risk and decision making.

Acknowledgements

We would like to acknowledge the support from family and friends who have recognised the time and commitment required to write a book. We also acknowledge and thank those leaders and managers who have been the subjects of our musings and on whose experiences we have drawn. We also express our appreciation to the commissioning and editorial support team at Policy Press for their flexibility and patience during the process of putting this book together, and to the peer reviewers for their constructive comments.

Foreword

This book explores how the concepts and ideas of leadership can be understood and applied in social work and social care. While there is a wealth of leadership theory and case studies in military, business, education and government services settings, there has been an absence of what place this body of theory and practice should have in social work and social care. If we want a vibrant, respected and effective social work and social care sector, it needs leaders and the exercise of effective leadership.

The concepts of leadership explored in this book can be applied at all levels and in all types of organisations that deliver social work and social care services. Personally I am particularly interested in the concept of practitioners as leaders. This helps us see practitioners as people who shape what they do, have the courage of their convictions, take the initiative and most importantly, see themselves as leaders of those they are helping in their journey of change and in their leadership role mobilise others to deliver help and support that makes a difference to people's lives.

Service users want services that are positive in their outlook and that they believe can make a difference and change lives. Providing this positive outlook is one of the key qualities of leaders. This book helps explore how these leadership concepts can be applied in a way that empowers users in a less traditional and directive way. The authors suggest a less prescriptive approach in relation to how work should be done and how outcomes are defined.

Given the centrality of service user experience it is vital that leaders in social work and social care understand how they create and influence the culture of the organisations in which they work. From a service user perspective the culture of the organisation can be critical to how they experience services. This is almost exclusively through their personal interaction with staff. This book explores the key role leaders and leadership throughout an organisation play in creating positive or negative cultures.

Finally the book helps us consider how the development of leadership can be fostered. It is clear that this needs to be a conscious process and that development can lead to improvement. This is critical in personal services such as social work and social care where the failures of leadership, often unconscious, can have such serious consequences for vulnerable service users. Conversely, good leadership throughout an organisation can have a tremendously positive impact for those who use social work and social care services.

Colin Green
Director of Children's Services and Chair of the Association of Directors of Children's Services, Families, Communities and Young People's Policy Committee

Introduction

Effective leadership and management are often cited as the key to successfully 'transforming services' in the context of policy developments, both in the UK and internationally. As a group of UK-based authors, we are inevitably influenced by our own context but recognise that good leadership involves a constant dynamic exchange of ideas and the willingness to learn through international developments. Our book draws mainly on a number of UK-based case examples as well as international ones, and we hope that you find the content flexible enough for your own context, wherever you are reading it from. Both social work and social care have faced and continue to face an unprecedented period of challenge and uncertainty. There is an ongoing drive to realign the approach to delivering support in a way that offers choice, flexibility, that is person-centred and innovative and that enables service users to access services in a seamless and empowering way. This requires the development of leadership capabilities at every level of the workforce as well as in the community.

This is by no means an easy statement to make as confidence in some areas of social work and social care has undermined trust and belief in the systems involved. Some critiques of current practice link poor management practice to poor outcomes for services users (DCSF, 2009, 2009a). Within the UK, for example, serious case reviews continue to cite management as a vital ingredient to the provision of safe and accountable outcomes of social work and social care services (CQC, 2009; Laming, 2009; DfE, 2010). These critiques occur within a context of emphasis on the role of leadership and management to ensure that social work and social care operate efficiently and effectively, are meeting 'consumer' needs, respond to the increasing marketisation of services and facilitate those engaged in delivering services to work across new organisational boundaries in transparent ways.

However, uncomfortable questions are sometimes left unanswered about the responsibilities of management for the effectiveness of frontline practice and the wellbeing of those they manage. While particular criticisms are present about the 'downside' of leadership and management in social work through a critique of neoliberal managerialism in care organisations, there is a paucity of empirical research relating to management and a relative silence on its role in the proactive development of practice. This book aims to interrogate some of these relatively unexplored areas in more depth. It looks more closely at the pivotal but challenging role leadership and management might play in improving organisational culture and thus practice, and aims to facilitate the voices of managers in how they go about establishing a more critical and realistic dialogue with staff and service users to promote genuine partnership; it also explores how sound management and leadership practice can be seen as a catalyst by which individuals, groups, communities or organisational performance can be critically and realistically evaluated. Some commentators have referred to aspects of this approach as offering 'deep value' (Bell and Smerdon, 2011). This term attempts to capture the value created when the human relationships between people delivering and people using public services are effective and the conditions are present that nourish confidence, inspire self-esteem, unlock potential and erode inequality and so have the power to transform relationships and services.

There are now a number of public bodies in the UK working on strategies to develop leadership and management within integrated services, for example, the National Skills Academy for Social Care, The Health Foundation and The King's Fund. These reflect a more concerted push for initiatives around leadership and management development within care services over the last decade and a desire to secure greater provision of accredited education and training. The type of leadership or a coherent model of leadership for social work and social care has not yet been systematically identified, nurtured and promoted, although this is at least now beginning to evolve. However, it is important to recognise that environmental, professional practice and policy contexts are complex and constantly changing, with the attendant need for managers and professionals to continue to evaluate practice and ideological frameworks. These trends call for a more diverse and informed knowledge base and literature focused specifically on the unique role of leaders and managers in social work and social care. The problem is that in most cases, these thoughts about leadership are not empirically derived but rather they are conceptual. It is in fact quite striking that what we know about leadership is on the whole mainly derived from informed belief. Leadership is also one of those concepts that attract a lot of derision as well as optimistic rhetoric, and thus there is an uneasy relationship with leadership in social work and social care given that it has been easier to lambast when things go wrong.

There is also a strong desire to ensure that any leadership and management education and training is firmly rooted in practice and work-based learning. In relation to the content of management education, the roots of social care and social work remain important for many, as the sector has developed initially within a public welfare framework where management and leadership practice must reflect expected ethical and moral behaviours, as well as increasingly being able to operate within a 'business' environment. This environment is constantly in a state of flux, however, so those leading people through change require good practical skills, an ability to engage in political discourse (personal and communal) as well acquiring, developing and updating their theoretical knowledge in the discipline of organisational and management theory. These essential knowledge and skills help to inform policy-driven interventions, to challenge as appropriate, as well as enabling managers to take on the role of mediators within relationships between government and its citizens. Genuine leadership will not only guide practice but will take on the challenge of promoting diversity, equality and justice in the way services are developed and supported in the community at a time when there is a move towards more individualised care and support.

There have been an increasing number of quality texts published over recent years that seek to define and articulate the role of leadership and management in social work and social care. These have tended to contribute to the discourses about the difference in leadership and management and particularly the challenges for social work management in finding its own voice within a growing managerialist agenda. While this book adds to this valuable collection, it also attempts to move beyond these debates by addressing some of the contemporary issues facing management that have not yet been fully developed. A particular feature of this book, therefore, is the broadening of discussion to include perspectives from other social science disciplines. It explores what might be learned as social work moves into several new and different phases and takes on new roles, particularly within an integrated environment with changing professional roles and co-production at its core.

In light of these complexities, this book has three main themes. The first involves exploring the concept of leadership in social work – what it is and what it is not. Leadership remains a contested concept and is one which cannot just be applied generically or cited uncritically. It is also a concept frequently associated with management but thinking about these two roles merits further debate in relation to their similarities and differences. Chapter One therefore takes a critical look at leadership in its different guises, going beyond the usual typologies offered. We have written on the basis that theories of leadership are not necessarily a bad thing and they have sometimes inspired research to test them and commentators to critique them. Chapter Two considers the cultural context for leadership and discusses theories on organisational culture; it examines the ingredients considered to be essential for a learning organisation in which leadership might thrive. Chapter Three brings us back into focus by looking at the vital role of service users in leadership practice. As a multiple authored book, we have identified that there are some differences taken by each of us in the approach to the different themes and topics, the theories that we have drawn on and the ideological models that support them. We hope you find these differences challenging rather than disconcerting.

The second theme focuses on the concept of organisations introduced in Chapter Two. Organisational theory is often about trying to understand phenomena such as strategy, structure and culture. These elements have become much more organic since the move towards integration and devolvement of policy implementation to a local level. There is increasing complexity that has an impact on governance and workforce planning, particularly when we compare these with traditional and less fluid organisations. Chapter Two, for example, unusually considers the concept of design and design theory and how this might extend our thinking beyond more fixed notions of how we more traditionally view organisations and particularly the relationship between organisational structure and design with culture. Chapters Five and Six explore the concept of workforce development and planning from both strategic and operation perspectives. These are integral to understanding how organisations function, given that 'people' provide the majority of resources for social work and the provision of support and care. It is vital that leaders and managers can appreciate how the workforce addresses these tensions as we move towards more self-directed and preventative approaches to support as well as developing systems of care or a more integrated and holistic approach from the strategic perspective. Chapter Seven explores some of the more 'tricky' issues and challenges for management and leadership, and builds further on the concept of culture by looking at a case study in which leadership failed. Not many books have looked at the concept of abdicated or failed leadership, and we have approached this case study using systems theory to provide a more in-depth analysis. Here we have examined the concept of power in organisations by exploring the particular phenomenon of 'dignity' within the context of organisational culture and leadership.

The final theme of the book looks to more practical issues focusing on how individual managers might more effectively lead practice by exploring possibilities for making a difference. This involves a chapter that examines the challenges of how managers provide formal and informal support to staff and service users. Chapter Six builds on specific case studies researched by the authors in the area of supervision, development of alternative communication structures such as more creative use of technology and effective user involvement strategies. The final chapter explores the notion of management 'skills' and how one learns to 'become' a manager. Building on theories of existentialism (Lawler, 2005), emotional intelligence and virtue ethics, readers will be encouraged to examine and reflect on their own leadership and management styles and those of others, and to think more creatively about the type of manager they aspire to be. In summary, the diverse contributions by the authors of this book express our high hopes for leadership and a realistic appraisal of some of its pitfalls – as they say, 'knowledge is power'. We hope that you find the topic of leadership as intriguing and complex as we have attempted to present it.

ONE

Leadership in social work and social care: a critical exploration

Introduction

As a general introduction this chapter examines the phenomenon of leadership, with particular reference to how 'leadership' might serve our purpose in social work and social care. Genuine discussion about leadership should be informed by the context for practice and examined through different lenses, for example, structural, organisational, professional and operational (Lymbery, 2001). Within social work and social care, leadership is perceived as fundamental to achieving new paradigms of care which shape the way in which future services are subsequently designed and delivered (van Zwanenberg, 2010). This language and the models that support them are not necessarily shared in the rest of the European Union (EU) or the world. A cursory look through any UK government policy document, however, that has an impact on care, demonstrates that as a metaphor, leadership is already deeply embedded in discourse about care provision. This chapter intends to provide a more critical appraisal by revealing the contested nature of leadership that merits further exploration. Leadership, for example, is significantly associated with the operation of power and influence and within the discourse around care – particular models of leadership have become highly privileged or preferred. This chapter aims to facilitate the development of alternative or more subjective viewpoints about how we theorise about leadership and its direct application to practice.

While we aim to give a basic outline of more common or frequently discussed models of leadership, our core purpose is to emphasise its relational aspects that are crucial to effective social work and social care. Similarly, we assert that the role and purpose of social work itself is highly contested, and so we should explore the reasons behind this. For example, leadership needs to be purposeful, so that social workers should have a clear idea about the purpose of social work. Lawler and Bilson (2010) refer to the role of theory in shaping the way we perceive the task of social work and social care, and the importance of acknowledging how theories shape (or not) the way in which we approach our work within the public and community sector. We can be neither neutral nor dispassionate when implementing policy but must focus on what motivates those working in care services and the associated values and ethics. Being honest and knowledgeable when reflecting on contextual and contributing factors, and thinking about what we are aiming to achieve when analysing leadership and management in our own profession, is therefore essential when imagining and constructing alternatives.

Why we are so concerned with leadership

The language of leadership commonly refers to 'being led' and 'leading', and draws and is posited on the framing metaphor of an image, or symbol, of a relationship of guidance or direction giving, and is traditionally associated with hierarchical structures (Bass, 1990). There are connotations of power from whoever's perspective leadership is viewed. The action of leading is seen as essential to espousing vision and promoting the values of a particular government policy or the aims of an organisation or profession. This perspective is also contentious and we return to the debates and critiques of this concept throughout this book. Within social work and social care, organisations face relentless new pressures to adapt, learn, innovate and constantly improve performance. Keeping up with rapid technological and other opportunities and threats requires greater integration across a range of organisational boundaries through increased collaborative or integrated working (Hafford-Letchfield, 2010). The latter has been accompanied by increased complexity as organisations consolidate and in many cases combine structures and resources to promote new ways of organising service delivery, with raised expectations coming from a consumer culture and among a complex array of stakeholder involvement. Leadership is associated with 'survival' in these competitive and progressive situations where single or small groups of specially gifted or positioned individuals lead through their moral, intellectual, interpersonal, material and political resources (Northouse, 2011). Typically, the types of leaders required in these scenarios are referred to as 'transformational', 'charismatic' or 'situational' (Bass, 1990; Northouse, 2011). Similarly, the person or people in such leadership positions should also be empowered by having sufficient room to manoeuvre or the authority to lead, alongside sufficient resources, time and support. This requires effort or commitment from those being led, which can benefit all those involved (Boehm and Yoels, 2008).

Until relatively recently social work practice was located within a 'bureau-professional paradigm', and while subject to change, leadership activity within social work remains largely shaped by this context. We also recognise that many of the ideas of leadership being explored within this text stem from the critical paradigm of neoliberal policy and reform.

Contemporary leadership in both social work and social care has attempted to respond in particular to outcome-based policies such as 'personalisation' policies in adult services (HMG, 2007) and 'risk management' and prevention within children and family services, both of which represent a challenge to the traditional practice paradigm (Munro, 2011). Social work leaders and managers are expected to take responsibility for leading these developments, and for managing emerging social care markets within the sector. As we shall see later in this chapter, more recently emphasis has been given to adopting a systems approach to organisational and service development by moving away from command-and-control models towards adapting and developing learning cultures that can in turn influence the way professional frontline practitioners are managed and supported (Munro, 2010). Adopting a dispersed or distributed leadership style should give people within the service and its providers the confidence to challenge poor practice. Moving away from heroic leadership styles (The King's Fund, 2011) focuses on the role that leadership might play in developing the organisation and its partnerships. Followership is also important. However, shared leadership is not without its dilemmas because distributing leadership tasks throughout an organisation and promoting organisational learning requires cultural change. This presents a dilemma for formal leaders who are required to both disperse authority and to act hierarchically (Williams and Sullivan, 2011).

Leadership in social work and social care – is there a difference?

There are differences between social work and social care in relation to leadership but a noticeable lack of discrimination between the two. This book is about leadership across the sector but explicitly refers to the unique contribution that social work makes within this sector. Dickens (2012) tells us that the alternative term 'social care' has arisen as a result of policy-making and political debate which may be considered distinct from social work, part of social work or incorporating social work in the way it covers all services, resources and support that social workers might plan, promote and arrange, including from communities and independent agencies. He further suggests that social care may also refer to the whole range of personal social services, and carries some connotation of ambivalence towards social work. This ambiguity initially helped social work in the UK to develop its professionalism, for example, by becoming a graduate profession. This enabled social work to define its knowledge base, role complexity and to establish accountability with the latter made clearer through the introduction of a clear regulatory framework. For example, two high-profile inquiries in social work (Laming, 2003, 2009) subsequently led to a 'root-and-branch' review of the profession in England and the reform of social work (Social Work Taskforce, 2009). Leadership responsibilities have to be supported by improved knowledge and practice skills relating to strategic planning, the commissioning of best value services and the delivery of high quality specialised services (Hafford-Letchfield, 2010). Likewise, on the provider side, leaders in social care need to be more savvy with an increased range of skills (Gallop and Hafford-Letchfield, 2012). This work has an added complexity brought about by partnership working which may require joint initiatives or indeed fully integrated agency working, and which requires opportunities for leadership within a multi-agency context.

Further, codes of practice within the four UK countries, England, Wales, Scotland and Ireland, have all specified key values for social care, which Dickenson (2012) argues serve to underplay the complexities of the social work role as they do 'not identify the central dilemmas of balancing care' (p 36) with the difficult judgements required, nor address the need to achieve change in the wider social circumstances of users' lives. These developments have been perceived as tools for government-led, top-down regulation of the workforce. The British Association of Social Work (BASW) *Code of ethics* (2012), which leans towards a value-based as opposed to a role-based definition of social work, perhaps reflect a more bottom-up bid for professional status and autonomy. However, the Association relies on social workers voluntarily signing up to these. The international definition of social work similarly emphasises the role of social work in working with the principles of human rights and social justice (IFSW and IASSW, 2000). All of these social work definitions and codes do not always sit well with the realities of statutory social work which experiences high levels of proceduralism, gatekeeping to resources and care–control dilemmas (Dickens, 2012). The development of the standards of proficiency for social work (HCPC, 2012) has done little to challenge government-led codes of practice.

Finally, the cumulative failure to recognise the organisational context and to underplay the realities of circumstances and very high levels of need presenting most social workers has reinforced another 'banal picture that misses the ethical, intellectual and political challenges of the work' (Dickens, 2012, p 40). Some progress was made through the Children's Workforce Development Council (CWDC) that stressed the demands and complexity of the work, observing that no other profession has to make judgements and exercise powers with such potential serious consequences (CWDC, 2009, para 14). The Association of Directors of Adult Social Work (ADASS) has likewise argued that social work skills will always be required in adult social care but need to be used in more direct, therapeutic work with individuals or in advocacy and community development work (ADASS et al, 2010). Leadership, and the acknowledgement of leadership, perhaps has a role here, not only as a vehicle to exercise the voices of practitioners and individual social workers, teams and organisations, but through the championing of the profession itself. The challenge for social work leadership is to stay open to new ideas, but to be clear and assertive about the complex dimensions and responsibilities of their profession and to be willing to take on leadership roles. This is cited as one of the drivers for establishing The College of Social Work (TCSW) in England (2010).

In summary, the many different interest groups in the care sector makes it important to recognise the overlaps, potential alliances and conflicts within and between them as well as tensions caused by official claims over the roles and tasks of social work by shifting power and control away from central government and towards local communities and individuals. We saw earlier how the rhetoric of leadership may not be genuinely aligned to the desire for empowerment. There remains a limited empirical basis for asserting the effects of leadership in social work in the face of the assertion that social work is practised in the spirit of evidence-based practice in order to see its effects (Tafvelin et al, 2012). Leadership has also been a missing ingredient in social work education, given its association with management. The inclusion of leadership within TCSW's professional capabilities framework (2012) as a required outcome throughout the social work career trajectory has, however, signalled one intention to tackle the development of leadership potential among social workers. Similarly, the emphasis on relationship-based practice has given more weight to the argument for supporting leadership in social work, setting the context and thinking about the exchange between leadership in social work and social care, and the impact remains to be seen. We now turn back to the broader context and the influence of systems on leadership within care itself.

Influence of public policy on leadership

Periods of unprecedented financial challenges through the radical reform of public services depend on a thorough assessment of how services can develop. As suggested earlier, this could be supported by continuing investment in leadership development at all levels, and points to the increasing importance of leadership across systems of care as well as within individual organisations. Developing leadership also requires a national and even international focus as well as a local one. There has not been a substantive review of the administrative demands placed on care service for many years, and much of the literature on managerialism has highlighted the essential rationalisation of these demands (Harris, 2003; Tsui and Cheung, 2004).

A number of government policy initiatives have had a complex impact on the management and administrative costs of care provision, for example, through private finance initiatives (PFIs), personalisation, the imperative towards social enterprise and the extensive outsourcing of a wider range of services, all with complex contractual and management arrangements including regulation (Hafford-Letchfield, 2010). While Connolly et al (2010) have demonstrated an association between higher management costs and better quality care, there have, of course, been a number of spectacular management failures in recent years which have documented extremely poor care within institutions and people's own homes (CQC, 2011a). It is important to recognise that professionals were previously regarded as arbitrators of quality, but in more recent times this has become the responsibility of managers and regulators. Many public inquiries and serious case reviews have specifically highlighted failures in both management and leadership (Laming, 2003, 2009), and propose radical new approaches to meet these challenges. These issues are discussed in more depth in Chapter Seven.

Reforms in the UK, for example, have encouraged a significant number of staff to leave the mainstream organisation, such as in the statutory sector, and to sell their services back through various forms of mutual and social enterprise, and the scale of these reforms makes the issues of leadership and management in social work and social care ever more important. We pick up some of these themes in subsequent chapters in this book when we reflect on the ways these become important, for example, through either managing change, putting up resistance or championing some of these approaches. There has been a move towards the commissioning of small independent private 'social work practices', the conception of which rests on three pillars. These are: consistency in corporate approaches via a more personal relationship between the service user/s and their social worker; the attraction of a 'professional partnership' to social workers demoralised by increasing bureaucracy; and the motivation for increased professional autonomy and owner-control of their partnership organisation (Carey, 2008). Carey identifies three proposed models within children's services as examples: a 'professional practice' (social enterprise) run by a 'partnership' of social workers legally independent of the local authority; a 'third sector' (not-for-profit) model run by a voluntary organisation; and a private sector (for-profit) model. This new entrepreneurial outlook seeks to relocate children's social work as a 'business' (Petrie, 2010) alongside 'opportunities for social workers to learn commercial and social enterprise skills' (DCSF, 2009, p 11). It follows the increased commodification of services to vulnerable people and within the social work and social care labour market, particularly in relation to the provision of senior management structures. These developments are underpinned by the government's commitment to contesting local government services and to remove barriers to other providers outside the sector, and in scoping out potential for new markets for the purposes of delivering care. These developments are not without criticism for their impact on children, families and the profession. As illustrated in the last section, the continuing denigration of any achievements in care so far further exploits themes of popular discontent with social work and its partner agencies.

Leadership as a vehicle for social justice

Within social work and social care, the creation of a climate of fear in which workers, including leaders and managers, feel unable to speak out against policies and practices which they know to be harmful to service users and the community has been identified as one of the more insidious features of managerialism (Cooper, 2005). This book seeks to critically review some of the key debates that underpin current policy and practice debates and the resulting pressures. We look more closely at this phenomenon when considering the concept of organisational design, culture and the concept of dignity in leading effective care services. Professional autonomy, such as the right to speak out, has been described as a casualty of the managerial revolution that has sought – on the basis of no real evidence – to portray social work as a 'failing profession' in need of reform (Lambley, 2011). By the mid-1990s that 'reform' had resulted in the replacement of a rich repertoire of social work methods by the single approach of care management. New Labour (post-1997) tackled some of these issues through the introduction of new forms of regulation and inspection which showed a similar distrust of professional social work, and made a powerful case for a return to relationship-based social work, drawing on collective approaches and based on values of social justice (Ferguson, 2007; Ruch, 2011). More recently, Munro's inquiry into the state of safeguarding services in children's social work documented widely the impact of working conditions on practice (Munro, 2011) and the need to review several aspects of the system simultaneously to achieve systems change. This has contrasted with some of the public discussions of senior UK politicians who believe that social work should be more practically focused (Conservative Home Blogs, 2012; McAlister, 2012). Again, effective change in the 'system' is seen to be dependent on achieving skilled leadership at a local level where practical knowledge of how the organisation works can be aligned to change. Attention to leadership education and development (considered in the final chapter of this book) is crucial here. In the UK, Munro's review, for example, found that most bureaucracy that limits the effectiveness of practice is generated and maintained at a local level including financial, procedural and personnel requirements. Like the earlier Laming report (Laming, 2009), the finger was pointed at local politicians and senior personnel whose behaviour and expectations must be focused alongside resourcing of frontline practice directly related to improving and supporting the frontline. Here leadership is seen to bind both leaders and followers (managers and practitioners), implying social commonality and commitment and thus a social responsibility (O'Reilly and Reed, 2010). It is implied that subsequent reorientation of accountability through the types of networks and alliances between these two partners can be built through such collaboration.

In short, it has been suggested that we are living with a discourse which remains deficient on social work and social care and its collaborative partners, coming from a strong neoliberal political ascendancy (Walker and Walker, 2011). The political function of this discourse tends to deflect attention away from the fundamental causation of perceived failures of social work and the contributory factors such as financial deficits, managerialism and defensive practice. This raises the question as to what contribution social workers, managers, practitioners and other professionals should be making to build a case against the scale, speed and change seeking to further individualise services and meter out some very austere and radical policies that are not always in tune with the values and ethics of social work and social care. Leaders, managers and those they lead have close proximity to the end users of the welfare state and the consequences of social, economic and political policies and political ideology. They observe first hand the negative impact on poverty and inequality, and could work with these constructively by taking a defensive stance combined with the framing of progressive alternatives. Some of these issues are followed up in Chapter Three concerning strategies of developing leadership within the community and with service users. The differences between social work and social care, the universal subordination of social work and social policy to economic policy and critiques of its variants under neoliberalism could form the basis for a more radical approach to leadership from a more central position by shifting power outwards and downwards. Much debate about social work and its stakeholders has focused on how we keep alive an alternative discourse on the purpose of care, advancing the case for social justice and making the case for the correlations between equality and wellbeing.

We are told with certainty that cuts in the public sector will be compensated for by growth in the private sector alongside the development of a 'Big Society' with the same anti-state underpinnings (Cameron, 2011). We are yet to see the empirical evidence for this. While the public sector is a crucial source of welfare and social justice, there has always been a growing critique that it also provides a source of injustice (Ferguson, 2007). Leaders and managers need to keep a sustained focus on the social consequences of government policy, particularly in relation to deficit reduction strategies, and to cross-examine the assertion of 'fairness', particularly in acknowledgements that we are very much involved in making decisions about core services within a devolved administration and in determining priorities. One example concerns spending reviews over previous decades that have led to occasions where the voluntary and community sector are cited with a degree of certainty and optimism. Developing leadership through investment in the infrastructure, and utilising the mainstream partnerships that voluntary and community organisations have had to develop with the state in order to survive, has provided access to representing the needs and views of service users, many of whom are the most marginalised in our society.

What traditional theories about leadership have to offer

Traditionally the knowledge base in social work and social care has derived from a range of social science subjects, which are then applied eclectically to practice, which is also true of its leadership. Social theory informs our understanding of social problems; social policy enables us to define the role and 'policy purpose' of social work; and management and leadership provides an understanding of how the organisation, management and the leadership of practice occur. Lawler and Bilson (2010, p 25) developed a framework for exploring management and leadership theories in social work using critical social policy, the rationale behind leadership development in social work, and in particular, its relationship to managerialism. Since the early 1990s critical management theories and studies have sought to bring together critical theory and post-structuralist perspectives as an alternative to the politics of managerialism and to link its techniques to neoliberalism. The literature on social work management has been developing narratives on management using different theoretical tools and political perspectives (Tsui and Cheung, 2004), and comes from a number of scholars seeking to highlight inconsistencies between experiences of frontline social work with the claims of mainstream managerialism; it has connected those experiences to broader explanations and theorising. Similarly, social theories offer us a 'value base' from which to examine the nature of social work and the theories that inform it. There are also a number of social and political movements that have demonstrated the role that service users and other stakeholders can play in defining and shaping leadership in social work.

Making sense of leadership through these conceptual frameworks is helpful when examining one's own leadership practice. Scholarship also refers to three roles that involve leadership, management and administration, which are interdependent. Yet in the public sector, politicians frequently refer to management as a pejorative as well as denigrated term equated with bureaucracy and from which the public also takes its cue following anecdotes about the merits of management. Let's explore this further.

Thinking through leadership and management

No discussion about leadership development would be complete without acknowledging the strong links made between leadership and management, or indeed the role of the 'leader-manager', which:

> ... demands a mix of analytic and personal skills in order to set out a clear vision of the future and defining a strategy to get there. It requires communicating that to others and ensuring that the skills are assembled to achieve it. It also involves handling and balancing the conflicts of interests that will inevitably arise, both within the organisation and outside it where ... a wide variety of stakeholders will have a legitimate interest. (The King's Fund, 2011, p 12)

Leadership also clearly requires considerable management skills such as marshalling the human and technical resources needed to achieve the organisation's goals, and ensuring the administration needed is in place. How we actually measure skill itself and its associated knowledge and values is likewise an under-researched and under-documented area (Gould, 2000; Crisp et al, 2003). Unlike leadership, management is essentially a practical activity and managers use a range of knowledge and skills within their practice. This integrative task involves achieving synergy, balance and perspective. Most management activity is undertaken through complex webs of social and political interaction involving a continuous process of adaptation to changing pressures and opportunities (Hafford-Letchfield, 2009). The development of management skills and the acquisition of insight into self, others and the process of evaluation of learning stem from many different stimuli. Determining an ideal structure for defining and measuring learning outcomes is challenging and requires testing the romantic notion that 'all is required is a brilliant manager' (Tsui and Cheung, 2004, p 441) to solve what are essentially very complex issues that have an impact on contemporary organisations delivering care services. Placing the management of services within clear fiscal and governance frameworks will inevitably have a significant impact on which specialist areas of practice and knowledge are deemed most valid for social work management and, consequently, what should be included in the leadership and management educational curriculum (Galpin, 2009).

There is a danger of over-emphasising technical knowledge, skills and dependency on which specialist areas of practice and knowledge are prioritised. Galpin (2009) asserts how this potentially overlooks the broader structural issues where skills are required to work effectively with issues such as discrimination, oppression and inequality within communities. We need to clarify how more effective work can be associated with particular styles of leadership. Ideally, the leadership and management curriculum should offer learner-managers a complex mix of intellectual discipline and practice development from which they are more able to critically analyse the structures, cultures, discourses and priorities within their environment. From here they can further develop their leadership and management competencies and skills and their abilities to critically reflect on their own practice, values and ethics. Management education should equip managers to make sense of the complexity and conflict inherent in the management task to enable greater responsiveness, innovation and challenges in delivering and improving services as opposed to an unquestioning acceptance of the status quo.

Aspirations towards more humanist or existential management (Lawler, 2005) are embedded in the aforementioned underpinning social work management principles that reflect its professional value base (GSCC, 2007) and the inclusion of personal and strong democratic elements in leadership development programmes. A significant shift in the power and status of service users and carers, from recipients of professional wisdom and judgements to one of co-producers and co-providers of care, requires a significant shift in power and status (Beresford et al, 2006; Carr, 2007; Galpin, 2009). To support staff and stakeholders to engage in these changing relationships, managers need appropriate engagement and negotiating skills (Gallop and Hafford-Letchfield, 2012). One factor may be the way in which leadership and indeed management might act as a buffer between politicians and service users. A survey of public sector managers by the Institute of Leadership and Management (ILM) (2010) demonstrated that of those most dissatisfied with the public sector, around half (48 per cent) put this down to poor or unsupportive management or leadership and other competence issues. A further quarter of respondents cited the failure to deal effectively with underperforming staff as a major cause of their dissatisfaction, alongside a perceived inability to motivate staff and inadequate senior management skills where interaction was poor, coupled with lack of understanding about the functions and responsibilities of other teams. While this study highlighted public sector managers' support for target setting, there was dissatisfaction about the lack of empowerment in setting realistic localised targets for their teams rather than having uniform targets imposed without consultation.

Managers often acquire responsibility for managing others, without the benefits of formal management training, utilising fundamental life skills combined with professional expertise combined with practice 'know-how' (Eraut, 1985). They need knowledge and skills for accurate problem definition, effective communication, conflict resolution, negotiation and the development of practical strategies. Getting the basics right, converting key concepts and principles into effective action and mastering these in practice as well as theory is required before considering and identifying advanced professional development needs in the management and leadership role. It also requires a clear vision about the role of management. The potential scope of managerial responsibility and role is so broad, however, that there are inevitably common core features as well as highly specialist ones (Hales, 1993). Key elements of the approach to management learning in social work are those that recognise the positive relationship between management development and organisational performance in the unique environment of care. Another essential element is the employment of critical reflective techniques in order to make sense of current complexities and to retain sufficient flexibility to be able to respond to unknown future developments (Fook and Askeland, 2007; Lawler and Bilson, 2010).

As we will see later in Chapter Eight, little is known about in-service training programmes for managers in contrast to the predominance of university-based accredited programmes. Blumenthal (2003, 2007) has pioneered the integration of managerial and organisational capacity-building in order to build a theoretical foundation for designing management development. He defines capacity-building as 'actions that improve non-profit effectiveness' (Blumenthal, 2003, p 9) in four performance domains, which include: organisational stability over time; financial stability with sufficient resources to meet fluctuations; quality and its impact on clients; and finally, healthy organisational growth. Blumenthal has a fifth dimension which is capacity-building relating to systems management, 'whereby there is a conscious effort to improve an organisation's skills and systems, or ... new management strategies or structures' (2003, p 55). These all point to the capacity to identify and support organisational leadership, to manage change and to develop a healthy culture. Therefore, within any management development or administration programme that typically addresses technical management skills, there needs to be multiple approaches to learning and use of different tools that make explicit and support the organisational goals and practice environment. It is clear that a number of perspectives on management emphasise issues broader than managerial skill sets, particularly in relation to developing the organisational environment and leadership capacity. These are considered more closely in the next chapter.

Social work managers are often charged with motivating employees to perform well in their jobs. While management skills may suffice for task-related issues, motivation and organisational innovation require leadership (Fisher, 2009). Some managers have learned to lead successfully based on their practice wisdom and personal experience through a practice-led approach (Sedan and Reynolds, 2003), but as a group, social work administrators may rely too heavily on these two facets. Classic studies of leadership have demonstrated that managers who conform to the tenets of one leadership theory or another, versus none at all, achieve more in their own eyes than those of their workers (Hall and Donnell, 1979).

Not all leadership emerges as a result of training and education. At an operational level, it is possible to gain a benefit from good leadership even if an integrated approach to leadership at strategic level is not present. By engaging staff, and nurturing simple actions that can be taken by leaders day-to-day, this can cost very little but make a real difference to performance and contribute to a culture where further improvements are likely (Roebuck, 2011). Research by Baker (2011) highlighted that long-serving leaders at the top of an organisation help to maintain strategic direction and ease transition where there is a high turnover of executive staff.

There are, therefore, many debates about the nature and style of leadership, its definition and disputes about its impact. Figure 1.1 attempts to demonstrate some of the more popular of these and their key features. In the first quadrant, we see that 'transactional' leadership is an approach that capitalises on stability and has a strong hold on maintaining the status quo and steering the way ahead. This style of leadership is useful for motivating people to improve performance and in achieving short-term goals. Transactional leaders focus on increasing the efficiency of established routines and procedures, and are mainly concerned with establishing and standardising practices that will help the organisation reach maturity, achieve efficiency and productivity.

'Transformational' leadership on the other hand, as seen in the top right-hand quadrant, engages more actively with followers, by focusing on higher order intrinsic needs, and by raising consciousness about the overall mission – the significance of specific outcomes and new ways in which those outcomes might be achieved. Transformational leaders will put the group interests first, by connecting with the follower's sense of identity and the collective identity of the organisation.

Figure 1.1: Leadership theories, models and styles

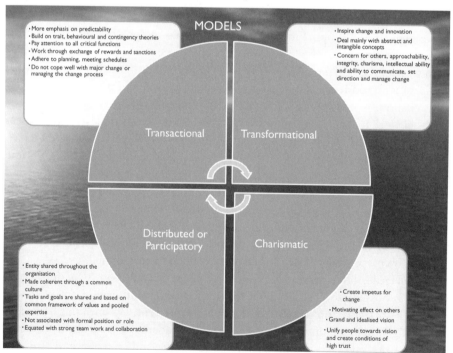

MODELS

Transactional
- More emphasis on predictability
- Build on trait, behavioural and contingency theories
- Pay attention to all critical functions
- Work through exchange of rewards and sanctions
- Adhere to planning, meeting schedules
- Do not cope well with major change or managing the change process

Transformational
- Inspire change and innovation
- Deal mainly with abstract and intangible concepts
- Concern for others, approachability, integrity, charisma, intellectual ability and ability to communicate, set direction and manage change

Distributed or Participatory
- Entity shared throughout the organisation
- Made coherent through a common culture
- Tasks and goals are shared and based on common framework of values and pooled expertise
- Not associated with formal position or role
- Equated with strong team work and collaboration

Charismatic
- Create impetus for change
- Motivating effect on others
- Grand and idealised vision
- Unify people towards vision and create conditions of high trust

Such leaders are said to often provide an inspirational role model based on trust, admiration, loyalty and respect from followers who are in turn willing to commit as a direct result of the leader's qualities. Transformational leadership is most often associated with dynamic change environments and what is commonly referred to as 'emotional intelligence' by being able to read the situation and get a response.

'Charismatic' leadership in the bottom right-hand quadrant mainly builds on some of these personal qualities required for change. Charismatic leaders are said to be very much in tune with building a group, whether it is a political party, a cult or a business team, with a focus on making this clear, distinct and sometimes superior, and from which they can create an unchallengeable position for themselves. The values of the charismatic leader are highly significant which, if well intentioned towards others, can elevate and transform an entire organisation, but similarly can be intolerant of others who challenge and become irreplaceable, which makes it difficult for succession planning. These types of leaders are probably the farthest from what is required in social work and social care.

In the left-hand bottom quadrant, 'Distributed or Participatory' leadership is the one most akin to the co-productive agenda. This seeks to share power and work in the most democratic way, and leadership is not associated with a specific position but is instead an attribute that arises in different individuals throughout the organisation. Distributed leadership focuses on leadership practice rather than specific leadership roles. These leadership practices occur when those in authoritative and subordinate positions interact with each other.

Discourses on leadership: rhetoric or reality?

So how useful are the above theories of leadership within our own sector? O'Reilly and Reed (2010, p 971) have suggested 'leaderism' as a discursive term to complement the evolution of neoliberal and new public management mechanisms and practices within public services:

> The emerging discourse of "leaderism" justifies the growing influence, not to say power, of an ideology in which a model of the "rational consumer", rather than of the "dependent client" or "informed citizen", is mobilised within policy debates and discourses that have fateful consequences for mundane, but vital, issues to do with the managerial and administrative practices through which scarce resources are allocated and deployed within public service organisations.

The discourse of leadership, they suggest, potentially contributes to three elements of policy reform being promoted. First, leaders are construed as change agents associated with leading transformational, system-wide change through practice that enables and facilitates reforms that will radically reshape the nature and content of 'public services' and the manner in which they are provided and consumed. Second, leaders are expected to potentially alleviate and absorb the endemic and inherent tensions between politicians, managers, professionals and the public by playing a major role in drawing them together in a unifying discourse that emphasises collectivity. Third, leadership is delegated to a wide range of stakeholders such as frontline staff, service users and carers, and innovative organisations, whose autonomy allows them to become authors of their own reforms.

The rolling back of the state has grappled with entrepreneurship, which prioritises devolved authority and service innovation within competitively designed environments. Emphasis on actively managing the culture of organisations seeks to align the beliefs and values of its members with those of policy-makers. Culture is a constant theme throughout the topics in this book, and we illustrate this in the next chapter by introducing the concept of organisational culture and the relationship of leadership to developing culture. According to O'Reilly and Reid (2010), the change of discourse to leadership attempts to re-define any tensions emerging from managerialism for the care sector by stressing the importance of establishing a passion for a common goal between leaders and those being led. 'Policy reform aims to achieve more customer-focused public services through the principles of standards and accountability, devolution and delegation, flexibility and incentives and expanding choice' (p 965). There is a strong presence of leadership discourse in how government represents reform. As a core lexical item in public service reform it is associated with the personalisation of services, such as those seen in *Putting people first* (HMG, 2007) and the Health and Social Care Act 2012, making leadership of these reforms the primary contributing factor to successful performance management and associated with 'excellence'.

Within this discourse, the representation of different people taking up leadership roles serves to locate accountability with them, rather than at the political level. The role taken by politicians, then, is one that enables them to set objectives and steer those implementing them from a distance. In this scenario, the majority of leadership will follow a functionalist line, and adopting critical perspectives enables us to develop alternative or more subjective viewpoints on how we theorise about leadership and its application to practice (Ford and Lawler, 2007). One might conclude that the rhetoric of 'leaders at all levels' in current organisations implicitly relates the role of leadership to positions of hierarchical authority, or those nominated. Some of these dynamics are embodied in the relationships between leaders and followers shown in Figure 1.1 earlier. For example, Ford and Lawler (2007) assert that the leadership aspect of a relationship is not necessarily recognised from the outset, but might only be defined as such in or after the process or as an emergent process as opposed to an individualised phenomenon. The essence of this relationship may be experienced subjectively and therefore not easily articulated. Ford and Lawler (2007) further identify that the regular conflation of management and leadership in the literature makes it more difficult to describe the relational aspects of leadership and how this might develop beyond the confines of management relationships. They thus introduce the concepts of existentialist and social constructionist thinking into the leadership debate, both of which encourage an analysis of the ongoing and relational acts between people that enable and give consideration to the ways in which certain aspects of leadership are produced and reproduced between leaders and followers:

> Existential and constructionist approaches then, form the basis of a quest for a shift in focus away from the myth of leadership and its potential alienation, deskilling and reification of organisational forms, towards the dynamics of "leadership" as a social process. Through this, individuals and organisational members are encouraged to interrelate in ways that encompass new forms of intellectual and emotional meaning, to experiment with new paradigms and behaviours and to discover more meaningful and constructive ways of relating and working together. (Ford and Lawler, 2007, p 415)

In conclusion, leadership cannot be discussed outside of its relational aspects and cannot be understood without a greater appreciation of its followers. This has implications for the way in which we conceptualise and think about leadership development, or the development of leaders. This cannot focus purely on technical competencies but must give attention to our ability to create climates in which individuals themselves can act to improve services. Chapter Eight explores these leadership development issues in more detail.

Leadership in integrated or multi-agency environments

The ability to work across boundaries and to persuade others over the right course of action has become more important than the cavalry charge on behalf of a single institution or better delivery for service users, by creating a cadre of leaders to address multiple or single needs. This post-heroic model of leadership involves multiple actors who take up leadership roles both formally and informally, and who importantly share leadership by working collaboratively. The focus therefore goes beyond personal behavioural style or competencies but is on organisational relations, connectedness, interventions into the organisation system, changing organisation practices and processes (Turnball James, 2011). Complicated relationships in multidisciplinary environments and integrated services require the negotiating of authority between professionals and managers from different professional backgrounds. The literature on collaborative leadership can be applied to both intra and interorganisational settings. It reflects the interdependence and connectivity in public management (although this is increasingly being reduced), and counters the limitations of traditional approaches to leadership, particularly those based on the primacy of hierarchy and heroic leadership. It involves managing power relationships and generating consensus (Williams and Sullivan, 2011).

The emphasis on working collaboratively offers the prospect of delivering outcomes and achieving synergy around social issues that are beyond the capabilities of single organisations. Leadership has been named as a one of the determinants of effective collaborative practice (Sullivan and Skelcher, 2002).

Learning about our partners – how they frame reality, what their roles and ambitions are, how far they are prepared to cede power, and for what purposes – is important in the search for collective action. According to Williams and Sullivan (2011), this leads to learning with others in pursuit of joint solutions to complex problems, particularly the premium of intersectoral learning and the development of new models of public service delivery in an economic climate of financial restraint. They suggest that organisational learning is linked to structural conditions such as cultures, power, relationships, norms and rules that mediate that process, which are linked to leadership style and interpretive approaches to learning that focus on this socialisation. The use of formal power in shaping and transferring organisational learning through different structures, systems and people also needs delicate and refined qualities to manage interpersonal relationships, based on individual qualities such as perception, empathy, discretion, subtlety, flexibility and decisiveness. These are debated more fully in Chapters Four and Five that discuss the development of the workforce. Leaders are required to evidence high-quality conflict management and interpersonal skills. Trust is important in promoting collaborative working, requiring leaders to have an open attitude, to emphasise long-term relationships and to respect partners' autonomy. In general, shared and distributed models have much value in collaborative arenas, particularly because of their rejection of hierarchical imperatives, their appreciation of dispersed power, especially in groups, and their emphasis on mutual learning, experimentation and reflective practice. Paradoxically, strong hierarchical leadership may be required in particular circumstances at particular stages of the collaborative process to achieve change by demonstrating considerable persistence to implement and embed strategic actions. There is an argument in favour of encouraging employees not to think in terms of success or failure, but in terms of learning and experience (Farson and Keynes, 2002).

Leadership as a concept in crisis management

Ongoing examples in social work and social care highlight expectations around effective crisis leadership that, according to Boin et al (2008), require political and administrative skills. Effective crisis leadership entails recognising emerging threats, initiating efforts to mitigate them and dealing with their consequences (Boin et al, 2010). In the wake of crisis, the public, the media and political opponents tend to exhort the need for crisis management skills. Once an acute crisis period has passed, re-establishing a sense of normalcy and communicating the issues to a public demanding to be reassured is usually marked by intense politicisation. While the crisis is still unfolding, the drama of accountability and blaming begins, either for causing the crisis, failing to prevent it, or for an inadequate response. Surprisingly little has been written about the wider political leadership challenges generated by these destabilising events such as the frequent public inquiries and serious case reviews in social work and social care that regularly gain public attention. It could be of interest whether leadership style can help explain the dynamics and outcome of these periods (Boin et al, 2010). A crisis opens up opportunities for challenging and changing the status quo. Leaders can push for change, reforms or defend the status quo, and there might be a battle about how the crisis is an indicator of structural failure.

Boin et al (2009, 2010) identify two factors in determining the outcome of post-crisis blame games: first, the extent to which blame for the mismanagement of a crisis is attributed to leaders and governments (by inquiries, the press, legislators); and second, the political astuteness of the blame management behaviour of leaders during and in response to crisis inquiries and the strategies developed to manage the impact and to interact with those involved, such as stonewalling or cooperating. Leaders have to negotiate a deeply entrenched tension by consolidating, restoring and showing faith in the security and validity of pre-existing social, institutional and political arrangements while simultaneously facing pressure to criticise and reform these same arrangements. Ducking, diffusing and deflecting responsibility are much more likely initial responses than taking responsibility and absorbing the blame that comes with it. Several tactics can be deployed to defuse criticism, by arguing for continuity and announcing measures to show that they have got the message (Boin et al, 2010, p 710), navigating this difficult pathway between an:

> ... open, reflective, responsibility-accepting stance that encourages policy-oriented learning but may leave them politically vulnerable, and a defensive responsibility-denying stance that may deflect blame at the price of undermining learning. (p 708)

We pick up these issues in later chapters in relation to the concept of dignity and organisational culture. These approaches may erode a leader's long-term legitimacy, requiring a mixture of agency, policy and presentational strategies in response. Psychological leadership research shows that political leaders who display distinct and comparatively stable leadership styles are a function of their more deep-seated personality structures and professional socialisation. Two dimensions of leadership style have been shown especially relevant in understanding leadership during crises: a leader's need for control and a leader's sensitivity to context (Hermann and Preston, 1994). The need for personal control or involvement in the policy-making process varies, leading some to be more hands-on and involved while others depend more on subordinates and their bureaucracies. This degree of control or personal involvement appears to be related to an individual's need for power where high power needs involve direct control and setting of agendas for followers and with minimal delegation. Visibility, however, also makes it harder to avoid blame. In contrast, leaders with less control needs focus mostly on critical decisions, and leave the implementation of these to handpicked subordinates whom they trust and rely on. Public perception is crucial to the style adopted. Being seen as 'less engaged' is more likely to lead to bureau-political conflict and to deflect blame. A leader's sensitivity to context is an important dimension as high complexity leaders will be more sensitive to external or multiple policy perspectives on a particular issue, and able to seek out alternative views, policy options and contingencies. On the other hand, this may lead to less decisiveness during crises.

Towards creative leadership and making a difference

The discussion in this introductory chapter leads us to question a repositioning of professionals and service users as leaders within our current structure and culture and direction of travel. It has potentially destabilising consequences for prevailing relationships, practices and routines, but how can these be mediated and legitimated? In short, are traditional leadership approaches likely to be appropriate for our purpose, and more specifically, do the emerging models of leadership offer any better solutions?

The concept of power is inherent to discussions about leadership and its capacity to influence others. Organisations typically exhibit power through the position or status that individuals or groups hold, particularly within its hierarchy. Power is exercised legitimately, as well as through the ability to reward or coerce (French and Raven, 1986). Personal power may stem from one's knowledge, expertise, competence and personal characteristics and is recognised in relationships. Creativity is the process of generating something new or original, and most interpretations view creativity as bringing together existing ideas to develop something new and of value (Steele and Hampton, 2005). Thinking about problems afresh from first principles may help to discover common threads, to experiment, rewrite rules, visualise future scenarios and to work at the edge of one's competence combined with the application of imagination – all are features of innovative leadership (Steele and Hampton, 2005). Creative people tend to reinterpret and apply their learning in new contexts and communicate their ideas in novel ways as well as keeping their options open. They are more able to learn to cope with uncertainty and to trust their intuition. The contribution of innovation in public services is essential for public value as well as for efficiency and benefits for individuals (Hartley, 2005). Creativity in high-pressured environments is possible if the pressure is interpreted as meaningful urgency rather than arbitrary deadline or management pressure. In social work and social care, the value of creativity depends on the extent to which it contributes to intended outcomes such as improved quality of life, sustainable communities and improved relationships involving trust and participation, increased user involvement and economic value (Steele and Hampton, 2005).

The third sector has long regarded creativity and innovation as important characteristics of their organisations and responses to social problems. Unconstrained by political direction and control imposed on the statutory sector, they come from the position of being free, independent bodies, to develop new ways of working. In practice, however, constraints and disincentives through the market mechanisms, overly prescriptive contracting arrangements and risk-averse decisions because of fragility has limited their potential for radical innovation.

Likewise, changes in social norms, affected by ideology, culture, developments in the economy and advances in technology, have had an impact on the way 'public value' has been defined. Changes in demography, diversity and social relationships have also made definitions of the 'public interest' complex (Steele and Hampton, 2005). Services therefore need to constantly review their objectives, strategies and purposes in light of these changes, and to guard against complacency or service provision being on a 'good enough' basis.

Rittel and Webber (1973) use the concept of 'wicked issues' to describe a problem that is difficult or impossible to solve because of incomplete, contradictory and changing requirements that are often difficult to recognise. Moreover, because of complex interdependencies, the effort to solve one aspect of a wicked problem may reveal or create other problems. It can be understood in many different ways and may be inseparable from other problems and demands creative solutions. Classic examples are economic, environment or political issues:

> The search for scientific bases for confronting problems of social policy is bound to fail because of the nature of these problems.... Policy problems cannot be definitively described. Moreover, in a pluralistic society there is nothing like the indisputable public good; there is no objective definition of equity; policies that respond to social problems cannot be meaningfully correct or false; and it makes no sense to talk about "optimal solutions" to these problems.... Even worse, there are no solutions in the sense of definitive answers. (Rittel and Webber, 1973, p 155)

Prompts for creativity include a crisis or severe problem, a search for improvement, new emerging needs or opportunities, or changes in the wider system of public policy. It also requires confidence and stamina to act beyond one's own remit. According to Steele and Hampton (2005, p 35), leaders need not, and should not, feel responsible for providing the creativity their organisations need, but they do have a role in fostering the essential ingredients and an environment in which the creative process is understood and supported. Leading by example by demonstrating their own curiosity about the causes of problems and alternative approaches and by maintaining a focus on outcomes and service improvement, they must exemplify an active approach to risk management, which supports innovation. Senior staff usually have a role in screening or filtering ideas. Celebrating the success even of a few small innovations can encourage a positive attitude for developing new ideas. Creative teams also have networks that extend beyond the internal workforce, drawing on different sources of expertise, and leaders can make time for discussions that encompass both operational and policy staff and bypass any turf wars as well as bringing in different perspectives and experiences of what needs to change. Developing external relationships, particularly around some of the 'wicked issues', helps to stimulate thinking and establish the climate for supporting proposed innovations that require interagency cooperation.

Summary

This chapter has provided a broad and wide-ranging introduction to some of the critical debates about what is considered 'leadership' in social work and social care. By drawing on a wider source of literature and diverse knowledge base, we can already see the complexity of the concepts associated with leadership. There are many wide-ranging debates about its true meaning and usefulness in achieving a vision for those we work with, particularly in relation to the fast moving socioeconomic and public policy environment. This chapter aimed to set the scene for the subjects discussed in more detail within subsequent chapters. Suffice to say, being a leader in social work and social care requires those taking up the role to stay with the courage of their convictions and to be able to cope with complexity. Hafford–Letchfield and Lawler (2010) refer to these as 'the emperor's new clothes'. Having a good knowledge and understanding about leadership and management theory also enables us to develop sight of what is directing or stimulating leadership. Sight becomes insight and in turn, prompts action. The folklore tale of the *Emperor's new clothes* is suggested therefore as one that resonates with many contemporary issues within care environments. While neoliberalism and new public management have continued to have an immense impact on the trajectory of professionals working in social work and social care, the unique skills, knowledge and values held by the professions form a key element of their specific approach that can give rise to innovatory and critically reflective action. Subsequent chapters in this book go on to examine specific issues within leadership and management practice, starting with a closer look at the contextual and environmental factors broadly visited in Chapter Two. We leave you to read on with a specific question in mind – are we just a witness to those changes going on around us, or are we able to initiate and move towards genuine change, a distinct and material, so to speak, set of new clothes?

TWO

Leadership in 'learning organisations': organisational culture and creativity

With contributions from Niall Daly

Introduction

Chapter One provided a broad introduction to some of the critical debates about what is considered 'leadership' in social work and social care. Leadership constitutes complex phenomenon dependent on a critical evaluation of its context. By drawing on a wider source of literature and a more diverse knowledge base, we now consider these complex concepts associated with leadership given the abundant literature on leadership. Wide-ranging debates about the true meaning of leadership and its actual usefulness in achieving a vision for those we work with are dependent on how leadership interacts with a demanding socioeconomic and public policy environment. This chapter explores some of the ideas associated with our understanding of this broader context. It discusses ways in which organisational theorists have characterised organisational structures and cultures, for example, and the impact of different cultures on organisational practice and how leadership might make sense of and have an influence on these. Within this book, this chapter is pivotal in bridging ideas about both operational and strategic leadership across different levels of an organisation, and signposts leaders to think about the organisational culture and thus the nature of the services and the teams in which they work. It highlights the differences in perspective from those working at the frontline, as well as frontline managers to senior leaders in organisations, in relation to a number of external and internal factors that influence how leadership is fostered, developed and supported. Metaphors can also be a good use of understanding better how organisations work alongside case studies that help to analyse and apply ideas about leadership. To engage with some of the more lucid accounts of leadership provided in subsequent chapters, this chapter therefore specifically considers the complex interaction between multiple aspects of an organisation and its various stakeholders (internal and external).

Systems theory is a particularly useful paradigm for thinking about the interdependency of organisations through its alliances and partnerships. This is referred to in a number of subsequent chapters. An important area within multi-agency and interdisciplinary and integrated working is communication, and the failure of communication is often cited within public inquiries as a response to mistakes, challenges and serious incidents. This is the subject of Chapter Seven when we look at the consequences for when leadership fails. According to Capra (2003), communication systems are constantly reinforcing themselves through multiple feedback loops. These produce a shared system of beliefs, explanations and values – a common context of meaning – that is continuously sustained by further communications. Through this shared context of meaning, individuals acquire identities as members of a social network, and in this way the network creates its own boundary. This is not a physical boundary but a boundary of expectations, of confidentiality and loyalty, which is continually maintained and renegotiated by the network itself. What Capra is referring to here is the hidden side of organisational life, particularly its culture and climate, which have a powerful influence on the development and delivery of services. This can also work negatively in reinforcing cultures where poor quality thrives and remains closed to challenges, as we shall see in the case study of organisational and systems failure in care leading to a serious case review.

Organisational culture

Culture is a key concept in the leadership literature, and a unifying theme running throughout this chapter and subsequently the book. Seeking to recognise and understand the concept of culture in its various guises and forms can enable leaders to develop ethical and value-based leadership approaches. Culture is often referred to as the glue that binds organisational systems and processes together to enable improvement to services, enhanced professional engagement, the reduction of conflict and enhancement of problem-solving and communication. Organisational culture is apparently unifying, and this strongly appeals to a leader or management's concern with projecting an image of the organisation as a community of interests. One example includes how paying attention to 'dignity' appeals to organisations working in the care sector as it is proscriptive and cautionary, given the nature of the work. Systems failure and abdicated leadership is an often-neglected facet of culture that inevitably leads to poor standards and unsafe climates for practice, as discussed later in Chapter Seven. Other facets of culture discussed here include the contribution of design principles, the relevance of professionalism and professional cultures, and through an overview of the types of organisational initiatives and interventions that can be used to support the transfer of knowledge to practice in order to ensure a healthy culture and the provision of safe and effective services .

Culture is one of the enduring buzzwords within the leadership and management literature and is seen to penetrate to the essence of an organisation. In popular terms, it is analogous with the concept of the organisation's 'personality' in relation to what or who the organisation is, its mission and core values (Hafford-Letchfield, 2011). Culture is a term originating from anthropology and refers to the underlying values, beliefs and codes of practice that make a community unique and distinguish the community from others. It is powerfully subjective and reflects the meanings and understandings that we typically attribute to situations and ways of solving them. The suggestion that there is a common culture, for example, in social work or in social care, has been the subject of growing research seeking to study certain aspects of an organisation, such as its climate and human resource management (HRM). Within the discipline of social work and social care, this has been stimulated by increasing recognition that achieving change cannot be achieved through organisational structural reform, its processes or emphasis on the different variables and roles in the workplace that emphasise efficiency and management to improve performance. James et al (2007) suggest the term 'organisational climate' to refer to the estimations that people have of their jobs, co-workers, leaders, pay, performance expectations, opportunities and equity, all of which have an impact on an individual's wellbeing and thus the culture. They argue that climate and culture are two different constructs, although within the last decade they have been discussed simultaneously in the organisational literature. Holt and Lawler (2005) develop the idea of organisational 'climate' in social work that, they suggest, provides a means of identifying and indicating specific organisational initiatives that might have a positive impact on service delivery over time (p 32), and that has the advantage of making service improvements amenable to management. They see the culture of an organisation as being rooted in its values system that provides an aggregate view of what goes on there. They suggest that focusing on the climate is more likely to increase amenability to change, even where this does not explicitly engage or reflect the organisation's value system. Visible features of organisational climate may be seen in its peer support, relationships with supervisors as well as rewards and incentives (Holt and Lawler, 2005).

Trying to understand and articulate factors influencing an organisation's culture and climate frequently features within serious case reviews and high profile enquiries in social care, and in the development of systemic approaches to social problems, as we shall see in Chapter Seven, which highlights cultural problems as key factors contributing to critical incidents or failures (Bostock et al, 2005; Cooper, 2005). The complexity of this area is reflected in the lack of consensus as to how to define 'culture', as every aspect of an organisation is, in fact, a part of its culture and cannot be understood as separate from it. Objective aspects may be tangible, such as rituals, leaders and stories about the organisation. Buono et al (1985) refer to its multidimensional nature, and subjective aspects which include ways in which people interact with each other, perform their work, and even their dress code, all of which are powerful determinants of individual and group behaviour. Gordon (1991) observes that an organisational culture 'is a product of successful adaptation to the environment and is, to a significant degree, an *internal* reaction to *external imperatives*' (p 404; original emphasis). Finally, Schein (1997) referred to the hidden and unconscious nature of culture. Put simply, culture is learned, shared and transmitted. The combination of assumptions, values, symbols, language and behaviours are those that manifest as the organisation's norms and values (Hafford-Letchfield, 2009). In practice, culture is contingent on relationships between service users, patients and citizens, staff and managers, which in turn interact with a wide range of dynamic factors such as professional status, class, ethnicity, gender, sexuality, and so on. These issues are picked up further in the next chapter on service users and leadership practice, and in Chapter Six on different models of support.

Although there may be several sub-cultures flourishing within an organisation, the cultural network is the primary informal means of communication. French and Bell (1995) likened this network to an iceberg, where what you see above the surface constitutes the formal organisation, consisting of structure, spans of control, rules and procedures and job descriptions. However, below the surface lies the informal and invisible organisation made up of grapevines, informal leaders, group norms and sentiments, emotional feelings, needs and relationships. These ideas are explored later in Chapter Eight, when we explore different ways in which cultivating a leadership style might shape organisational culture. Conversely, a sound philosophy, vision and management and leadership style that models values and creates a system where staff feel valued and rewarded is seen as important to creating a healthy organisational culture (Hafford-Letchfield, 2009).

Growing interest in organisational culture lies in the recognition that this may be an important factor in successful management and leadership, and asserts that one needs to understand, monitor and actively manage the culture of an organisation. This highlights the limitations of the managerialist perspective when talking about the feasibility of managed culture change. Chapter Eight on leadership development explores specifically how far education and training can influence the way in which organisational culture can be managed by promoting distributive and collaborative approaches. There is significant potential offered in tapping the potential offered by actively studying organisational culture. This provides a non-mechanistic, more flexible and imaginative approach to understanding how organisations work. Likewise, Wilson and Rosenfield (1990) distinguish two schools of thought here: first, the analytical school, which stresses the context and history of the organisation and how culture acts as a socialising force controlling the behaviour of members, and second, what they term the 'applicable school', which asserts that culture can be utilised to secure commitment to central goals and as a means of managing successful organisational change.

Different faces of organisational culture

Culture can vary at different levels, so leaders and managers may need to recognise the potential for conflict arising from multiple stakeholders, each of whom will have their own agenda or vision and be working from a different perspective and with a different set of criteria or expectations. Observations suggest that few large and complex organisations are likely to be characterised by a single dominant culture as opposed to pluralistic cultures. Where organisations are not differentiated along clear occupational lines, such as in integrated environments, there will be a number of co-existing sub-cultures. According to Scott et al (2003a), sub-cultures may share a common orientation and similar espoused values, but there may also be disparate sub-cultures that clash or maintain an uneasy symbiosis. Scott et al

(2003a) identified three types of sub-cultures in complex organisations vis-à-vis their organisational functionality:

- *Enhancing cultures:* these represent an organisational enclave in which members hold core values that are more fervent than and amplify the dominant culture, for example, specialist or expert teams that constitute centres of excellence.
- *Orthogonal cultures:* an organisational enclave that tacitly accepts the dominant culture of the organisation while simultaneously espousing its own professional values, for example, clinicians within an integrated service who maintain allegiance to their own professional body.
- *Counter-cultures:* an organisational enclave that espouses values that directly challenge the dominant culture, for example, resistance by specialists or disciplines to broader management diktats or to the limitations of professional freedom as a result of overzealous management.

These examples reveal the 'unwritten rules' within an organisation that are one of the most powerful ingredients of culture, and are described as such because they are not often openly discussed in meetings or in formal documents. This absence of discussion or infrequency of debate can lead to rules being rarely questioned or challenged, as demonstrated in the organisational case study on 'dignity' in Chapter Seven. Further, unwritten rules are usually shared by most, if not all, the members who work in a team, and provide a common way for everyone to make sense of what is going on around them, to see situations and events in similar ways and to behave accordingly. All of these factors combine to have a powerful influence on how people behave at work, often without them realising it.

Another classification introduced by Handy (1999) has offered the following typologies that are easily recognisable in the types of large bureaucratic, often statutory, services in social work:

- *Role cultures:* highly formalised, bound with regulations and paperwork; authority and hierarchy dominate relations. It has a typical pyramid structure and is easily recognisable within a number of statutory services in social work.
- *Task cultures:* the opposite, preserving a strong sense of the basic mission of the organisation; teamwork is the basis on which jobs are designed. The structure tends to be more flexible and matrix, perhaps aligned with the aims and values of a community-based voluntary sector organisation.
- *Power cultures:* have a single power source, which may be an individual or a corporate group. Control of rewards is a major source of power, utilising a web-like communications structure, and may, perhaps, be recognisable within the third sector.

Cultural differences between departments or services within an organisation can consume much of its energy, and where there are disparities, or a lack of clarity, these differences can contribute to resistance to change. Johnson (1989) talks about formal and invisible power structures, the latter of which enables people to bypass formal procedures for decision-making and the holding of informal or invisible power that can be used to block change. Reiterating and making explicit the formal structure of work and its relationship with the overall organisation also helps to clarify the different levels of responsibility and to establish the direction of the service. The formal structure may have to change in order to achieve a transformation in the way work is done. Resistance to change often reflects a lack of trust and needs to be overcome through careful listening and explanation to reduce misunderstanding.

Johnson (1989) also talks about an organisation's control systems and adapting these to accommodate new ways of working. Moving towards a culture of listening, supported by improved communication and training for those involved, promotes recognition that change does not always follow a rational, linear pattern of decision-making often assumed at a more strategic level. Organisational policies and actions must reinforce what is communicated, and behaviour must match the rhetoric. Even in organisations with strong cultures, the social distance between strategic or senior management with those working directly with service users can be both wide and tenuous. Given that culture is said to emerge from the natural social interaction of those working in the organisation, and evolves and emerges over time, it is thought that some organisations have the capacity to transform themselves from within by addressing these communication voids and are shaped to suit strategic ends (Senge, 1990). The increasing use of appreciative inquiry (AI) (Cooperrider, 1998) within social work and social care (Bostock et al, 2005) acknowledges the need for a different approach. One can begin by developing an awareness, understanding and insight into the history of an organisation, as well as the key events or contexts that helped shape its identity (Schein, 1997).

According to Handy (1999) who has written a lot about organisational theories, there is a much greater emphasis on the relationship between the four aspects of an organisation to which we should be giving our attention. Handy conceptualises these four aspects as people, systems, the task and the environment. Handy refers to this as a 'systems approach to management theory' (p 186). There are also a number of influencing factors that determine the culture of an organisation, namely, history and ownership, size, technology, goals and objectives, the environment, and, of course, the people. Moves to capitalise on research into organisational culture, and methods used to manage and enhance positive cultures within social work and social care (Bostock et al, 2005), have particularly focused on the idea of working towards becoming a 'learning organisation' through adopting methods such as AI, where the value of positive cultures is described as an important ingredient in the way organisations evolve and learn. This is discussed in more detail later in this chapter.

In summary, organisational culture literature is divided into two broad streams that capture the discussion so far. One approaches culture as an attribute or something that exists within an organisation, alongside structure and strategy. The second regards culture more globally by defining the whole character and experience of organisational life for which culture is a metaphor. The distinction between the two has important policy implications (Scott et al, 2003a) in terms of whether, like other attributes, culture is capable of being manipulated to satisfy organisational objectives and as a means of re-engineering an organisation's value system. By contrast, in taking a systems approach, culture becomes the defining context by which the meaning of organisational attributes is revealed. We look at some of these differences when we examine the application of the principles of design to the transformation of organisation systems. We also assess how features of culture inform thinking about the impacts on our own objectives for leadership, and the relationship between leadership and culture.

Working below the surface: adding in psychoanalytic perspectives to systems theory

We have touched on systems theory and some of the associated concepts, in particular, culture and climate. The application of psychoanalytical concepts to organisational systems theory enables us to think in more depth about some of the unconscious processes that occur in communication in groups and organisations, and provides a rich and powerful model to apply to organisational difficulties. Alertness to the emotional undertow of organisational life can be a powerful source of information for managers and leaders in enlarging understanding, reviewing performance, foreseeing challenges and opportunities, and guiding decisions and action (Armstrong, 2004). The capacity to work in a way that attends to resistance and negative processes in organisations, combined with systemic approaches, has been described by some theorists as 'working below the surface'. By hypothesising about the emotional experience of organisations one is able to shed light on the challenges and dilemmas facing the organisation, and provide a source of understanding and insight into the forces that determine its nature and ultimately its fate. As we saw in the debates about leadership in Chapter One, it could be argued that the rolling back of the welfare state has since resulted in more competitive, mistrustful and paranoid forces within society that can be mirrored and perpetuated within social work organisations. For example, globalisation, intensified by the IT revolution, increased mistrust, exemplified through the introduction of managerialism and new public management and business principles. These have led to increased mistrust, accompanied by rigorous and imposed criteria of performance management and accountability.

The degree to which the boundaries of an organisation are made more permeable has allowed both the creation of partnerships across boundaries and the intrusion of external authority structures. An example of this lies in the many new agencies of inspection, regulation and performance management that represent greater government intrusion across this boundary. A decline in the individual's trust in care organisations, including professional bodies, together with a competitive environment has perpetuated fear that an organisation will compete to seek its own ends rather than the benefit of its users and community

(Cooper, 2005). This change of environment brings problems and issues to leaders and the processes they need to adapt. In Chapter One it was suggested that some concepts of leadership are idealised (O'Reilly and Reed, 2010), and questions were raised about how they might actually adapt to be more effective and creative. Some have argued (Armstrong, 2004) that a great deal can be learned from the individual's emotional and irrational response to the organisation and by moving away from conceptualising these as a source of disturbance in organisational functioning; if we regard emotional experience as a rich source of information, much is to be gained.

In considering leadership, those working in unstable, intrusive environments may look to their leaders for support that requires the leader to mobilise personal qualities, including a capacity to create a psychological contract between leaders and followers. Cooper (2005), for example, asserts the need to 'read beneath the surface' in his analysis of the outcomes of a report following the public inquiry into the death of a young child, Victoria Climbié, at the hands of her carers in the UK in 2000. Cooper uses a psychoanalytic approach to analyse some of the dynamics involved in this inquiry, and makes links between the disjuncture between public policy, organisational climate and individual frontline practice in relation to safeguarding children. These have been picked up by Munro (2011) in her subsequent systemic approach to safeguarding work with children.

Cooper (2005) highlighted the common discourse that can occur in the public and community sector, for example, the everyday acceptance and understanding of how stories are told and retold about organisations. Discourse analysis research primarily studies the way abuse of social power, dominance and inequality is enacted, reproduced and resisted by text and talks in a social and political context. Those interested in critical discourse analysis aim to take an explicit position, and thus want to understand, expose and ultimately resist social inequality. Having access to or control over public discourse and communication is an important 'symbolic' resource, as is the case for knowledge and information. Most people only have active control over everyday talk with family members, friends or colleagues, but this control is more passive when it comes to media usage, as illustrated by Cooper. In most situations, ordinary people are more or less passive targets of text or talk, for example, in the way their managers or other authoritative bodies refer to them or inform them of what they should be doing. On the other hand, members of more powerful social groups and institutions, and especially their leaders, have more or less exclusive access to, and control over, one or more types of public discourse. Thus, leaders and managers in the care sector are often seen as being able to control discourse, both within the organisation and in the way the organisation is expected to respond to politicians, policy and other public political discourse. Controlling and determining the definition of the communicative situation, deciding on the time and place of the communicative event, or on which participants may or must be present, and in which roles, or what knowledge or opinions they should (or not) have, and which social actions may or must be accomplished, goes hand in hand with leadership roles. We now turn to look at AI, a method used to promote a more systemic and conscious approach to communicative action which is increasingly being adopted within social work and social care, and that can be used by leaders as a more empowering approach to managing change (Bostock et al, 2005).

Appreciative inquiry

Using concepts of design to stimulate creativity in social care

Research has highlighted the importance of people feeling motivated by their work through involvement and challenge, even where high pressure exists, and asserts that creativity can still occur if the time pressure is interpreted as meaningful urgency rather than arbitrary deadlines or management pressure (Steel and Hampton, 2005). Cooperrider (1998) described how positive images are capable of generating direct action, and his identification of the 'positive principle' (Cooperrider and Whitney, 2001) referred to the utility of positive feelings for building and sustaining momentum for change. Other studies have demonstrated that the ratio of positive to negative talk is related to the quality of relationships, cohesion, decision-making, creativity and the overall success of various social systems (Fredrickson and Losada, 2005), and builds on theories of broadening and building positive emotions to develop resilience as well as generative change that is useful in organisational development interventions.

In Chapter One we compared the functions of management with those of leadership, suggesting that leadership is different in the way it seeks adaptive and constructive change. Different situations may call for different types of leadership behaviour, and as we have seen so far, leaders should adapt their styles to the situation and to the motivational needs of those they are leading. Communication skills from a distributed or participated leadership perspective tend to utilise techniques and approaches that harness the potential for being curious and by remaining neutral in order to maximise the participation of those they work with and to encourage their participation. AI is one such approach associated with positive psychology, and has been used to challenge the problem-orientated approach historically used in public and community services, particularly in relation to inquiries into serious incidents.

David Cooperrider and Suresh Srivastva developed AI in the 1980s as a framework for initiating or managing change, focusing on the positive, personal and organisational attributes that may fuel change. It is an action research model to empower and liberate from the bottom up, and also a change management tool to simultaneously discipline and control (top down). According to Cooperrider and Shrivastva (1999) it seeks out the best of *what is* to help ignite the collective imagination of *what might be*, which is why it refers to 'dreaming' in the process. Earlier we looked at the importance of organisational culture. AI attempts to engage with a capacity-building process that begins by valuing the organisation and the culture in which it is embedded, by:

- learning about the organisation – its relationships and environment;
- identifying through questions and curiosity and building on existing strengths rather than examining in detail problems and deficiencies;
- putting organisations back in touch with their 'deepest living values';
- helping the organisation to create its niche by identifying its collective hopes and dreams and then designing a process for realising them.

It is not unusual in public sector organisations to note that there are sometimes differences between espoused and lived values in everyday events, which is usually due to the difficult and challenging demands that confront social work and social care. Cooperrider and Shrivastva (1999) have defined the key principles (or beliefs) of AI as being based on, first, the constructionist principle, built around a keen appreciation of the power of language and discourse of all types. These include words to metaphors and narrative forms, which create our sense of reality. Cooperrider and Shrivastva (1999) asserted that our realities are constructed on the basis of our previous experience. Second, there is a principle of simultaneity by which they refer to the types of questions we might ask. These questions set the stage for what we find and what we discover, so again, the power of questioning is revealed here. This source of 'data' in turn becomes the linguistic material, the stories, out of which the future is conceived, conversed about and constructed.

Three other principles are described within an AI approach. The 'poetic principle' refers to the stories told within the system that we are in and how this is constantly co-authored and open to infinite interpretations about the past, present and future. Like poetry, this provides a creative and constant source of learning. The 'anticipatory principle' aims to make best use of the infinite human resources that we have, for generating constructive organisational change. This emphasis on the collective imagination and discourse about the future is thought to be capable of guiding the current behaviour of the organisation. It builds on the idea that what we anticipate determines what we will find, in a kind of invest to save type of approach. Finally, the 'positive principle' of AI follows the process in which the image of reality is enhanced and to plan actions that can be aligned with the positive image achieved.

Table 2.1 summarises some of the key differences between problem-solving and AI.

Table 2.1: Key differences between problem-solving and appreciative inquiry

Conventional problem-solving	Appreciative inquiry
Identification of problem	Appreciating and valuing the best of 'what is'
Analysis of what course to take	Envisioning 'what might be'
Analysis of possible solutions	Dialoguing/determining 'what should be'
Develop action plans where the basic assumption is that an organisation is a problem to be solved	Innovating/creating 'what will be' where the basic assumption is that an organisation is a mystery to be embraced

The stages of AI are often abbreviated to the 4Ds: *discovering*, which enthuses feeling; *dreaming*, which inspires imagination; *designing*, which invokes innovatory concepts; and *delivering*, which commits to making things happen in practice.

> By beginning with discovering what already works well, we capture positive feelings about achievement and contributions which have already really made a difference. By making space for dreaming, we free the imagination to envisage an ideal future. This utopian exercise lifts us out of the immediate problems we are striving to resolve and inspires fresh perspectives and solutions. By next harnessing creative thinking at the design stage we are enabled to generate options that would help make our dream a reality and reconceive the way in which we operate. And by culminating in sustained action, individuals, teams and whole organisations are mobilised to deliver lasting change. (McAllister and Luckcock, 2009, p 31)

Appreciative leadership

Within an AI approach everyone is involved in the process by working, learning, changing and acting together, and this is one method that facilitates the participatory and distributed leadership discussed in Chapter One. AI has gained currency in social work and social care because it enhances morale where participants work together and contributions are valued. Managing mistakes and challenges is a popular area to introduce AI as it regards these as opportunities for learning, and pending long drawn-out inquiries traditional to the public and community services, change can begin straightaway as opposed to waiting for an externally imposed verdict (Bostock et al, 2005). Rather, reporting and dissemination are outcomes from the process of AI, resulting in shorter timescales and cost-effectiveness. More importantly it does not seek to identify individuals as problems, but in a systems approach it looks at the interdependence between individuals, their teams and organisations, where the climate facilitates each person's input, opinion and feelings. As the term implies, creating a shared vision is prioritised where contribution to this is gladly received and appreciated. The constant demand to improve services and to improve outcomes for stakeholders is an imperative for appreciative leadership.

Performance management and inspections regimes hold us to account by confronting us with the gap between progress and outstanding issues. This can lead to more defensive responses and to losing our sense of idealism away from placing people at the centre of change processes. AI does not start from a defensive position and has many applications, for example, in coaching and mentoring, more productive team meetings, team and service development, multi-agency work and service user engagement. Some critics of AI have highlighted the contingencies that affect it given that AI does not magically overcome poor communication, insensitive facilitation or unaddressed organisational politics. Bushe (2010) argues that the core of AI lies in its generativity, and that it is therefore potentially transformational, particularly at the dream phase. Others have cited the importance of planning after the AI event by integrating it into their organisational processes or capturing significant benefits following the AI summit, and to make it part of their process rather than projects (Stellnberger, 2010). Narrative is an important factor given that service improvement is a continual, iterative process. Being able to see what the team has talked about, what they have done and how that relates to positive improvement is an important part of validating the work and sustaining the effort. Bushe (2010) argues that the 'positive nature' of AI alone is unlikely to overcome all the obstacles it might face, and consequently wisdom from traditional organisational development needs to be applied competently, that is, AI is still vulnerable to all the organisational change variables. In creating awareness around issues and obstacles that could interfere with an AI intervention, an organisation gains a position where it can identify these more easily and, if necessary, develop approaches and strategies to counteract them. Finally, despite its increasing application, AI remains under-researched in terms of critique, and Grant and Humphries (2006) suggest that combining an evaluation of AI with critical theory may bridge an apparent paradox between the negative associated with the former and the positive focus of the latter. They suggest an integrated use of AI and critical theory that they call the 'critical appreciative process' (CAP) to deepen insight and recognition of the complexity in human endeavours.

Creative cultures and the principles of design

Most people understand creativity, at a general level, to be the process of generating something new or original or by bringing existing ideas together in a different way to develop something new and of value. Daly (2010) has explored the application of concepts from the discipline of 'design' more frequently associated with the innovation, construction, evaluation and distribution of 'products' and the possibilities for social work and social care organisations. He proposes that we take on board the influence of design theories and methodologies in connection with the construction, development, delivery and evaluation of social care services, together with an exploration of organisational structure (Daly, 2010). The capacity to think about problems afresh from first principles, to discover common threads amidst the seemingly complex and disparate, to experiment or visualise different scenarios, these are some of the features of more creative approaches to working through contemporary social problems. Even if creativity does not result in innovation or yield successful outcomes, creative thinking can still add value by leading others to think differently, and as illustrated in the discussion about learning organisations, an unsuccessful innovation can also lead to learning (Steele and Hampton, 2005).

Charitable bodies such as the Design Council (www.designcouncil.org.uk) have asserted the promotion of broader concepts of design to transform communities, business and the environment, and suggest that this approach creates value by stimulating innovation, improving the built environment and tackling complex social issues. The application of design principles offers a more creative approach to problem-solving with the power to tackle complex and pressing social issues by coming from a more person-centred perspective, common to those principles currently driving social care, to encourage new perspectives and to generate powerful ideas as opposed to a traditional, linear approach. The design approach is different in the way it uses a pragmatic approach to solving challenges, recognising that people need practical help to overcome barriers or to move towards making ideas more tangible through an iterative process of testing and refinement. As is common with approaches used in design, prototyping from the start leads to real and rapid impact. Designers, for example, take time to identify those who are affected, to understand their needs, wants and capabilities, and build on ideas of collaboration (Design Council and Warwick Business School, 2012).

These may echo with the challenges that face leaders in social work and social care where new policies might be implemented instrumentally without sufficient discussion about how they might be implemented more creatively. There are some clear examples of these in social work and social care, such as the challenges experienced in the implementation of personalisation in social care (Hafford-Letchfield, 2010), and taking forward relationship-based practices in safeguarding work and other areas of government reform to take ideas forward. Jumping from research to practice and grappling with evidence-based practice has been a major challenge where social work academics are criticised for not making research findings or evidence available or accessible enough (Gordon et al, 2009). Similar critiques of practice assert that practitioners neglect evidence and research (DCSF, 2009) calling for an iterative process that expands on our knowledge of both people and the environment and embedding design principles in research from the start so that projects are built on empirical evidence from human behaviour and building more crucial partnerships. This approach is exemplified in 'paradigm-busting' (Leonard and Frankel, 2012) thinking, in examples of how design approaches might work in relation to collaboration around social problems. These might include different approaches to health and wellbeing in communities where there is a challenge to reduce the incidents of deaths from lack of activity, such as cancer and diabetes (Lee et al, 2012), against the influence of inactivity from more sedentary lifestyles. Design can develop new ways in which people can be active at work to reduce health risks and increase productivity. Another community example might be where half of men and a third of all women between the ages of 18-24 are classified as binge drinkers (IAS, 2010), looking at how the design of community social spaces can be used to break down and challenge norms in certain social groups to create more positive norms and to keep the social benefits of sharing a drink (Design Council and Warwick University, 2012).

Thinking through design: a case study

The following case study provides an opportunity to look at the concept of design in social work in more detail. Social care and design both use 'practice' methods that include end user views and expectations. However, they also experience difficulties in evaluating outcomes because the experience of receiving *care* and *design* is 'personal'. Some examples need to be provided and some discussion about the challenges this presents for design and social care. This needs to be balanced by research into what people say they want from design and social care. The way in which care services are organised, managed and delivered has, over time, developed from largely bureaucratic, hierarchical structures, to increasingly flexible, innovative and responsive services that reflect the needs and requirements of people using those services. One of the main responses by governments has been to look to the private sector to increase user choice and quality by fostering competition. Design has aided this transformation, along with other social science subjects that have informed and affected the way in which services have been designed. However, it has been policy developments that have brought service users, patients and clients into direct contact with the practice of professionals who deliver services, thereby creating a new context for professional practice. Increasingly 'end users' experiences' are 'factored in' to the way in which professionals and those leading and managing services organise and run services. Day et al (2000), for example, have illustrated how the design of the physical environment is being increasingly recognised as an important aid in the care of people with dementia, and has been shown to have a therapeutic effect in promoting wellbeing and functionality.

The photograph of the two pathways (see Photograph 2.1) illustrates a common difficulty and tension within design. The landscape designer designing and constructing this footpath has placed a sense of aesthetics above predictable outcome. The two fences represent boundaries and are physical barriers clearly demanding compliance. Within these hard boundaries there is considerable room for choice. A softer boundary has been constructed by the paved route that follows the curve of the outside fence and is more aesthetically pleasing to the eye. The smaller informal path on the left illustrates the actual path of the user. Such paths are termed 'desire lines'. By prioritising aesthetics over usability the designer has, perhaps inadvertently, created a more aesthetically displeasing end result. This image could also be used to examine and illustrate the use of influence and power, and how users have reconstructed this by making practical choices. In this example, the users have a choice. They can clearly see where they are supposed to go, but make a choice. They create a 'workaround'.

Photograph 2.1: Taking an alternative path

Daly (2010) suggests that there are adequate design solutions to this problem. These would fall into four broad categories:

1. Do nothing: let the public's collective feet decide the path, as they are going to do this anyway. The disadvantage of doing this would be one of utility and aesthetics – the roughly worn informal unpaved path would become waterlogged and muddy in the rain and unpleasant to use.
2. The design process could be extended and the designer could wait to see where the public's feet had collectively worn a path, and then pave this with a hard surface; the practicality of use would be achieved, but probably at the expense of a general sense of aesthetics.
3. One could enforce the aesthetic, by planting low sharp-leaved or thorny shrubs on the left-hand side of the paved path, preventing all other routes. A water feature would achieve the same effect.
4. Alternatively, the problem could be seen as an opportunity to synthesise pragmatic consideration, user feedback and aesthetic considerations. Such a solution would seek to extend the paved area to include both the formal and informal path and to align the edges of this with the curve described by the fence.

Failure to create a solution would produce an inadequate design, but is not uncommon. Fortunately, users of misplaced paths are usually free, within some limits, to create alternative solutions. This is frequently not the case when inadequate pathways and processes are created within systems delivering social care services. Instead, both user and professional can be forced down a pathway they are reluctant to travel in order to get to the service at the end. Such practice often creates tensions, conflicts and inefficiencies that obscure the creation and delivery of adequate services. There could very well be logical and pragmatic reasons to force a process down a particular pathway. To stretch the analogy further, the landscape designer insisting the path follow the curve of the fence on the right may be doing more than satisfying a sense of aesthetics; it may be that a particular hazed is to be avoided, drainage could be inadequate and the designer is concerned for travellers' comfort. Similarly, forcing both professionals and users to tightly defined pathways of assessment and provision within social care settings may have the best of intentions; these could include monitoring purposes, financial constraint or preventing solutions being prematurely selected. However, in both scenarios, where users are channelled it will be important that the reasons for doing so are overt. Not being open about intent will say much about the relationship between designer and user. Such a relationship is made poorer by avoiding opportunities for feedback, participation and co-construction. The only feedback that is likely in such circumstances is non-compliance or not using a service.

Piecemeal design and the dangers of adding too much

Few would argue that it is important for services to respond to changing need and for continued improvements to be made; however, there can be a danger of adapting and adding to a service which may be improvements in themselves, but could well be dysfunctional or inefficient when the service is examined in its entirety. It is difficult for leaders and managers in social care charged with the responsibility to improve services and to ever increase efficiency to know when to make adjustments to services, when to add extra components and when to redesign the whole service from scratch. The call to redesign services, for example, following the recommendation from Munro (2011) to the UK government in relation to child protection services, must be taken as just that, not merely improved or added to, but redesigned and reconstructed. However well intentioned, piecemeal reform can, over time, if not monitored closely, produce counterproductive results. The ability to adapt to changing needs as these occur can highlight the flexibility of an organisation and is seen as virtuous. Indeed, responsive service provision and reflective practice have become a 'mantra' in the field of social care. Such adaptability would need to be informed by the interrelating functions of the whole organisation rather than 'add-ons' that seem to be adequate solutions at the time.

Fostering an organisational learning climate and knowledge transfer

Organisations that embark on explicit and organisation-wide learning strategies have been referred to by Senge (1990) as 'learning organisations', although this does not take into account the role of spontaneous, accidental and unplanned learning through the day-to-day life of the organisation. We have already alluded to the direct relationship between climate and culture and how it enables managers to achieve the above areas of competency and capability. James et al (2007) suggest the term 'organisational climate' to refer to the estimations that people have of their jobs, co-workers, leaders, pay, performance expectations, opportunities and equity that have an impact on the individual's wellbeing. The way in which people describe environmental objects in relation to themselves is seen as important aspects of culture. Some of these issues are referred to above in the discussion of organisational design issues. Environmental objects are not only physical, but include variables with a subjective, judgemental component that can be operationally defined, for example, a climate for learning. Senge (1990) wrote that a 'learning organisation' values, and derives competitive advantage from, continuing learning, both at an individual and collective level. He proposed that people put aside their old ways of thinking (mental models), learn to be open with others (personal mastery), understand how their organisation really works (systems thinking), form a plan everyone can agree on (shared vision), and then work together to achieve that vision (team learning). Given that leadership theory places great emphasis on the interaction between leaders and followers (Bass, 1990; Avolio et al, 1999), enabling managers to develop an authentic approach to leading is cited as desirable and effective in achieving positive and enduring outcomes in organisations, but poses a challenge to teach and assess. Within the current climate, unless leadership education strives towards a more transformational experience, its effects may readily dissipate, leaving behind just fine rhetoric. Authentic leaders are thought to be those who know and act on their true values, beliefs and strengths, while helping others to do the same by establishing a climate and culture for learning. How managers develop these concepts in practice raises the question of whether leadership can be taught, and which models or styles should be emphasised. Pedagogic approaches in leadership development that draw on the arts (Leonard et al, 2013); Hafford-Letchfield and Harper, 2013), or on psychodynamic perspectives (Menzies-Lyth, 1979; Ruch, 2011) as well as a sound evidence base, may provide tools to help facilitate these areas of capability, and are discussed in more detail later, in Chapter Eight.

The proliferation of collaboration in and between the public, private and not-for-profit sectors is typically viewed as offering the prospect of delivering outcomes and synergies seen as multiframed and resistant to conventional and optimal solutions (Williams and Sullivan, 2011). As organisations acquire knowledge about the management of collaborative processes, about each other's cultures, operating systems, management styles and ways of organising, this interorganisational knowledge transfer becomes important to capitalise on, in its own right. Williams and Sullivan (2011) have explored what form leadership should take to address the challenges arising from the particular demands of promoting and sustaining effective learning and knowledge management processes within such a collaborative context, and whether models, process and tools can be transferred between different sectors when they are very different. The literature is comparatively silent on the role of learning and knowledge transfer with a lack of focus at an interorganisational level, particularly given that theories about leadership are also frequently contextualised within single organisations. There is debate around whether learning is an individual or collective phenomenon where some have argued that knowledge is only created by individuals and it is the role of organisations to support them as opposed to individuals who are active agents of organisational learning (Hafford-Letchfield et al, 2008). Theories of organisational learning include an analysis of structural conditions such as cultures, power, relationships, norms and rules that mediate the process; different levels of learning such as technical, systemic and strategic; and different types of learning, as described in Argyris and Schon's (1990) single and double-loop learning theories. Again, this has become a theme in subsequent attempts to reform social work and the reclaiming of professionalism and its contributions to organisational practice (Munro, 2011).

Learning and promoting a culture of safety

Earlier discussion on culture suggested that leadership has a role in promoting systematic learning and improvement that is visible and tangible to frontline staff by being present and active, and consistent participants in the dialogue. Those working in the front line routinely deal with defects and barriers to their ability to deliver optimal care, which leads to shortcuts and what Leonard and Frankel (2012) refer to as 'workarounds'. These reflect the inherent system failures evident at the front line of care, and can be valuable sources of learning which, if not capitalised on, can normalise shortcuts in safe procedure and reinforce the perception that leaders are not really concerned about these problems. Leonard and Frankel further suggest that leaders can profoundly influence a culture of safety through their support of a learning system – a visible structure that captures the concerns and defects from those providing services at the front line – which demonstrates that leadership is interested in their concerns, the information is acted on, and, when the issue is resolved, that there is systematic feedback to the people who gave them information. They describe a robust safety culture as the:

> ... combination of attitudes and behaviours that best manages the inevitable dangers created when humans, who are inherently fallible, work in extraordinarily complex environments. (2012, p 3)

They further put forward the following attitudinal and behaviour norms as offering protective factors of which leadership becomes the keeper and guardian of the learning system that promotes these:

1. Psychological safety that ensures speaking up is not associated with being perceived as ignorant, incompetent, critical or disruptive by treating people with respect when they do (leaders must create an environment where no one is hesitant to voice a concern and caregivers know that they will be treated with respect when they do).
2. A sense of organisational fairness, where caregivers know that they are accountable for being capable, conscientious and not engaging in unsafe behaviour, but are not held accountable for system failures.
3. Working towards a learning system where engaged leaders hear service users'/ patients' and frontline caregivers' concerns regarding defects that interfere with the delivery of safe care, and promote improvement to increase safety and reduce waste. This should involve a visible display of the issues important to the delivery of safe, high quality care, information that reflects the work done to improve safety and how it is being tested, and active dialogue among caregivers in working to drive improvement. Leonard and Frankel (2012) describe this as a visibility board, but different methods could be used to support this process, such as debriefing to close the loop and sustaining team behaviours.

Reason (1998, p 295) highlights that safety culture 'is a concept whose time has come', stating that there is both a challenge and an opportunity to 'develop a clearer theoretical understanding of these organisational issues to create a principled basis for more effective culture-enhancing practices.' It is vitally important to social work and social care in how we conceptualise and identify the organisation's safety culture, as this represents a critical factor influencing multiple aspects of human performance and organisational safety. Chapter Seven focuses on the concept of 'dignity' in an organisational context, and highlights and develops the idea that a culture of safe care requires the enduring value and prioritisation of service user, staff and public safety by each and every member of the organisation, no matter at what level. Using a systemic lens to examine the consequence of when leadership fails, we reinforce the extent to which individuals and groups must commit to personal responsibility for safety; act to preserve, enhance and communicate safety concerns; and strive to actively learn, adapt and modify (both individual and organisational) behaviour based on lessons learned from mistakes and serious case reviews. In summary, a culture of safety combines key issues such as personal commitment, responsibility, communication and learning in ways that are strongly influenced by senior leaders but must include the behaviours of everyone in the organisation that builds on the capacity for distributory leadership.

Summary

This chapter has considered the issues of culture and climate examined largely through a systems approach, and considered the relationship of context and different aspects of culture in achieving a distributed and participatory approach to leadership. This is developed further in Chapter Three where we consider service users and leadership practice through a conceptual framework of co-production. Distributed leadership cuts two ways. On the one hand, it involves devolution of authority downwards, and on the other, it involves an evolution of accountability upwards (Huffington et al, 2004). This is more than delegation of leaders to their followers, but a systems approach brings into view the boundaries and capabilities of the organisation as a whole in relation to one's own group sphere of decision-making and action. This means keeping in mind the whole as well as the sum of its parts. Some of the key skills that leaders require are related to being more aware of what leverage they have in any situation and having the tools to find out the different story lines at both the macro and micro level. Thinking through these has led us to look the importance of narrative in social work and social care, and specifically at different types of hypothesising and questioning, as illustrated in the application of AI. All of these are linked to inquiry and reflection in practice to achieve what Northouse (2011) referred to as 'authentic leadership'.

THREE

Service users and leadership practice

Introduction

As an active researcher, and an 'on, off' mental health service user for 20 years, Carr (2010a) suggests that while she doesn't know much about leadership theory, she does have knowledge about the impact of good or bad leadership on service users. When commenting on the decision to close a local emergency mental health clinic, Carr stated: 'This may well have been a tough decision for the leaders involved, but perhaps not as tough as the decision to stay alive when living had become unbearable' (Carr, 2010a, p 21). Closing an emergency service, she further suggests, 'shows how leaders can become detached from the human consequences of their style, values, decision making and exercise of power' (Carr, 2010a, p 20–24). For service users like Carr, leadership needs to demonstrate humanity and social justice as well as empathy with service users who are living their lives in difficult circumstances. Recent policy developments argue for greater involvement of service users in power-sharing and decision-making; this can be very challenging to deliver in practice, however, particularly when service providers may be reluctant to share power, or when they are suspected of neglecting or abusing a vulnerable child or adult. These tensions (care and control) are evident in many areas of care work. In reviewing leadership and management theories, Lawler and Bilson (2010) developed a theoretical framework that is used in this chapter to explore leadership from a service user perspective. The framework allows for some consideration of the different leadership and management approaches used, and reflects on service user experiences of leadership. The review of certain theories makes it possible to understand how leaders might become detached from the human consequences of their decision-making, and to identify which approaches might prevent this. Prior to this examination, we review some of the key research underpinning how we have conceptualised and utilised service user expectations and experiences so far.

Service user expectations and experiences

During research carried out in England into what adult service users thought that leaders and managers in adult social care services should do, the participants identified the following principles:
- Treat us with respect, and support our choices.
- Enable us to access and/or manage the services we need.

- Understand what dignity means in very practical terms and make it a reality.
- Show the way, keep people on board and together.
- Listen to us, make change happen and get results through the best us of people, money and other resources. (Skills for Care, 2008, p 1)

These views reflect an approach to leadership and management practice that is participative and informed as well as rights and valued-based. In Chapter Seven there is a greater consideration of what is meant by 'dignity', but for now it is important to highlight how ideas about dignity, respect and choice inform service user expectations along with the need for staff who can demonstrate effective management and leadership. Other research into the experiences of children in England using care services and their expectations from social workers and the service revealed the following requirements from social workers:

- Respect our individuality.
- Give us more say in planning our care.
- Enable us to have more influence over decisions about contact with our families.
- Provide easier access to social workers when we need them.
- Enable us to be treated the same as any other child. (CWDC, 2012, p 33)

The children in this study also said that they wanted someone who was willing to listen to them, to show empathy, to demonstrate that they were reliable (keeping promises, turning up on time, and so on), who would take action, respect confidence and view them as a whole person (not just talk about the problems they faced) (CWDC, 2012). These expectations highlight the importance of humanity in relationship-based work, and the link between effective management and service leadership (for example, 'show the way' and 'take action'). Both examples also mirror what Carr (2010a, p. 22–24) was articulating earlier. Leaders need to make the right decisions, demonstrating human and emotional skills, and engage in power-sharing with service users. In order for this to happen, leadership practices need to be dispersed, and be related and responsible rather than remote and transactional. 'If the top is still holding onto power, how the bottom can exercise any?' (Carr, 2010a, p 20). The introduction of government policies that aspire to give service users more control, power and choice, however, has challenged the traditional view of 'heroic' leader and opened up debates about how service users can be engaged in changing the culture, structure, delivery and types of services. It is therefore timely to examine ideas about leadership from the perspective of people who use services.

It is clear from the research findings that the experiences and expectations of adult and children's groups differ in some ways (for example, the degree of independence expected), but there is some consistency (for example, the need for dignity, respect and empowerment is notable in both groups, and there is a requirement for those delivering services to be responsive and to ensure that services are tailored to individual needs). Service users are a diverse group, and as a result they expect and are likely to experience services differently, and engage with services differently. Simmons (2009) developed a model that illustrates the 'subjective' and 'objective' aspects of service user involvement, which can help us to understand these differences and to examine the impact on dispersed leadership practices.

Figure 3.1 demonstrates Simmons' model (2009) of user involvement. According to Simmons (2009), service users can be grouped as either auto–exclusion (A) or delegation (B). In the case of A, they are *individuals* who identify themselves as having a voice, but may not care enough about the service or want to use their voice, while in the case of (B), service users may see their influence as one step removed, that is, they seek to use their voice via politicians or senior officials. These perspectives contrast with *collective* approaches that emphasise service users who see themselves as directly connected to a service (C), making rational choices about their needs and services, and may use a complaints system if things go wrong. Service users who see themselves in a participative process (D) are more likely to work with service providers on specific service user issues.

Figure 3.1: Simmons' model of user involvement

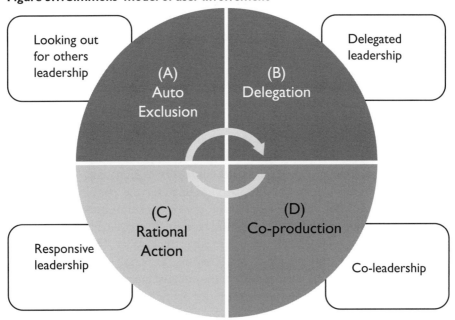

Source: Adapted from Simmons (2009)

If we take this model and think about it in terms of the leadership expectations of service users, it is possible to differentiate between the different service users and the expectations they have of services. Looked-after children, for example, may not consistently engage with services during their time in care (A), but may need leadership from professionals or other workers who can 'speak for them' until they can, or want to do it for themselves. In the same way, there may be good reasons why older people in care services may prefer to delegate the responsibility of designing their care to others, for example, terminally ill patients (B), but they may need workers to ensure good quality care in these circumstances. These are important distinctions because it is assumed that customers are 'active participants' who are making rational choices about their care, whereas some service users are unable or unwilling to act as customers. Vulnerable people do not always make rational choices, for example, an abused and/or neglected child may be reluctant to talk about what is happening to them. The worker will need to be engaged in leadership to protect the most vulnerable and to ensure that their needs are identified and met. In quadrants (C) and (D) the leadership approaches are defined by the nature of the relationship between the service user and the service; for example, the customer, concerned with the transaction between supplier and themselves, may wish a speedy response to a query or complaint (C), while in the case of (D), the service user may wish to co-design a complaints process to improve the way in which services are delivered. In all of these examples it is possible to consider the customer/service user as a leader of their own care, and to see a leadership role for the staff who come into contact with them. Simmons' (2009) model allows us to think about service users as a diverse group, with different needs and expectations. The model reminds us that social workers will adapt their practice to reflect the context and expectations of those receiving care services. The leadership practices that are needed, therefore, are different in all four quadrants, but the approach adopted by social workers recognises the principles of social justice, human rights and empowerment, even though these elements will be worked with in different ways.

Beresford's (2007) research into the role and tasks of social workers highlighted what service users and carers valued most about the social work approaches reflecting on three elements. First, service users said that they valued social workers who adopted a social approach (seeing service users and carers within a broad social context and responding accordingly); second, social workers who engaged in relationship-based practice (the use of a relationship to build trust, empower and support people's self-empowerment); and finally, those whose personal qualities made encounters a positive experience (warmth, respect, non-judgemental, treating people equally, listening to people, being trustworthy and open, and so on). These elements bring together qualities of humanity and respect but are informed by an understanding of service users' lives. Beresford's (2007) research also highlighted what service users didn't like about social work, which included a perceived increase in social workers' use of power and control in response to political demands, particularly in relation to children and families.

The report raised questions about whether social workers should be engaged in helping individuals to transform their lives, particularly when the requirement to change might be a condition for a service. It highlights how it is possible for a diverse range of people to have different views and expectations of social work, reinforcing the position that social work is a contested activity. For social workers, the challenge is to ensure that individuals are treated fairly and well. Professional leadership must therefore be informed and practised appropriately.

Payne (2005, p 10) developed a model of social work that identified three approach]es to practice, which is now explored in relation to professional leadership. While these approaches are presented here as discrete dimensions, in reality social work roles may reflect a combination of any of the three outlined in Table 3.1.

Table 3.1 : Three approaches to practice

Approach	Characteristics
1) Maintenance	Helping to deliver or ensure access to a service
2) Therapeutic helping	Helping to achieve potential growth and development
3) Transformational	Helping to address inequalities and to effect change

Source: Adapted from Payne (2005)

If we look at Payne's maintenance approach (1), it might be argued that this is a functional role as it supports a transaction between a customer/service user and a supplier. However, a social worker will be aware that anyone they come into contact with may belong to any of the categories identified by Simmons (2009), and as such the service user will require a tailored response from them. Social workers are trained to use a relationship-based approach, that is, 'the professional relationship is the medium through which the practitioner can engage with and intervene in the complexity of an individual's internal and external world' (Wilson et al, 2008, p. 7). When undertaking an assessment, for example, the social worker will be aware that the time allotted for the assessment may be short, and that the outputs from the assessment may appear transactional, but the social worker will engage in leadership behaviours. Dustin (2007, p 85) gives an example of a care manager who used her professional discretion to take a day out of her schedule to move a man from his home to a residential facility, saying that, 'He needed time to accept and adjust to this fundamental life change.' For some social workers employed in therapeutic helping roles (2), the leadership role requires the worker to enable individuals to develop personal insights and to achieve personal change. This may, for example, involve working with a service user who is seeking support to stop harmful behaviours such as substance misuse. Social workers can work with individuals in a therapeutic relationship and helping role to support an individual to make the necessary changes they need to achieve. There is an expectation that social workers will support individuals to achieve change rather than impose change, but there are circumstances where social workers may have to exercise control, for example, where a court might require parents to change abusive behaviours to keep children safe, or the children will need to be removed. These situations require a social worker to work in a respectful way with the family, providing members with the necessary support to enable them to change. Leadership practice that uses a relationship-based approach to build the necessary trust and self-belief that can bring about change is in keeping with social work values. In adopting the transformational approach, (3) workers may be involved in challenging social and structural inequalities which require professional leadership, for example, supporting women who have experienced domestic violence and/ or abuse to get a home after leaving an abusive partner and spending recovery time in a refuge. In all three dimensions the leadership practice will be negotiated through the relationships developed through practice. In summary, service users and workers will be affected by, and in some circumstances will be able to affect, the context within which care is provided, and we now turn to look specifically at the impact of the context in which leadership is practised in relation to these relationships.

Context for leadership practice with service users

As already outlined in previous chapters, the policy context within which leadership is practised in social care has been changing. There have been two key global developments that have an impact on service users. First, social movements, such as 'disability rights', have demanded that governments ensure equality and social justice in every aspect of public life. This has generated legislation and policies that recognise limited service user rights, for example, the right to be assessed. As we have seen in earlier chapters, alongside this, neoliberalist ideas have supported the development of social care markets as a way of delivering consumer choice, independence and control. This development has transformed some care organisations into 'quasi-business institutions', and some services have developed in response to customer demands. Not everyone, however, has welcomed these developments. Harris (2003) argues that in care markets where customers pursue their own interests, this may be at the expense of others in cash-strapped care systems. In addition, consumerist approaches and practices do not transfer power or control to service users, but rather providers must ensure demands are met. This does not sit well with some service user movements where democratic principles are valued and service user participation is expected, but in consumerist-based services participation may be limited or denied. By contrast, democratic approaches are concerned with relationships between people, and service user participation is associated with citizenship, and is valued by service user movements and groups (Beresford, 2000; 2003). Lawler and Bilson (2010) take the view that the competitive management and leadership approaches that are necessary for organisations that are focused on increasing market share are not appropriate in social work. For-profit businesses need leaders who can exploit opportunities, but most people would take the view that vulnerable service users are not simply a business opportunity. The introduction of policies such as *personalisation* (HMG, 2007) in England has created spaces for the development of new and often unregulated services, which may be purchased by customers with personal budgets who then manage the service. In contrast, Ranson and Stewart (1994) say that for some service users, the option to choose a service is not available to them, although they access a service, for example, prisoners. It is for these and many other reasons that leadership is context-specific and needs to be tailored to the specific situation.

According to Tony Blair (2010), many politicians support market-based care solutions as a pragmatic choice. As the British Prime Minister who, during his own government, accelerated welfare reforms in the UK in the 1990s, Blair took the view that the government and the private sector needed to work together. He recognised that while the values and ends might differ between these two groups, what mattered for citizens was 'what works', even though this was untested and there was little, if any, evidence of what did work. As a consequence of such policy decisions, social workers now deliver a diverse range of services in new ways. Some social workers complain that these developments are unhelpful as they are unable to spend time in direct work with service users (Dustin, 2007; Munro, 2011), despite service users saying that they value the contribution that social workers can make to their lives (Beresford, 2007). In child protection work critics have argued that these changes can have negative consequences for the protection of children (Munro, 2011). However, for some service users, the availability of personal budgets and the ability to commission personalised services has been a welcome development. It would seem that the value placed by a service user on exercising personal choice, and being a leader in their own care, is dependent on their individual circumstances and expectations.

A framework for considering leadership practice

The challenges facing professional and management staff in ensuring appropriate leadership practice has two final considerations: the organisational context for practice and the approach adopted by the individual leader. As Carr (2010a) has already identified, the decisions made by leaders in organisations can have a huge impact on the lives of service users, and the emerging contexts for practice can introduce different kinds of leadership practices. Lawler and Bilson (2010) clustered leadership and management theories into four quadrants. For example, they asked about the influence of organisational forms on management and leadership and its focus on the individual, such as the characteristics or traits that effective managers and leaders may need to have. Lawler and Bilson (2010) identified two distinct approaches within each of these: rational objective (approaches that attempt to objectify knowledge in an impersonal, detached manner) and reflective pluralist (a range of perspectives and interests, unpredictability and uncertainty). In this first example, the organisation is the main focus along with rational–objective approaches used by leaders and managers, which are reviewed in terms of the possible impact on service users.

The Audit Commission (2008) suggested that leaders must adopt proactive strategies in their work with service users and carers, which, in the case of older people, meant targeting resources and making sure that worker effort maximises the impact and outcomes from these resources. The report detailed an approach to service development for older people, which reflected concerns relating to the expected increase in the number of older people in the population and limited funding to provide care services to this population. Using rational–objective approaches leaders and managers are interested in simplifying complexity and building a strategy that is predictable and easily understood. The report illustrated the strategic approach, as illustrated in Table 3.2.

Table 3.2 Approaches to service development for older people

1) Understand, engage and mobilise communities to help themselves	Largest group of older people and low cost activities
2) Age-proof mainstream services to support independence	Large group of older people and low cost
3) Develop services to promote independence	Smaller group – medium costs
4) Provide social care	Smallest group – high costs

Source: Adapted from Audit Commission (2008, p 33)

This approach allows for service user engagement, for example, at the first level, where organisations may develop strategic plans that are informed by the needs of older people. However, it assumes that individuals will fit the demands of the organisation, and will be relatively passive consumers whose needs and demands are easy to predict and manage. Even where consultation is undertaken, the services will be predetermined to fit within a 'bureaucratic rationing paradigm' rather than a 'person-centred' or 'personalisation paradigm', reflecting the need for economies of scale and prevention, to keep costs low. Service user engagement takes place through surveys and other research methods, and this is used to promote self-help literature and is expected to attract little cost. At the second level, municipalities or local government offices may wish to consult with users of services to design services to meet a wide range of community needs. In doing so, planners can 'age-proof' (ensure the services are accessible to anyone of any age) existing and new services so that mainstream services are adapted to support independence. This again attracts low costs. At level three, there may be a need to proactively develop services that prevent individuals from participating in community life and losing independence. One example is illustrated in Camden, London, where local leaders have worked with Transport for London to develop services that provide personal mobility vehicles to older people. This new service is designed to promote independence among a group of older people who, it is believed, will, without targeted interventions, become 'dependent', resulting in high-level care needs. There is clearly a financial cost to developing preventative services, but it is anticipated that this will result in fewer older people needing social care that attracts much higher costs. The fourth category is a high cost option, to provide social care. The overall goal will be to ensure this service is used only by the few, provided by largely market-based services and paid for in part or in full by the individual, where this is possible.

The adoption of rational-objective leadership approaches makes sense if efficiency and economy are the overriding factors. However, this overly rational approach to human systems can be problematic because of the underlying practice assumptions that are made. Service user needs are complex, and strategies that assume service users want and desire independence ignores the realities of some service users' lives. Some people may operate independently in some areas of their lives but they may be dependent in others, for example, where older mental health service users may be independent in terms of their mental health needs, but may be dependent in relation to requiring help with their children, or vice versa. There may be unintended consequences from this rational-objective approach. Leaders may become distant from any personal responsibility of this service model and rather than focus primarily on what is needed, may find themselves focusing on what can be afforded. While rational-objective approaches *may* have an adverse impact on service users, however, it is these approaches that currently dominate social care.

We have a second example to illustrate how the organisation remains the focus but leadership is explored using reflective-pluralist approaches. A learning disability partnership board in England recruited adults with learning disabilities onto its board to improve local planning, commissioning and the delivery of services to adults with learning disabilities. The board has been proactive in tackling barriers to participation, which has led to many service developments. The workforce development sub-group produced a guide (2007) to advise on how to involve service users in choosing and developing staff, which was informed by service users working on the sub-group. The guide outlines best practice in engaging service users in staff inductions, ongoing learning and development, appraisals and in providing feedback for staff probationary reviews. Service users across the care service have been engaged in training to understand their rights as customers, and new systems were put in place to help service users to exercise those rights. In developing a responsive and sensitive complaints process, for example, the authority has engaged its customer relations staff in piloting a complaints service. One hundred adults were given a postcard, which can be posted to the customer complaints team, if a service user has a complaint. A special pin number has been printed on the card, which identifies the service user. On receipt of the card a customer relations staff member contacts the service user and deals with the complaint. In framing adults with learning disabilities as customers, the authority hopes to design and deliver services that maximise participation in mainstream service provision by removing known barriers to participation. Significant time and effort has been put into ongoing training for staff to change the culture and attitudes of workers so that they enable and empower service users to make choices and to live more independent lives.

The degree to which service users are engaged in shaping service provision is greatly increased if service users are engaged in strategic decision-making groups. A leadership approach can support co-production strategies and accept the need for organisational learning and some uncertainty. This enhances the potential for the system to engage service users to help design the support and care which is then made available to other service users. However, participation on the board is limited by its size. In the above example of a learning disabilities partnership board, service users set up their own expansive consultative system to ensure that they could engage as many people as possible in decision-making processes . However, it is clear that decision-making in care systems isn't completely 'open' because board membership is restricted, so some form of representation is required. As a result strategic boards will, to some extent, reflect the interests of those agencies and individuals they represent as well as the interests of individual members of the board. The degree to which participation and its associated power is dispersed is therefore context-specific. For the learning disabilities partnership board, participation allows scope for a plurality of perspectives and interests as well as engaged leadership, although the overall focus is on improving the performance of the organisation through its work with service users.

In contrast to a focus on organisations, Lawler and Bilson (2010) reviewed the literature on leaders. As discussed in Chapter One, they suggest that much of our understanding about leadership has been shaped by idea of the lone 'heroic' leader, and researchers have been preoccupied with identifying the characteristics or traits of effective leaders over many years. More recently, research has been focused on understanding how transformational leaders engage followers. Research by Alimo-Metcalfe and Alban-Metcalfe (2005, p 65) used grounded theory to identify transformational leaders, rejecting the charismatic or heroic models of leadership. They identified over 2,000 constructs, generating 48 groupings, which formed the basis of a pilot questionnaire. Six factors were finally identified, as illustrated in Table 3.3.

The six factors informed the development of a transformational leadership questionnaire, which can be used to evaluate leader capabilities. Alimo-Metcalfe and Alban-Metcalfe (2005) suggest that leaders in a UK context were seen not

Table 3.3: Factors identified in transformational leaders

Factor 1	Valuing individuals (genuine concern for others well being and development)
Factor 2	Networking and achieving (inspirational communicator, networker and achiever)
Factor 3	Enabling (empower, delegates, develops potential)
Factor 4	Acting with integrity (integrity, consistency, honesty and open)
Factor 5	Being accessible (accessible, approachable, in-touch)
Factor 6	Being decisive (decisive, risk-taking)

Source: Based on factors identified by Alimos-Metcalfe and Alban-Metcalfe (2005)

---

as heroic leaders, but more as 'leaders as servants' (Greenleaf, 1996), unlike in the US, where leaders are described as 'distant heroes'. However, this and other similar research adopts rational, scientific methods to identify particular characteristics that in the end need to be interpreted, as leadership is a negotiated and context-specific activity. In this research, Alimo–Metcalfe and Alban-Metcalfe (2005) were able to draw on the work of Stone et al (2003) who had argued that transformational leaders were committed to organisational objectives, while servant leaders were focused on followers. Only through a commitment to followers were these leaders able to achieve the organisational objectives, drawing on subordinate outcomes. They argue that servant leaders could sculpt a shared vision and develop shared meaning when people came together, and 'the constructs of leadership emerging from our data also placed great importance on being sensitive to the agenda of a wide range of internal and external stakeholders, rather than seeking to meet the agenda of only one particular group' (Alimo-Metcalfe and Alban-Metcalfe, 2005, p 63).

The questionnaire produced from this particular research adds to many 'management tools' that have been developed by to support organisations to identify outstanding individual leaders. However, there are critics of these developments, rejecting this mechanistic process, and Carr (2010a), for one, stated, 'I shudder when someone mentions "toolkits" in the context of leadership and management in health and social care; tools are for mending machines and I am a human being; so is everyone in the mental health system, including people in leadership positions' (Carr, 2010a, p 21). What are missing are the aspects of leadership that incorporate the relationships between workers, managers and service users based on democratic (rather than consumerist) ideas of 'social justice, power sharing and decision making that involves the people it is likely to affect' (Carr, 2010a, p 21). In this way, leadership can be viewed as a construct to be negotiated and defined by stakeholders. This view of leadership fits more comfortably with what Lawler and Bilson termed 'plural-reflective approaches'.

In considering what kind of leader is suitable for social work, Lawler and Bilson (2010) suggest that leadership needs to be principled, that is, respectful and responsible. They suggest that these two principles help to promote reflection on actions and these increase the capacity for compassion and concern, which Carr (2010a) highlighted is important to service users. These principles recognise the different expectations and experiences of service users. Lawler and Bilson (2010) acknowledge that management and leadership roles in social care are not easy, and that there is a need for 'a framework that is relativist and complex because this is the nature of the world in which social work managers and leaders must act' (Lawler and Bilson, 2010, p 179). They suggest, therefore, that those approaches that fall within the rational-objectivist category (which are dominant) are generally less suitable than those that recognise complexity, reflection and plurality of perspectives. Given the range of organisational forms that are emerging, there is a need for empirical studies to explore this further.

Participatory approaches in leadership

Service user-led organisations have been emerging in the new policy landscape over many years now. These organisations are often organised and operate very differently to the hierarchical structures characteristic of traditional care services, and embed principles and practices characteristic of service user movements which, according to Beresford (2000) and Begum (2006), can be collated into four categories:

1. Self-selecting (members decide for themselves whether they belong to a particular group)
2. Being organised and run by service users themselves
3. Being focused on campaigns 'on rights issues' that unite different agendas
4. Being focused on developing new forms of knowledge to challenge widely-held views about service users and carers

These characteristics reflect an approach that is participative, proactive, inclusive and developmental. In terms of Lawler and Bilson's (2010) framework, the organisation and its management practice fits within those quadrants where complexity and uncertainty need to be worked with, and leadership is negotiated and co-constructed. 'Expert by experience' is a term that is often used to explain the perspective brought to organisations by users of services. Some of the challenges that workers and service users experience in this process are summarised here:

- *Conflict:* where this experience conflicts with management, professional and organisational agendas, those leading participatory processes need to ensure that the service user perspective is valued and no one view dominates another. This may be difficult as achieving organisational objectives is a primary goal, and these goals may conflict with service user goals and concerns.
- *Meaningful engagement:* if service user participation is to be meaningful, therefore, service users need to engage early on with other group members, to be able to present their perspective and avoid tokenism, particularly at service level where experiences can inform and define the problems, issues and tasks. Without a service user perspective other stakeholders may well impose their beliefs or ideologies on a process that may be hard for service users to challenge.
- *New boundaries and openness:* organisations need to understand and be explicit about the challenges they face when they seek to work in participatory ways with service users. Service users are not bound by the limits of organisational culture, professional and or management world views, and this diversity is important. Service users are well placed to challenge those delivering services because they have knowledge about what it feels like to receive services, advice or support in their own experience, and more broadly.
- *How views are gathered matters:* how service user experiences are gathered and used is important. In the first example in this chapter on older people's services, limited research methods were proposed, while in the second example on

learning disabilities service participation was through direct involvement (and wider consultation).

- *Emotional empathy:* service user participation can provide a rich source of knowledge and experience to inform and lead thinking in new ways, but requires those engaged in designing change to be able to take risks with ideas and to be able to put themselves in other people's shoes to explore any new ways of thinking.
- *Taking part:* some service users may struggle to articulate their views, either because they have a particular health condition, a language difference or find it culturally difficult to challenge others, and in order to successfully take part, information needs to be clear and accessible, and confidence-building experiences may be needed.
- *Power issues:* service user participation can be greatly increased if issues of power are discussed in an honest and open way, and service user participation is rewarded in the same way managers and professionals are rewarded by paid work. However, these requirements may generate resistance within organisations where staff are unused to working with and valuing diverse interests, as well as more open approaches to power-sharing and decision-making.
- *Rewards:* in customer-oriented services where participation is confined to developing the service to improve satisfaction levels, other forms of rewards and possibly more narrow forms of engagement between customers and providers may emerge.

In co-production processes the participation of service users is combined with workers' and managers' experience to explore problems, and collectively, to develop appropriate solutions. However, co-production work can be fraught with challenges as vested interests, budgets and value conflicts between stakeholders can emerge to destroy stakeholder groups if the group is not safely contained. One example of an emerging service that was successfully co-produced was in London. The NHS and the local authority in Camden came together with service users, carers and community members to develop new services for mental health service users. They planned to increase the number of people who would have access to a personal budget by providing a new way to assess, plan and provide support services that would promote and support self-directed decisions. The council planned to develop a range of options for support and advice, which would include paid staff to relatives, volunteers and support provided by user-led organisations. To achieve this Camden promised to work with partners to develop a framework for commissioning that they would roll out to other service areas. These participatory approaches were incorporated within best value developments, which were outcomes-focused, and service user participation was critical to defining appropriate outcomes. Participatory approaches gave a wider group of people the opportunity to have some influence in the decision-making process and the actions that followed (Kirby et al, 2003).

Clearly leadership involved a degree of power-sharing and the inclusion of diverse perspectives, to generate decisions and actions supported by people who would be affected by those decisions. This approach directly includes the voice of the service user, but, as we have seen earlier in this chapter, sometimes the service user's voice has to be presented by others. It is possible to combine 'humanity' with work processes that enable everyone to get the job done, and the leadership approach needs to be able to accommodate diversity to ensure the inclusion of service user perspectives. This is a different kind of leadership to that provided by the heroic leader. Distance leaders will struggle to promote the leadership that is likely to lead to 'social justice, power-sharing and decision making that involves people it is likely to affect' (Carr, 2010a), unless they can create a culture where this is possible, and review how leadership might be distributed. Rational-objective management and leadership approaches are unlikely to deliver this.

Another model widely used to 'assess' degrees of participation is Arnstein's (1969) ladder of participation. The ladder has eight rungs and on the bottom two rungs are 'manipulation' and 'therapy', which are essentially light (or non-) forms of participation. Rung three is the first real level of engagement (informing), but the decision-making power is still held with professionals and managers, while rung four (consultation) suggests that service users' and carers' voices will be heard, but they remain unable to participate in decision-making. Rung five (placation) is a higher level of engagement, but service users and carers still do not hold much power over decision-making, while rung six (partnership) begins to engage stakeholders and allow negotiations to take place. The top two rungs, delegated power and citizen control, increase the power and decision-making of stakeholders until they have full power and control. This model has been criticised for creating the impression that service providers should always strive to give service users and carers full power and control (McLaughlin, 2009). One of the strengths of the ladder, however, is that it identifies different levels of participation, and is therefore a useful framework to explore what is meant by participation, and degrees of participation. The model brings to the fore discussions about where decision-making takes place and who holds, and who doesn't, power within partnerships, and the nature of the power relationships between stakeholders. This becomes very evident when the complexities of real life are discussed, and it may be possible that some service users may want greater levels of involvement in service design, raising issues about control. There are many other models that identify ways in which participation might be encouraged and supported, but it is clear that understanding what is meant by participation needs to be articulated and understood at the start (Tanner, 2009, in Harris and White). As new forms of care provision emerge it will be important to be able to distinguish between different types of services, service users, their expectations and experiences, and leadership approaches used. Service users and carers may expect service providers to share power with them, and where this is appropriate they may take on organisational and individual leadership responsibility, while in more consumerist-focused institutions, innovation, quality improvements and increased market share may provide the incentive for service user participation. However, it remains unclear how the role of customers in a demand-led model may have an impact on the sector. Carr (2010a, p 21) suggests that the greatest challenge for leaders will be to 'take responsibility for the impact of their decisions on others, to recognise the invaluable asset of common humanity throughout the service system and build spaces in which productive relationships can flourish.'

Summary

This chapter has reviewed the expectation and experiences of service users to develop an understanding of service user perspectives on their care experiences, enabling some discussion on the importance of dispersed leadership that recognises diversity and can respond appropriately. Professional leadership takes place in systems where the role and tasks of social work have been undergoing change, and while much of what social workers do is valued and supportive of dispersed leadership, there are areas of practice that are contested and challenging. In organisations that adopt largely rational–objective approaches to leadership practice, limitations can arise, as the focus is largely on organisational outcomes, which the leaders anticipate will meet service user needs. However, the assumptions made about uniformity of services are problematic, whereas in organisations where there is more scope for working with diversity and opportunities for learning from working together leadership practices are enriched. Services that are developed with service users require less of a heroic leadership model, although some thought is needed as to what kinds of partnership arrangements are made with diverse groups and how any difficulties might be contained. In all the models that have emerged there is a need for social workers and other leaders to be principled and engaging. These are considerable challenges. Lawler and Bilson (2010, p 180) say that while they do not believe 'there is one correct way to undertake management and leadership', they do believe 'in the human potential to understand complex situations and to respond with creativity and passion.' This needs to encouraged by organisations that value and respect individual differences and support practices that enhance and develop the very best leadership that is widely dispersed throughout organisations.

FOUR

Leading strategically: organisational strategy and managing people

Introduction

The effective leadership of people and organisations is complex, requiring knowledge, skills and understanding across a number of disciplines in addition to appreciating the context of social work and care organisations. To facilitate understanding of this complexity, this part of the book focuses on people within organisations and therefore the next two chapters include debates from management and organisational theory, while seeking to locate these debates within leadership in social work and care. This is an area that has not been extensively explored within contemporary social work literature, or certainly not in seeking to critically locate social and care workers within strategic organisational contexts and environments. Where current literature has explored these issues, the focus has been on those at frontline management with less attention on those organisational aspects that are involved in the development of strategy and its implementation in the management of organisations. This chapter's approach takes a critical macro view of changing organisational contexts in which leaders and managers seek to deliver care services at a senior level in these agencies. It has important considerations for leaders, professionals, commissioners and regulators in seeking to understand the nature and impacts, intentional or unintentional, of organisational strategy.

Social work and care enterprise

The discipline of human resource management (HRM) covers a wide range of organisational and worker activities and processes, and as a result this makes the subject both complex and confusing for many frontline managers and staff. This situation is often compounded by the relatively little attention given to the development of people systems, with poor workforce intelligence available to support the management of such a diverse environment as in social work and social care (Evans and Huxley, 2009). To successfully manage large organisations, it is important to understand the workforce, staff recruitment (Evans and Huxley, 2009; Curtis et al, 2010), retention challenges (LGA, 2009), staff burnout (Collins, 2008; Hamama, 2012) and the importance of promoting good people management and evidence-based practice (Evans and Huxley, 2009). This importance has been underlined by efforts in England, for example, within the care sector through initiatives such as the Integrated Local Area Workforce Strategy (InLAWS) (Skills for Care, 2007), Social Work Taskforce (2009) and the *Capable, confident, skilled* strategy (Skills for Care, 2011a). These efforts have also been driven by the current UK Coalition government's policy to increase the use of private sector organisations in the delivery of what was once considered traditional state care services.

The inevitable increase in the number of organisations makes it more difficult to ensure national initiatives are implemented unless they are regulatory requirements. National development of social work and care human resource organisation has often been limited, with work being concentrated on reviewing how the profession should be structured and remunerated (LGA, 2009; Social Work Taskforce, 2009). As a result, the application of strategic human resource and more operational human resource management has not been included in the curriculum of qualifying social work training or in many post-qualifying programmes, and appears to be under-researched in this sector. More recent years have seen greater attention being focused on the leadership and management of frontline social work managers, but strategic questions for social care organisations remain under-investigated. The following two chapters aim to contribute to this underdeveloped area by drawing on research and writing from outside the sector, and contextualising within this area.

At the time of writing, while there are efforts to develop strategies, policies and tools to support social care workforce development, much of the current work may not be drawing on the full range of critical work in HRM, especially given the complexity of the sector. For instance, can these initiatives be successfully applied at national, regional levels, across statutory and independent (private and non-profit-based) sectors? If so, what are the diverse strategic, financial or operational requirements of organisations, their workforce, citizens and service user groups? It is therefore important that leaders, managers and workers in these organisations critically reflect on the challenges, debates and opportunities to manage and encourage people in this diverse environment for the effective delivery of care services.

Organisational context in social work and social care

The operating environment, policy context, financing and structure of social work and social care has undertaken substantial changes in the UK in the last two decades and is likely to continue. The implications are for reduced state provision and increased provision from the private and not-for-profit sector, with the inevitable changes to organisational focus, strategy and greater use of private sector business management techniques. Alongside the structural changes there have been workforce challenges in recruitment and retention (LGA, 2009), concern about low pay (Hussein, 2011), scandals involving poor care (CQC, 2011a) in addition to changes to the regulatory and business environment (Harris, 2003). Collins (2008) underlines the importance of development at an organisational, in addition to an individual, level, to support social workers in dealing with stress, establishing appropriate coping strategies and ensuring practice resilience. The focus on much of this chapter is on those strategic workforce issues that have an impact on staff, the organisation and users of services.

Organisational change in the UK is not new, and we need only to consider that there was a time when social work was undertaken largely within the charity sector before consolidation within local government employment, along with the responsibility for all statutory social work being invested in local authorities (Seebohm, 1968). Social work then became part of the local authority workforce, together with an ethos and commitment to universal services ensuring that the Poor Law was considered an issue of the past. At this time in history, the use of public services for the delivery of care was seen as preferable to that provided by market forces (HMSO, 1970). This approach to the structure of services resulted in the unification of funding, with service provision being seen as a way of facilitating greater equity in service delivery together with better financial and political accountability (Glennerster, 1992). This important consolidation utilised bureaucratic hierarchies and professional control of the services (Clarke and Langan, 1993). However, the location of social work within local authorities rather than the NHS resulted in a more fragmented approach to the development and planning of the care workforce. This altered as a result of structural changes that were introduced via the National Health Service and Community Care Act 1990 that included the outsourcing of services to the non-state sector and increased use of care market initiatives and competition. These changes to social work have altered the structure of the organisational enterprise landscape in which care is provided, as well as the context in which social work and social care services are delivered. Social work and social care, as well as the leadership and management within the sector, therefore also needs to be viewed within a strategic organisational perspective if it is to ensure that the systems, processes and staff within organisations support good quality care.

Importance of 'managing people' in organisations

The strategic management of an organisation's workforce needs to takes a considered view of how human resource policies and practices are aligned with the organisation's strategic 'business' focus. This changed 'business' environment for care organisations requires a much greater understanding and use of commercial organisation skills. Much of the literature on strategic workforce management originates from what was considered 'manpower' planning which was, in turn, followed by ideas of the importance of effective human management (Peters and Waterman, 1982) and the subsequent frameworks that shaped thinking about the strategic role of HRM (Beer et al, 1984). It is important to note that many of these ideas and theories of both HRM and strategic workforce management are contested, and for the latter, concern has been raised as to whether the term is conceptually coherent (Bamberger and Meshoulam, 2000). Authors such as Snell

(1996) view workforce management processes as being more outcomes-focused in order to support organisations to achieve 'competitive advantage' against other organisations in the care market. In this context of care markets, care companies or services need to ensure that they have a competitive edge over rivals to generate more income or profit. In contrast, others (Ulrich, 1997; Bamberger and Meshoulam, 2000) believe that strategic workforce management attempts to unify the social, human and intellectual capital to achieve the strategic goals of the organisation. Critics therefore question whether these widely used management concepts of HRM and strategic workforce management are associated with either undertaking organisational processes or whether they are more aligned to the achievement of organisational outcomes. The development and use of strategic workforce management within social work and social care agencies are most commonly viewed as an organisational cycle or process, the steps of which feed and follow one another (Figure 4.1).

Figure 4.1: Organisational processes and steps

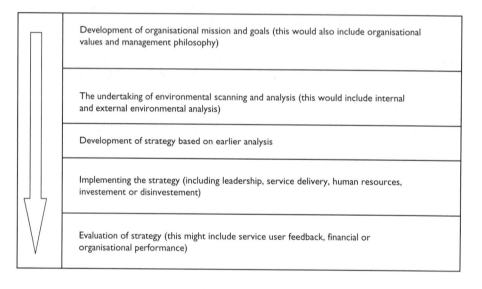

Development of organisational mission and goals (this would also include organisational values and management philosophy)

The undertaking of environmental scanning and analysis (this would include internal and external environmental analysis)

Development of strategy based on earlier analysis

Implementing the strategy (including leadership, service delivery, human resources, investement or disinvestement)

Evaluation of strategy (this might include service user feedback, financial or organisational performance)

Most organisations state that their staff are their most important resource asset and that those staff are critical to the organisation's survival (Boxall and Purcell, 2003). This, together with the nature of care services provided, underlines the importance of human resources to the care sector for the delivery of effective and good quality services. However, the management of this critical resource must go beyond the selection and retention of well-trained, competent and committed staff but also include the role, culture and interrelationship between those staff and the organisations for which they work. As we have already highlighted, the external commercial environment and the wider context in which these care organisations operate results in 'business' threats to them such as globalisation, competition, failure of care and regulation and austerity. These external threats as well as internal organisational challenges such as shortages of key staff and expertise make a case for greater importance to be placed on coherent strategic workforce management across the social work/social care sector. The sector is large as well as diverse, and for some organisations and services, a dedicated workforce strategy or HRM expertise may not be available due to the perceived costs of these services, or they may have been outsourced to other agencies (Cornes et al, 2010). Complex national organisations may equally find themselves seeking to support a diverse range of staff such as social workers, occupational therapists, unqualified sessional workers working across multiple sites on regional, national or even international organisational boundaries. Within all organisations the role and strategy of workforce management can be implicit rather than being explicitly stated (Gratton et al, 1999). As a result, for many organisations, HRM exists within a highly complex business environment which may have been influenced historically through a variety of organisational interpretations, internal politicking by key staff and informal work practice.

The care workforce

Successful human resource processes have been highlighted as important to improve the overall outcomes for health systems (Martinez and Martineau, 1998; WHR, 2006), and this is likely to be the position for social work and social care organisations. Within this stratified care workforce we should recognise key HR distinctions between the professions such as social work and occupational therapy and that of the 'unqualified' social care workforce, in that the former requires both an appropriate degree-level qualification and it may mean the title of the profession being preserved such as 'social worker'. This protection of title ensures its use is limited to those individuals who are appropriately qualified and registered in the UK. Since 2005, Section 61 of the Care Standards Act 2000 has protected the title 'social worker' in England. In contrast, many social care workers tend to receive on-the-job training, and their role often involves offering more personal care. Despite this complexity, there has been a dearth of critical perspectives on the role of strategic workforce planning across the sector. The reasons for this underdevelopment may be as a result of the lack of priority given to people management and workforce planning until more recent times. Historically debate has largely been confined to education levels and the use of the workforce in this sector, such as the role of social care support staff. As we saw in Chapter One, the reductions in the use of qualified social workers and the use of less qualified staff to reduce costs has been operationalised. This has resulted in the development of new roles such as advanced mental health practitioners (AMHPs) (DH, 2005), care managers and social care assistants. These changes have often occurred without the wider organisational debate on the context and impact of identity in social work, the role and function, nature and structure of the services. The social and economic ideological standpoints of social and care work, the wider social and economic changes that are occurring within society and social work's professional relationship with other caring professions are other areas that often get scant organisational attention. As a result, for many organisations there has been little investment in understanding the complexity and effectiveness of managing this resource, its working conditions (which may include ongoing professional development), compensation, professional leadership and the policy environment in which it is required to operate.

Organisational design, cost and productivity

A clear priority for many organisations is to secure their future viability, and this is increasingly magnified by the competition with rival organisations and services. This priority has been underlined by recent requirements for UK care regulators to pay increased attention to care providers' financial health (DH, 2013a). It is therefore unsurprising that within this context many organisations are concerned with service costs, productivity and the management of these factors (Godard, 2001; Boxall and Purcell, 2003). For organisations that produce products for sale, the cost of this production is essential, but for service organisations, cost-effectiveness is viewed in a similar way to production costs (Batt and Doellgast, 2005). This results in many organisations attempting to develop broad strategies to contain these costs through mergers, the greater use of automation, changes to staff skill mix, and so on. We can see this cost consolidation in economic sectors such as fast food restaurants and retail shops where the sector competes on cost through the use of employment models involving low pay with few opportunities for personal development. Some have gone on to suggest that the domiciliary care sector of social care in the UK has taken a similar approach (Patmore, 2003). Indeed, Hussein (2010) highlights the pay of direct care workers is on or near the UK National Minimum Wage and at a similar level to non-care-providing ancillary workers in other sectors of the economy. As a result, it is not uncommon in this type of employment for employers to offer low commitment workforce management that emphasises adequate service delivery (just meeting regulatory demands) rather than high quality, due to their services being seen as price-sensitive and organisations wishing to reduce their overall cost of delivery. In contrast, higher levels of workforce commitment may be provided to less price-sensitive services where either risks of error with serious organisation consequences or high level of skills are required (or can be utilised to differentiate a service and a higher cost), and the provision of higher levels of pay and training helps to ensure the better use of skills (Boxall and Purcell, 2003). This market differentiation may occur when organisations offer a range of price plans or top-up levels for higher levels of service. In addition, high performance workforce systems are often associated with those HR practices that encourage the development, recruitment, selection and retention of staff (Zacharatos et al, 2005). These higher commitment processes are important in organisations where leaders are able to build organisations that encourage employees to be motivated and support the delivery of organisational goals (Whitener, 2001). This focus on cost-effectiveness has wider implications than just low commitment employment, and may result in tension between employers and employees (Boxall and Steeneveld, 1999). For instance, smaller organisations may find their financial viability threatened by organisational and market requirements to employ higher levels of a skilled workforce when they can least afford it. They may also find it difficult to cope with challenges such as workforce skills scarcity or being unable to afford the levels of skills required in their enterprise, thus resulting in workforce instability, resulting in retention and recruitment problems.

Leaders within organisations may also be challenged to maintain employee motivation and practice as the interaction between employees and managers may be arbitrated by workforce policies (Purcell et al, 2003; Bartel, 2004). For instance, as we have seen in previous chapters, policies and practice may be decided at a senior level and communicated downwards, but implementation is then mediated by individuals, practice and culture throughout the organisation. There are implications for national strategic workforce initiatives in the care sector given the significant changes to its structure, financing and organisation due to a greater plurality of employers operating in a competitive marketised care economy. The impact of increased venture capital and offshore companies based in tax havens into the care market is only just being recognised (Milmo, 2012). However, broader changes in social work have included that of training as well as policy initiatives such as individual budgets for service users to buy their own care (Carr, 2010). While Chapter One explored many of the debates on how these initiatives might reduce bureaucracy, it should also be recognised that within this context many employers may be seeking to evaluate the economic viability of their chosen area of service delivery. As a result of perceived high labour costs and person-based services, many organisations will have considered how to improve productivity and ensure cost-effective employment. The organisational aims and objectives, together with their service delivery models, will involve differences in their economic organisational and service strategy (Batt and Doellgast, 2005). For instance, those organisations that have entered the care market to maximise their profits may undertake different organisational strategies than those that are not primarily focused on profit margins.

Organisations whose business strategy requires that they maintain high staff skill levels are more likely to make use of higher pay, careful staff selection, and invest highly in internal staff development, while organisations that see themselves as being in a very margin-based (cost-sensitive) competition are likely to have low commitment to people management (Boxall, 2003). Those organisations with a cost-focused strategy are more likely to see their operational strategy to supply adequate (meeting minimum national regulatory requirements) rather than exceeding regulatory service standards as a result of the organisation having positioned itself to provide cost-effective (cheaper) services that sector service users or service commissioners may demand. For example, outside of this sector, many low-cost airlines use this economic argument as the rationale and business strategy for their low-cost services, that is, people pay a low cost but do not expect all the services such as 'free' meals provided by more expensive competitors. Some may argue that these cost savings are not only evidenced in 'no frills' but can also be seen in the organisation's response when things go wrong. This will become a crucial strategic concern within the care sector, and as we saw in Chapter Three, it links directly to who is considered the 'customer' and the commissioning of statutory care services. This suggests a greater need for leaders to critically consider the needs of all stakeholders, including the implications for vulnerable service users, which extend beyond simplistic strategies of tick-box management and the over-reliance on regulatory systems in the purchasing and commissioning of services.

Leading in competitive market-based environments

Management concern with financial and organisational viability of care organisations has given rise to considerable debate in the business literature about how organisations can maintain 'competitive advantage' by using strategic workforce planning (Boxall and Steeneveld, 1999). As we have already explored, organisations operating in cost-sensitive environments may implement a variety of business strategies; for example, where the business environment is extremely price-sensitive, many have used relocation to lower-cost labour countries to manage costs. Further examples may include the relocation of call centres to overseas countries where direct costs are seen as being lower. However, for the majority of social care providers, this strategy may not be possible, but it is not beyond the realms of possibility that functions such as local authority call centres may be relocated overseas in the future.

Call or contact centres

The use of call or contact centres has increased across all businesses and services in the UK and internationally. This type of organisation usually provides a contact point through which all contact with the organisation is routed, in order to centralise and manage contacts and to provide information. The key in this process is that of communicating with callers (this can be via telephone, email, online chat or fax), understanding their needs and delivering services quicker. For many commercial organisations the use of call or contact centres has been used, particularly in the development of contact centres where all forms of communication are used to manage their relationships with customers. While call centres have often been good at measuring efficiency, critics have argued that they have paid less attention to the qualitative measures that improve services within organisations and for their 'customers' (Tayles et al, 2002). Indeed, measures often seen within call centres include the numbers of call answered, calls waiting in a queue to be answered, number of calls answered in the last 10 minutes, numbers of free agents able to take calls, and so on (Gilmore and Moreland, 2000). Anton (2000) goes further by identifying that performance measures often include the average speed for calls to be answered, queue times, numbers of people who receive a satisfactory resolution in their first call and the number of abandoned calls, the average time taken per call and the speed in which a call is answered. Feinberg et al (2000) reviewed 13 critical operational determinants in 514 call centres, but only found that two of these 13 determinants had any statistical significance on caller satisfaction, namely, percentage of calls closed after the first contact and average abandonment of calls, the implications of this being that for many call centres, staff are still seen from a Tayloristic viewpoint of undertaking pre-defined tasks.

The use of call centres based in the UK, for example, has not been without controversy, with social workers involved in the Liverpool Direct call centre complaining that this development resulted in deskilling and reduced opportunities to undertake their professional social work (Coleman, 2006). The implementation of this service model resulted in social workers striking over what they saw as an erosion of social work values and professional practice (Ferguson, 2007). Employment systems and low-cost HR practices, where Tayloristic work design is viewed as cost-effective, are omnipresent in those organisations where reduced labour costs are used to gain cost advantage (Boxall and Purcell, 2003). Within these organisations, Tayloristic work design is often associated with attempts to improve efficiency and labour productivity, and often includes techniques such as the standardisation of tasks. However, international relocation as a strategy often provides only a temporary advantage, until other organisations in its sector do likewise, and currently within the statutory sector such relocation may currently be considered politically unacceptable. Alternative strategies involve improving workforce capability and organisational processes in order to gain organisational HR advantage (Boxall, 1998).

Responding to care market changes

The recognition of the impact of changes to the care market is likely to result in a variety of intended and unintended consequences. However, it is possible to recognise a trend for organisations to view the care market as having an assortment of various and divergent service needs, which in turn might be organised or conceived of as different service user market or business segments in organisational business speak. Organisational strategy in a more highly developed care market might therefore be to provide different levels of services to different groups of service users. For instance, the development of long-term care insurance products may in time result in different levels and quality of services being available for different care market prices. This is much the same way that food producers may manufacture similar brands of breakfast cereals, each of which are aimed at different sectors of the breakfast market. These developments link directly to successive UK government initiatives to implement neoliberal market reform and the promotions of consumer choice in care services. This trend can already be seen in studies of US older people's care homes in which they recognised different market segments, and the resulting organisational attempts to utilise different workforce strategies and competition to meet these demands, for example, training, pay, staffing levels and career structures to attract higher value market segments (Eaton, 2000; Hunter, 2000). However, literature on the effect of this form of market impact is extremely limited in the UK, resulting in the need to draw on the experience of other economic or business sectors.

In a study of Dutch and German management consultancies, two broad strategic types of organisational workforce management were identified – those that offered standardised solutions (more concerned with efficiency) and those that promoted professionals' ability to be more user-focused and to respond more imaginatively to problems (Doorewaard and Meihuizen, 2000). The former were characterised by more bureaucratic models of workforce strategy, while the latter sought to recruit dynamic workers, with retention being achieved through the provision of challenging high discretion work (Doorewaard and Meihuizen, 2000). Other authors (Herzenberg et al, 1998) developed a framework in which they categorised workforce strategies according to four systems of work; these ranged from professional high discretion systems (with little intrusion from Taylorism) to that of labour-intensive and unskilled systems. In a mixed large market that has high value-added market segments, such as older people's care, there are increased opportunities to offer a broader range of workforce strategies (Boxall, 2003, p 14) according to service user preference due to the ability to provide a range of services at different cost levels. In these differentiated economic care markets there is the possibility of providing a variety of professional skills in the workforce, as the argument can be made for greater strategic workforce investment based on the costs and marketing of service provision, this argument being on the basis that there are areas of the organisation's business that are either highly profitable or involve higher risk, and so require greater workforce investment. In this way it may make it economically justifiable to serve those different market sectors and develop appropriate HR to meet those needs. As a result of the shift to care markets, care organisations are increasingly aligning their business strategies with their workforce strategic policies to ensure not only that their costs ensure sustainability and organisational workforce flexibility, but also that they meet consumer and regulatory demands. This is a clear challenge for organisational leadership as there is frequently a tension between managerial control, professionalism and employee motivation, the latter having a significant impact on commitment, motivation and adaptability.

Organisational strategy

For all organisations at a business management level, strategic workforce decisions will inevitably depend on the tactical analysis that is undertaken for the future of the organisation, the structure of its workforce and the organisational choices made by managers in order to achieve the businesses goals. It is important for leaders within organisations to be able to understand the demands of service users and to ensure that the organisation and its workforce deliver these needs.

This inevitably requires leaders to understand a range of factors that might be influencing service delivery, including the internal decision-making process of the organisation. We have already explored some of the distinctions made between leadership and management in Chapter One, and here we have a closer look at understanding the roles of managers and management systems with an organisation. When reviewing the unique nature of social work in Chapter One, we considered the ethical codes illustrated in the international statement about the purpose of social work (IFSW, 2004) which recognises the profession's respect for the inherent worth and dignity of all people, and the responsibility therefore for the profession to defend all people's psychological, physical, emotional and spiritual integrity and welfare. Chapter Two encouraged a reflective and critical approach to analysing organisational structures and processes. The distinctive values held by the profession link to its professional identity and should be embodied within the organisations in which social work is practised. As a result, the processes of decision-making should seek to be inclusive and reduce conflicts in the implementation of the profession's core values and principles.

Organisational strategies can be formulated at a number of levels within an organisation, but key strategic choices are often made at the most senior level. Given the critical status of this book we therefore should inevitably question how these decisions are made, who makes them and the reasons why they might be made (McLoughlin and Clark, 1988). We have already identified, in preceding chapters, the impact that managerialism has had on care services, but we also need to recognise that management as a task and role has its own ideology, values, beliefs and visions of the organisation (Pollitt, 1990). While the need to continually improve productivity to ensure organisational viability is often driven through the greater use of technology and structural reform, this can normally only be achieved by greater workforce productivity. Recent reforms in the sector mean that managers often have a critical role in the development, implementation and evaluation of productivity, with success in achieving this being viewed as wholly dependent on the quality and professionalism of the managers (Pollitt, 1990). The underlying assumption of the approach is that when management is good and objectives are clear, staff are highly motivated, bureaucracy is reduced and that this would best be achieved through the use of good commercial practices imported into public sector organisations (Pollitt, 1990, p 7).

Power in organisations

The importance and distribution of power to achieve these outcomes is therefore seen as key in achieving organisational outcomes. A variety of methods are often employed within organisations to ensure order and direction among a workforce that often has divergent and conflicting interests, making organisations inherently political. However, this perspective conflicts directly with the ideas often held by professionals that organisations should be rational structures in which members are seeking common goals (Morgan, 2006, p 150). As a result, there are often considerable linkages between organisational political systems and management, and in order for leaders to be effective, the political context of decision-making and culture are important (Morgan, 2006). For instance, this can be seen in democratic organisations that require all stakeholders to be represented in decision-making processes through participative management approaches. While this might not be widely used in the UK, examples can be viewed within Europe through the use of supervisory boards (Cernat, 2004; Adams and Ferreira, 2007) or the use of worker-directors in Denmark and Norway (Hans Böckler Foundation/ European Trade Union Institute, 2004). These approaches may therefore have more in common with international values of social work and the promotion of participatory involvement.

The social work practice context within Europe often follows different traditions from that of the UK; for instance, in Germany, this is often linked to educational systems and social pedagogy in which people are supported throughout their life stages through combined initiatives of education and support (Treptow, 2010). These practice traditions are important as there are variations at a European level in the application of social work, but also differing implications for professionalism, funding, theory and law. In undertaking international comparisons of social work governance it is therefore clear that the contextual nature, development, training, regulation and configuration of services are as important as the roles, position (that is, level of self-determination), external support and self-help capacity of those receiving support. It is therefore difficult to draw together any detailed international comparison without exploring these complexities in more detail. However, the participation of workers alongside service users and citizens on supervisory or management boards may be an area for further consideration in relation to the democratisation of social work practice models and service delivery.

The role of strategic workforce management in addition to HRM are important as these approaches will often be used to support decision-making in respect of workforce structures, policies and the approaches to organisational development and even social work/care work output. Earlier in Chapter One, more detailed background on leadership debates was explored and this provided a useful opportunity to reflect on the experience of organisational working and leadership. For instance, many people talk anecdotally about how in their organisational structures, workforce cliques, coalitions of power and culture are created within an organisation, which may result in teams or departments becoming preoccupied with their own objectives or seeking to advance their power and influence (Morgan, 2006). Within this context, this may result in managers promoting or appointing staff to key positions to consolidate their own power or to promote their interests within or without organisations, and as a result, has important implications for conflict within organisations over issues such as budget allocation and workloads. For social work managers there may therefore be an additional layer of being seen to 'play the game', while at the same time attempting to achieve good outcomes and to resist changes that challenge their professional values and ideology (Aronson and Smith, 2011). All these factors make the workplace a more complex political environment in which today's leaders are required to work. The use of procedures, policies and rules are another way that organisations attempt to introduce rationality into the workplace, but these efforts may be thwarted by the same initiatives being used by managers or employees to obtain or influence organisational power. It is therefore important for leaders to recognise that organisational power and processes can be used, abused or negotiated to obtain greater person or organisational power and influence. Aronson and Smith (2011) highlight the frequent struggle for managers dealing with divided professional identities while trying to achieve more progressive professional and management outcomes.

People and democratic management

Workforce leadership has become an important consideration for most organisations following the relatively recent recognition of the importance of people to the success of organisations. Strategic workforce management in contrast to the operational management of people draws on theory developed from HRM and more broadly, strategic management of organisations (Boxall and Purcell, 2000). As already highlighted, it is important that there is coherence between the 'business' strategy of the organisation and its strategic workforce development; however, a further dimension is that of people and their relationship to the organisation's corporate strategy. The role of workforce development in this context is to facilitate the organisation to make the maximum use of the different skills and experience of its workforce to achieve its strategy, as well as to ensure consistency in workforce policies to support achievement of the organisation's goals (Boxall and Purcell, 2003) – by way of an example from earlier discussions, the importance of frontline social work and care workers demonstrating leadership, being more entrepreneurial and facilitative in their professional supervisory relationships with staff. However, staff can find these demands challenging, especially as a result of new public management demands for demonstrable compliance and outcomes and reduced risk, while simultaneously expecting a range of targets and auditable paperwork requirements to be met.

The use of strategic workforce management does provide a possible approach to achieving improved competitive advantage for organisations, and as a result this has been a key motivating factor for many organisations to engage with it. Critics of this approach, however, suggest that strategic workforce planning is a variation of management control, designed to draw the worker into the organisation and maximise their commitment but offering little back to the individual in return. As a result some have argued (Walton, 1985; Evans and Huxley, 2009; Curtis et al, 2010) that organisations should move towards greater commitment to their workforce and abandon control in their management. This argument is based on the premise that, in the high commitment workforce models explored earlier, workers exercised greater self-control over their performance and behaviour. In turn, this resulted in lower workforce turnover (Meyer and Allen, 1997), and for workers provided more autonomy, control and inherent job satisfaction. These critics argue that the use of self-control by individuals or workforce teams results in higher commitment and external control without the need for extensive managerial oversight, systems and technology. In addition it also provides the workforce with the same level of autonomy normally afforded to the organisation's managers. In many ways this philosophy is echoed in what some might perceive as the radical work of Ricardo Semler (Haijtema, 2007), who facilitates his Brazilian employees to set their own hours, wages, choose their managers and has all pay and company performance published within the organisation. For many managers this would be seen as a high-risk approach, and within a western management perspective be considered as threatening and unlikely to result in effective organisations. However, within Semler's organisation, Semco, this strategy has resulted in the company expanding in the middle of a recession and lowering its staff turnover (Haijtema, 2007). The contrasting approach is normally based on western management models that seek to achieve organisational outcomes through the use of performance management and management control. This latter approach supports managers and leaders to maintain management control and tries to increase performance using these methods to gain high levels of organisational motivation and competence as the mechanism through which managers seek to direct workers' efforts (Guest, 2007).

Promoting staff commitment

Understanding how the process of formal workforce management policies and processes have an impact on the performance of people is under-researched, although it is widely believed that the mechanism may work via its impact on the behaviour and attitudes of staff. As a result the relationship between the person and the organisation is likely to be a key factor, and this is often viewed within the workplace as a psychological contract between the employer and staff members. The contract assumes that this unwritten psychological convention provides a mutual benefit through the exchange of skills and commitment to one another. This psychological bond between both parties provides implicit promises and obligations to fair treatment, payment for improved service, and implicitly promises in return flexibility to meet the demands of life and families (Conway and Briner, 2005).

In recent years changes to the socioeconomic business environment, working practices and the constant drive to achieve organisational productivity have changed the nature of organisations and workplaces. The social work 'business' has not been immune to these changes as organisations and the workplace have been subjected to the increased influence of neoliberal economic policies, and the drive towards a market in the provision of social welfare services (Harris, 2003). These changes to the workplace have resulted in some authors suggesting that to fully understand the importance of the psychological contract, we need to understand the complicated association with perceived fairness and trust as well as the belief in either party to achieve these, together with their perceived fairness of the contract in relation to other members of staff (Guest, 2007).

The contract is one example of the interaction complexity between people and their employers, which needs to be understood by leaders in order to facilitate people to give their best and to achieve good outcomes for service users. For many workers the expectation has been that in exchange for their loyalty and achieving high performance that they would achieve upward progression within their workplace. However, changes in work environments and organisational culture mean that for many, this expectation no longer exists, and that for their commitment and good performance, they might now be offered the possibility of undertaking interesting work and development (Herriot and Pemberton, 1995). As a result, for non-managerial staff there has been a move away from the previous psychological contract of a 'fair day's pay for a fair day's work' towards pay being based mostly on workers' perceived contribution to the workplace (Herriot and Pemberton, 1995). These changes have also resulted in informal workplace norms developing such as a long hours working culture. The higher reliance on flexible working by employers, smaller workforce establishments and a greater preoccupation with work–life balance has resulted, for many, in this psychological contract being negotiated between the worker and their immediate line manager (Rousseau, 2001, 2003). This suggests a greater need for line managers and frontline leaders to be clear about their roles and obligations as organisational agents, in light of the impact that these informal arrangements can have on both the individual or the organisation. However, the impact of increased use of new public management tools in managing the workforce makes this increasingly difficult for both parties.

Bowen and Ostroff (2004) highlight the importance of leaders in supporting workforce management approaches to enabling the psychological contract, especially as most staff identify leaders and value them in the overall context of the organisation climate. This approach links workforce policies, practice and the psychological contract in order to achieve organisational performance. While frequent breaches may occur, violation of this contract often has serious negative consequences (Robinson and Morrison, 2000), with lower workforce commitment, reduced job satisfaction and increased workforce turnover (Conway and Briner, 2005). For organisations wishing to develop, effectively recruit and retain good staff, it is necessary to view strategic workforce planning, policy and management practice in its totality, and ensure coherence between policy and practice. The longer and more intense working hours in the UK often results in less time for recovery and reflection by the care workforce (Green, 2001), and has inevitably resulted in higher stress levels (Karasek and Theorell, 1990). It is well known that high stress levels over protracted periods of time may result in staff burnout, increased risks of workplace injury, lower levels of performance, poor mental health, reduced concentration, health-related problems, and may also result in higher staff turnover (Arrington, 2008, p 13). Good workforce management policies and processes would seek to address these concerns, and even for employers who are more concerned about economic viability and meeting minimum standards, they would normally try to reduce the factors that might result in immediate litigation, ensure increased workforce stability and development and that meet regulatory standards.

Recruitment and retention

Leaders within organisations who are seeking to engage and empower their staff must therefore also have an awareness of the potential impact of these organisational processes, so that there is an alignment between the development of coherent workforce policies and practice, the values and ethos of the care sector and the staff undertaking care work. In studying direct care worker turnover and vacancy rates, Hussein and Manthorpe (2011, pp 6-9) identify a number of issues and trends that link to many of the issues explored so far. Their study identified a number of factors that would be of concern to leaders, service users and the organisations that deliver care, and include the following:

- Stability of the workforce appeared to be related to whether the employing organisation was based in the profit or non-profit sectors, with the greatest staff turnover being that in the for-profit sector.
- Turnover rate of staff in the sector was around 25 per cent, which is significantly lower than the hospitality and catering sector (34 per cent), but remained significantly higher than the turnover for the economy as a whole (15.7 per cent). Vacancy rates for private care providers, however, remained the lowest, resulting in them having low numbers of staff vacancies but an extremely high level of staff turnover.
- The size of the organisation has implications for workforce management systems and styles of management. Larger organisations demonstrated lower turnover rates (16 per cent), but this may also link to the first point above, as many of the largest organisations would have been public sector organisations. This, perhaps, has important implications for proposals to promote the increased use of personalisation.
- Lower rates of turnover were observed in organisations that provided healthcare services, that is, nursing as part of social care in comparison to other providers in social care alone. Turnover rates were the highest in children's care services, adult residential care and adult domiciliary care settings.

These findings are corroborated by recent data from the UK that suggests that turnover rates for care staff are high, with differing staff turnover rates across the profit and non-profit sectors (Skills for Care, 2010). Additional changes to the workforce have resulted from European Union (EU) integration and higher numbers of staff from what was previously Eastern Europe being employed. This internal EU migration of care workers is directly related to the enabling of free labour across the EU and the new Eastern European members joining the Union rather than publicity initiatives (Hussein and Manthorpe, 2011). As a result, workforce management to ensure diverse recruitment and retention across the sector is important, rather than organisations seeking only to minimise staff vacancy levels. The importance of these retention and recruitment factors for the care sector is underlined by Castle and Engberg (2005), who demonstrated a correlation between these workforce indicators and quality and turnover of nursing aids (the UK role equivalent to that of care workers). While the development of resilience in social workers in training may provide some individual protection, the context of the work environment remains important, as well as the design and development of organisations (Kinman and Grant, 2008).

Organisational and professional leadership

As a theme throughout this book, different aspects of leadership have been emphasised in terms of challenging our thinking about what we understand and consider to be its role and importance in the care sector. Within this chapter it is used to consider aspects of service delivery, management of the workforce and more broadly, within organisational strategy. The lenses through which we understand and theorise leadership comprise a number of different models that include trait, behaviourist and contingency theory, but it is transformational leadership that has been seen as important in professional services (Martin et al, 2010). Leadership through this lens is most frequently seen as a way to transform the way that staff view not only themselves but also the organisation they work for, underlining their importance to the success of the organisation, highlighting the importance of individual skills requiring individuals to take responsibility for their own development and performance, and last, to motivate staff to work to achieve their own as well as organisational goals (Martin et al, 2010). Within this chapter we have been chiefly concerned with the importance of leadership in relation to workforce planning, management and the strategic orientation of the organisation. The debates reviewed so far may be seen to mirror much of the critical literature debate on the differences between leadership and management, with some (Senge, 1990; Agashae and Bratton, 2001) clearly connecting leadership with learning and organisational change. There are no doubt 'business' risks for organisations operating in competitive environments in respect of the potential for the loss of a focus on core values and ethics, especially when targets and cost policies are overly prioritised and considered the sole form of outcome measurement.

Social learning theorists (Bandura, 1977, 1986) view learning as being undertaken vicariously, which inevitably highlights the importance of organisational culture and workforce experience as providing important learning points of reference to assist staff in moderating their own behaviour. For instance, there are important lessons for all staff in organisations in the way in which people are responded to when they unacceptably achieve what they perceive to be organisational goals. As we will see later in Chapter Seven, successive investigatory reports into public care scandals continue to highlight organisations where unethical, or even criminal, behaviour is either tolerated or implicitly accepted (Higgins, 2001), and which may have also been accompanied by weak leadership, organisational isolation and a culture of learned helplessness that accepts poor care standards as a norm. This link with organisational culture and workforce management has been identified in healthcare performance, but the exact relationship between the factors has been difficult to specify (Scott et al, 2003a) and isolate. Serious case reviews in social care have highlighted factors that include organisations' 'mirroring' of family dysfunction (Sidebotham, 2011) and excessive procedural compliance (Munro, 2010). Prokop et al (2010), as part of the London Safeguarding Children's Board, highlighted that many national reviews also lack detail on organisational culture and capacity, emphasising that this is a factor that needs to be given much greater prominence in reviews. These findings suggest that the problem of poor care extends beyond rogue staff and is much broader than the development of 'leadership'. This has prompted others (Magill and Prybil, 2004) to suggest that some of these organisation and workforce challenges can be addressed through emphasising a greater coherence between 'business' practices and ethical values, but given the range of interlinked workforce management factors explored in this chapter, it is unlikely that this alone will resolve these challenges. We return to these issues with a more systemic analysis in Chapter Seven.

Importance of workforce diversity and equal opportunities in organisations

The challenge for organisations to balance the need for workforce development with organisational strategy and implementation extends beyond social work and social care organisations. The commercial pressures on organisations require them to almost continually analyse, review and plan the size, skills and diversity of their workforce to meet changing commercial, regulatory and strategic business needs, and to retain an appropriately trained and experienced workforce. These strategic workforce considerations in the UK have, in recent years, been within a dynamic sociopolitical policy and economic context which requires almost constant environmental scanning to meet the new organisational challenges being presented, that is, personalisation, marketisation, changes to regulation and subsequent reviews of the social work profession.

Within the social work and social care sector the majority of revenue costs are for staffing as a result of the highly personal nature of the services delivered, and as a result these are costly, either directly or indirectly, for organisations or commissioners. This context creates uncertainty for many employers' workforce planning and management practice. The shortages of qualified social workers has resulted in this professional group being able to exercise greater choice on where and when they work (Moriarty et al, 2011a), with many having opted to work for social work private agencies. The lack of focus previously on robust development and the retention of critical staff often contributes to higher stress levels and workloads in already under-resourced teams. In turn, this can contribute to higher stress levels and further pressure and increasing consideration for those existing workers to leave that employer. These challenges, together with those of meeting the needs of vulnerable population groups, regulatory requirements, national and local performance targets, the need to achieve financial stability, contingency planning and ensuring effective workforce management, underlines the importance of effective leadership. This should be combined with wider consideration and the valuing of employee roles, the effective use of strategic workforce planning and implementation to support and deliver good quality care services.

To ensure good quality services the development of a diverse workforce is needed to support the delivery of the organisation's objectives, supported by Equal Opportunity Employment (EOE) along with a raft of employer policies and practices. The importance of this diversity is underlined by globalisation and the multiplicity of service user needs, employment of migrant and indigenous co-workers, all of whom may have different cultural and social identities, nationalities and ethnicities. It is important to recognise that globalisation, migration and colonialism have had an enormous impact in promoting multiculturalist (Friedman, 2005) and workplace diversity. These factors have had an impact on workplace diversity, but may also encourage ideas of outsourcing work internationally to overseas workers that is likely to be viewed as threatening to an existing organisational workforce.

The use of migrant labour to meet particular staff shortages has been one strategy towards resolving an immediate staffing crisis. It may also result in cross-cultural challenges stemming from the diversity of the professional backgrounds of care staff (Moriarty et al, 2011). Simplistic solutions to meet efforts to achieve quotas for particular employees are often not helpful. For instance, Goldstein (2002, p 765) found that employing Black social workers to promote equal opportunities among Black service users led to increased stress in those employed Black workers. As a result, organisations and leaders may need to develop a skill-based rather than ethnicity-based philosophy while challenging the homogenisation, interpersonal and institutional racism that may be experienced by Black staff (Goldstein, 2002).

Challenges in diversity and progression can be seen in those studying qualifying social work, where male students, students from Black and minority ethnic groups and students with self-reported disability had poorer progression rates (Hussein et al, 2008, p 1588). While recognising the importance of cultural competence, social workers felt frustrated by organisational constraints, and an overall individual stance detracted from systems and organisational responses needed to deliver services to multicultural users of service (Harrison and Turner, 2011). Within the UK, the implementation of the Equality Act 2010 (HMSO, 2010) has strengthened and simplified the discrimination laws, sought to protect disabled people and to prevent disability discrimination. The Disability Equality Duty was implemented in 2006 in which all public authorities were to promote the equality of disabled people as staff, visitors and consumers. However, progress appears to have been variable, and a higher priority needs to be given by organisations if changes to cultures and service provision are to be achieved (Pearson et al, 2011). As a result, the long-term impact of the equality legislation is therefore uncertain, but leaders should seek to ensure that its implementation meets both the spirit and letter of the legislation.

Service users and workforce management

The previous chapter explored current initiatives for the involvement of service users in shaping, evaluating and collaborating in partnership with care services, especially in the interfaces between the different care sectors. Policies such as 'personalisation' have been proposed as an attempt to be more service user-centred, and taking a co-productive approach in developing support, one of which has been the use of personalised and individualised budgets to enable independence and self-directed support (Carr, 2010). Ongoing collaboration and integration to improve service user experience in the public sector (Huxham and Vangen, 2000) has been promoted through legislation and policy at a macro level (Martin et al, 2009), integrated services and organisations at the meso level (Glendinning, 2003), and across professional teams at a micro level (Hudson, 2002).

Chapter One examined the implications for leadership in integrated and multi-organisational environments, cited as essential to improving the quality of outcomes (DH, 2008). Critics such as Marchington and Grugulis (2000) have cautioned against this assumption, while others such as Finn (2008) identify that a predisposition to reproduce openness, opportunities for joint learning and exchange may be negated. Others highlight the risks of managers aligning individual professional motivation through processes of socialisation to the system that they serve (Ezzamel and Willmott, 1988; Sewell, 1998). Interprofessional cooperation can therefore also suffer from organisational culture where government policy and professional institutions work against efforts to encourage greater knowledge between institutional and occupational groups (Currie and Suhomlinova, 2006).

In many ways, the parallel development of service user involvement with interprofessional working have both shared a common goal of improving services, quality, safety and making services more user-focused. UK policy initiatives such as the *Next stage review* encourage greater partnership between professionals, users and carers (DH, 2008b). The importance of these initiatives can be viewed where service users and carers are being drawn into cross-professional working through joint service design and management, shared decision-making and equality of influence (Chadderton, 1995; Rutter et al, 2004). It is almost inevitable that this involvement will result in challenges beyond that of recognition and financial compensation for their time (Turner and Beresford, 2005) to users' review of public service governance (Contiandropoulos et al, 2004; Barnes et al, 2007; Martin, 2008). This work is important as we reflect critically on how we design processes to involve service users and carers in processes that are already sceptical of the service's ability to ensure non-hierarchical and cooperative working relationships of professionals. El Enany et al (2013) also highlight the professionalisation of service users where, through a combination of self-selection, socialisation and cultivation by professionals, unrepresentative involvement may develop and might result, as with managers, in a range of service politicking. These difficulties are often compounded by external pressures, that is, performance targets that draw staff towards their own organisation's needs and processes, especially in an environment where the only contact between service users and professionals was through formal meetings that are likely to prevent relationships developing or result in complicit relationships.

Impact of strategic management on the workforce

Strategic workforce management is a key issue in contemporary care organisations, and leaders need to understand and provide support in those areas that are important to an employee's work experience as well as their relationship to the employer's policies and practices. For leaders to influence the motivation, commitment and development of care staff, it is important that they not only consider the strategic and operational concerns of the enterprise, but also the role of all leaders, line managers, including managers operating behind the front line, organisational process and strategic workforce implementation. The links between professional leadership and relationships between the employee and the line manager are clear. Strategic decisions by the leader and organisations and their impact on staff members are important. The decisions can be experienced in a number of ways by the organisation's workforce, through a combination of impact on staff numbers, the nature of the job role and design, use of technology, skills, as well as the types of people that undertake the work required by the organisation. As already explored, organisational values and culture are powerful influences on organisational performance and care quality. This highlights the importance of workforce management and leadership being viewed within a wider context of 'people management'. The importance of leaders and line managers in mediating between the organisation's policies and practices links directly to staff members' personal experience and their perceptions of the psychological contract, trust, leadership and trustworthiness. For most large organisations there will often be variations in how workforce policy is implemented, with successful implementation mostly depending on individual managers and leaders, with the inevitable knock-on impacts on work satisfaction and organisational loyalty (Guest and Conway, 2004).

Across social work a variety of studies have identified challenges in staff retention and turnover as a result of high caseloads, low pay, poor supervision, increasing bureaucracy and a poor sense of appreciation all being cited as key reasons for staff leaving employment (Garthwaite, 2005; Eborall and Griffiths, 2008; Curtis et al, 2010). In the UK, the Local Government Association (LGA) (2009) has highlighted important changes to the profession, and that there are significant levels of discontent, despite attempts made by many statutory employers to support initiatives to encourage recruitment and retention. The LGA (2009) report identifies significant shifts to the social work workforce in recent years in that it is now predominately female (80 per cent), with 32 per cent of new entrants in their twenties (2006/07), 13 per cent of the children's workforce comprised of agency staff, with staff turnover at 11 per cent in 2005. Spolander et al (2010), in their scoping of a social work career framework in the West Midlands, highlight that career lifestyles in the profession are increasingly uncertain, and the continued use of traditional approaches to workforce management in this sector was unlikely to be successful in the future. While the assessed and supported year in employment (ASYE) and newly qualified social worker (NQSW) development schemes (Skills for Care, 2011) may arguably support recruitment and promotion of new entrants, there appears to be an ongoing risk of workers leaving the profession four to five years' post-qualification (Spolander et al, 2010). The use of initiatives such as 'golden hellos', payment of professional fees and flexi-time (LGA, 2009), together with retention bonuses, may have unintentionally increased social work mobility in urban centres due to the financial attractiveness and promotion incentives of moving to a nearby employer. This suggests that many of the issues explored in this chapter are factors worthy of further critical reflection and leadership.

The strategic management of organisational HR is important for those providing care services, along with suggestions that social and psychological contracts between employers and employees are breaking down (Kochan, 2001). The use of integrated and value-driven strategic workforce development and leadership enables organisations to move beyond the rhetoric of developing 'knowledge-based economies' so that strategic workforce planning becomes meaningful for the organisation, staff and all stakeholders, including that of users of their services.

The imperative for 'lifelong learning' enables organisations to increase their commitment to invest and support education and training within a marketised business environment. This requires organisations and their leaders to develop greater externally focused relationships to support education and training such as those with universities, colleges, professional associations and trade unions. However, the increased use of outsourcing workforce management functions adds a further layer to this already complex work environment, increasing the challenges of organisational target and functional culture, challenges in integrating and promoting reflective leadership and management, and making the retention of key skills within the organisation more difficult.

Summary

This chapter has sought to explore many of the strategic challenges of workforce management by exploring the complexity of strategic business considerations, organisational culture, leadership and organisational viability. These issues are seldom drawn together for discussion and debate within the social care literature, but their importance in contributing to effective service delivery is hopefully not in doubt. The need to extend beyond the challenges for frontline leaders and to critically reflect on the processes and roles of those behind the front line in social work and care is important. However, it will be necessary for organisations, HR professionals, trade unions, managers, leaders and workers to be much more analytical, critical, reflexive and skilled in developing and implementing systems seeking to enhance performance and service delivery. These debates will no doubt help to build different understanding of the workforce and their impact on users of services, as well as contributing to organisational and care sector learning.

Work such as that by Kochan et al (2005) suggests that the direct involvement of staff in the development, implementation and oversight of workforce systems often helps to reduce the gap between employee and employer interests. It is important to recognise their importance in other economies, such as Germany and Japan, in facilitating workforce improvements and management. This joint investment and development may also help to meet the agenda of achieving work–life balance and go some way to supporting personal and family needs (Bailyn and Fletcher, 2003), developing training opportunities for social work students (Brown, 2002) and facilitating a motivated and committed workforce. The role of power in organisation decision-making, and in employee and employer relationships, is also important but often not discussed openly within organisations. However, it is important that social and care work is undertaken in an open, honest and transparent way to ensure that these initiatives to develop staff and work processes can be utilised effectively, and reduce the fear that whistleblowing may diminish individual career prospects (Drago et al, 2006; Rosenfeld, 2007). Efforts by TCSW, BASW and other associations in the UK care sector seeking to increase professional engagement needs to be both critical and also promote collective responses in the social work profession.

FIVE

Managing the workforce: operational and tactical strategies

Introduction

In taking a wide-ranging critical review of leadership and management in social work and social care, our journey so far has taken us through a number of related and connected issues for people and their organisations. For example, we have considered challenging and important theoretical and practice-related debates and suggestions on the future way forward for care to be delivered. This chapter builds on the strategic workforce issues raised in Chapter Four by focusing on the operational and tactical levels of workforce management. This is the place where many of us may have more direct experience with the direct operational challenges debated by leaders, practitioners and managers about the social work and social care workforce. This chapter therefore continues to critically review key workforce-related debates necessary for leaders and managers involved in operational service delivery. We should recognise right from the onset that the ground for debate and discussion in this regard is very broad, and as a result, we will narrow these to areas related to operational workforce debates to enable a more in-depth exploration. This chapter therefore narrows its coverage to critical debate and theory that often encompasses HR development as well as critical management theory, to facilitate our deliberation on the operational workforce challenges for leaders and their organisations. Chapter Seven then develops some of these challenges in more detail, and focuses on these more specifically in practice terms. In recent years there has been an underlying assumption that the coordination of large organisations, including social work or social care agencies, requires a permanently appointed occupational group of managers, that this group of staff are the best equipped people to undertake this role and should therefore be remunerated more than those providing direct services. This orthodoxy has been seldom challenged, and as you read this, you may already be wondering why we are even raising such a self-evident debate. This debate has been exacerbated by the implementation of neoliberal economic theory, as historically professionals including social workers had enjoyed considerable autonomy and discretion (Harris, 2003), and had exercised lead roles in the coordination of services. However, critical management writers have questioned how as an occupational group managers have been able to assert that their expertise is indispensable, especially in questions about quality and the achievement of financial balance, and how politicians and financiers of private sector agencies have accepted this argument. This primary focus on finances, quality and outcomes has supported the drive for greater organisational restructuring and the increased power of the private sector in the delivery of services (Harlow, 2008). This has led to some suggesting that these organisational changes have had an adverse impact on social work, compounded by weaknesses of workforce planning as a result of poor workforce intelligence (Evans and Huxley, 2009).

The workforce challenge in operational contexts

Social work and social care finds itself battered by a number of crises ranging from poor workforce planning (Evans and Huxley, 2009), inadequate staffing such as residential care (Unison, 2004), elevated levels of occupational stress, large workloads and deficient resources (Houston and Knox, 2004), job dissatisfaction (Evans et al, 2005) and staffing vacancies (Fleming and Taylor, 2007; Eborall and Griffiths, 2008; Curtis et al, 2010). Other areas of unease have included concerns about the privatisation and regulation of care home resources (Scourfield, 2011) that at least, in part, have powerful links and implications for workforce strategy and management explored in the last chapter, and explored at an operational level here. While social workers comprise a relatively small number of the approximately 1.77 million people working in social care (Fenton, 2011), they are important group with responsibility for enacting statutory duties and further important roles such as acting as gatekeepers and signposters to other care services, often within a context of statutory local authorities in England and Wales. In addition to these important roles, as a profession social work is increasingly shaping, developing and implementing marketised social care services, often as a direct result of government policy. The profession has therefore been at the forefront of marketising services that were previously provided by the state or charities through policies such as *A vision for adult social care: Capable communities and active citizens* (DH, 2010). This environment of change has had implications for the recruitment and retention of the workforce, with the LGA (2009) highlighting poor retention of children's social workers in comparison to teachers, 9.5 per cent compared to 0.6 per cent, with an annual turnover in social work staff at 9.6 per cent. Their report highlights that solutions implemented to manage these shortages have encouraged the training of social work assistants to increase the numbers of social workers in the workforce, the procurement and implementation of IT systems to drive efficiency, workload management policies, in addition to increased training for support staff to undertake wider roles (LGA, 2009, p 13). In addition, some groups of the workforce continue to be marginalised, for instance, the domination of men in senior management positions, women working in lower-paid and lower-status positions, and poor levels of succession planning for Black and minority ethnic staff (Baginski et al, 2010). This working environment provides challenges for the sector in recruiting, developing and retaining its workforce in order to meet rising challenges and expectations from service users' regulators and service financiers. The implementation of neoliberal economic and new public management reforms across the social work and social care sector has resulted in a significant reduction of generic social work practice, at least where community teams in local authorities have ceased to relate to geographic communities. In addition to this reduced community practice, the relationship with professional practice has been broken down into its various constituent parts, for example, reception, assessment and provision (Harlow, 2008) focused by performance targets and pre-determined service frameworks (Penhale and Parker, 2008; Sinclair, 2008). This increased use of Tayloristic work design of the social work process has significantly reconfigured the way that services are delivered. This has included the use of specialised workers who provide limited levels of input or care as part of their contribution to a chain of care, before the 'case' is handed to the next specialised worker or team for their input (Dustin, 2007; Harlow, 2008). Each part of this process may be subject to performance monitoring with the inevitable chain of auditable paperwork, and has prompted criticism that less bureaucracy, reduced performance management and fewer centrally driven targets are necessary (Munro, 2011). A further example of the drive towards management efficiency and control, use of technology and attempts to utilise scientific management to improve resource predictability can be seen in the increased use of call centres in the sector (Coleman and Harris, 2008), while commentators such as Munro (2011) have called for a number of practice and management areas to be rationalised and simplified, including abridged inspection processes, improved social work expertise and easier access to social work advice. Through building on the strategic workforce management debates raised in Chapter Four, critically exploring the challenges experienced in HRM within this sector, we aim here to transcend the challenges of individual organisations and business units, to critically review the operational and tactical organisational challenges. A committed workforce with organisational strategies that promote staff satisfaction, evidence-based solutions and good HR practice (Evans and Huxley, 2009, p 265) is an acknowledged way of addressing challenges in the sector. The HR policies explored in Chapter Four will inevitably be subject to interpretation by individual managers within an organisation. This interpretation could also involve active subversion on the part of either managers or staff. The challenge of implementation is often compounded by policy development throughout the organisation's history, which can result in managers not always being able to explain the reasons why a particular policy was developed. As a result, workforce policy and strategy within any organisation can be considered complex, subject to a variety of political and economic pressures with inconsistency in application, especially across large organisations, as well as being subject to organisational and personal politicking.

Developing the workforce

The establishment of management frameworks to support an organisation's workforce development has been surprisingly recent, with key structures such as the Harvard framework only being put forward in the 1980s (Beer et al, 1994).

This links workforce policy to the employer's business strategy in order to improve organisational effectiveness, and to promote stakeholder requirements (Beer at al, 1984). Stakeholder enhancement is a key requirement for most organisations. This linking of business strategy with implementation should also promote and support teamwork, shared values and loyalty to the organisation. The tacit purpose of a workforce strategy is to promote consistency in its approach, despite the earlier criticism levelled regarding inconsistency in implementation and the disapproval of the use of scientific management techniques in social work and social care. Following the publication of the Harvard architecture framework, other alternative frameworks (Dyer and Holder, 1988) have attempted to analyse management goals along a number of dimensions, namely, that of contribution (employee behaviour), composition (head count, skills mix, staffing ratios, and so on) and commitment (level of employee commitment). Dyer and Holder's model (1988) emphasises similar requirements to that of other frameworks in that there is a need for consistency in application, but it also promotes how workforce 'inducement', 'investment' and 'involvement' need to be linked to the organisation's external environment. Within the social work/social care environment the linkage between supervision, leadership, job satisfaction and workforce retention are well established (Coomber and Barriball, 2007; Mena and Bailey, 2007; Chen et al, 2008). As the work of Munro (2011) highlights, this external environment has a significant impact on both the day-to-day and strategic operation of organisations in the social work and social care sector as well the motivation and retention of staff. For most frontline managers of large organisations, their involvement with HR policies and processes would conventionally involve recruitment, selection, retention and appraisal. However, the impact of workforce policies extends considerably beyond this, and also includes organisational culture, the structure and organisation of work and the management of people. Given the variation and extent of for-profit and not-for-profit organisations, it is not possible to clearly identify one dominant HR framework in use today. Despite this, most management programmes seek to align staff work policies to that of the organisation's goals and utilise systems and processes that they feel are the most appropriate to do this.

Managing and leading performance

We identified earlier that the rise of new public management and neoliberal economic policy reform has resulted in increased measurement of performance in organisations, in both for-profit and not-for-profit sectors. The increased use of these systems is often championed as forces for driving service improvement, facilitating greater accountability as well as efficiency enhancement. This focus on performance has been a significant political driver in the last two decades in western societies (Ingraham, 2005). These policy imperatives, with their socioeconomic and political drivers, have created the need for greater accountability and transparency (Munro, 2004a), resulting in the establishment of national benchmarks and standards leading to frameworks, procedures and processes of audit and inspection. The use of performance management in social work and social care has not been without criticism, not least where the achievements of targets have been prioritised above quality of service (Social Work Taskforce, 2009; Munro, 2010). This is a paradox, as many supporters would argue that performance management is a mechanism of seeking service quality. The process of service quality assurance (QA) is one where systems and processes are put in place to provide assurance of quality in the delivery of services or products, such as care services (Hafford-Letchfield and Chick, 2006). While the QA process can be subject to interpretation, its main aim in the care sector is to improve care to service users, by regulating aspects of care delivery as well as professional services, and for influencing resource allocation and practice development (Hafford-Letchfield et al, 2006). These models of organisational performance have been developed from a positivist, mechanistic and rational model of organisations (Morgan, 2006) that suggests that structures and processes can be analysed objectively, described precisely and so managed objectively. These performance systems have an impact on both managers and staff directly through the linkage of the performance framework to the organisation's goals, resource allocation, organisational processes and finally, outputs. In Chapters One and Four we explored the ideas that link these processes through a variety of objectives, plans, performance indicators and performance management systems. Normally we would also expect that this type of performance system would link directly to a governance framework that represents stakeholders, interest groups and commissioners (and others with a variety of interests), along with variable levels of power and influence (Talbot and Johnson, 2007) in the organisation. To understand organisational performance it is important to understand the structure of both performance systems as well as the governance of the organisation (Talbot and Johnson, 2007), but it should also be broadened to include the culture. This latter area is one that we will return to and explore in more detail later in this chapter. For many organisations, performance systems can be developed and implemented based on a variety of recognised frameworks, but conventionally, regardless of its origins, they normally involve the following attributes:

- *Efficiency:* this is mostly concerned with evaluating the level of resources used to deliver a service, that is, this might include measures such as bed occupancy rates in a residential unit.
- *Economy:* this attribute normally involves appraising levels of expenditure required in order to deliver a particular performance outcome, that is, level of expenditure of home care adaptations or home care services per head of population.
- *Effectiveness:* this is achieved through the assessment of the outputs or outcomes of a service, that is, the number of family placement breakdowns of children placed in foster care.
- *Acceptability:* this is normally measured through the surveying of service users' experience of care services. This is often measured routinely through reported experience and complaints.

- *Access:* the gauging of the speed and ease of accessing services, that is, length of time taken to complete an assessment.

However, in addition to the critiques of performance systems, all have weaknesses in both design and use. These can be grouped into a number of categories (Smith, 1995; Freeman, 2002) as follows:

- *Reliability:* this questions whether the indicator is an accurate measure of what you are seeking to measure. Problems encountered with reliability might include whether the collection and interpretation of data is undertaken consistently and accurately. Additionally, the data may rely on a proxy measure (is this measure accurately measuring what you think it is?), whether it is accurate and frequently recorded on an IT system.
- *Validity* of the measurement might include questions about whether the indicator measures what it is designed to measure. For instance, if we measure rates of discharge from 'step-down beds' (for example, occupying a bed when people don't need medically to remain in hospital but who still require further rehabilitation before returning home), does this target measure the effectiveness of care and discharge planning or in contrast, might it indicate poor quality due to high levels of usage or be a measure of a lack of available resources in the community?
- *Attribution:* can the performance be attributed to the organisation or to another agency or process? For instance, rising levels of complaints can be viewed as poor quality; alternatively, it may be the result of good complaint recording and the active promotion of the complaints system, or possibly even more assertive and discriminating service users.
- *Comparability:* most indicators are used to form a basis for comparison either across time or between organisations. However, it is debatable whether performance measures can be compared where there are different organisational characteristics or where there are changes in the wider societal, economic or political environment.

Performance is often viewed or promoted as being a neutral attribute in QA models. For instance, it is a result of intentional acts on the part of the workforce or organisation, but when it relates to the quality of achievements, it may be conceptualised as either competence or capacity (van Dooren et al, 2010). Critics therefore view performance management as being strongly ideologically driven by neoliberal and new public management perspectives of organisations (Clarke and Newman, 1997). This has resulted in the suggestion that the performance approach is an imperfect tool with weak and mixed effects (Hood, 1998; Pollitt et al, 2010), while others who promote performance measures would no doubt point to the success of reduced waiting times for care as a positive outcome. However, regardless of which performance system is used, there will always be aspects of care systems and professional practice that will be unmeasured, with the attendant risk that these areas are either neglected or don't receive adequate resources. Organisations concerned about needing to demonstrate improved performance may also undertake 'gaming' the system to achieve short-term positive performance outcomes. This may result in care system distortion, that is, thresholds may come to be viewed within the organisation as an end in itself or an indicator of either maximum or minimum levels of effort (once the measure is achieved, the focus can be moved elsewhere), distort local care needs in order to meet national targets or the implementation of short-term policies that may be less helpful in the long term.

Notwithstanding the considerable criticism and concern of the use of this type of control in performance systems (Pollitt et al 2010; Munro, 2011), it is clear that these systems have an ongoing impact on the workforce within social work and social care organisations. Despite these critical approaches, for many statutory and non-statutory sector organisations, performance management and QA have become integral aspects of modern organisational life, the assumption being that performance-based systems help to drive improved services and accountability, despite concerns that this approach also decries the values of professionalism and caring. These systems have now become so prolific that even when not required by regulators, performance systems are needed to satisfy commissioners of service delivery. This further underlines why culture within organisations is such an important factor for leaders. Dubnick (2005) states that staff performance management systems contain the implicit assumption that 'competent' staff would be more likely to generate both higher levels and better quality outputs. In contrast, performance is normally equated with the output of the organisation (Dubnick, 2005).

As a result of these assumptions and discourse, the former 'competence' perspective results in an increased emphasis on developing and supporting staff competencies across the sector. Within some organisations, performance is viewed in such a way that the output measure is considered most important, and that as long as this performance output remains positive, it wouldn't matter how they were achieved (van Dooren et al, 2010). Supporters of this approach to performance management argue that it is only when performance is achieved through a combination of results, quality and quality of the inputs, that is, competence and output, that performance is considered sustainable (van Dooren et al, 2010). They believe that effort therefore needs to be put into ensuring that all these measures remain positive as a result.

Workforce appraisal

We have returned a number of times to the theme of QA and performance management, and have identified that these organisational systems and processes often link at both strategic and operational levels. At this interface the interpretation and key focus of staff is ensuring their delivery, and this therefore links directly to the appraisal and retention of staff. It should be noted that a key difference between performance management and appraisal is that the former is often part of an ongoing process while the latter comprises snapshots taken at specific intervals. For example, performance appraisal could be undertaken annually and will often involve evaluating the progress an individual has made over the year and agreeing new goals for them to meet in the following year. In order to develop and apply a performance appraisal system, a number of interlinked processes are often required:

- There needs to be a clear identification of the required job performance. In reviewing the job performance of an individual employee, a key requirement is identifying what the manager/supervisor should be looking for when appraising the individual. Scrutiny of the individual's job performance may be challenging due to the reliability of observation, for instance, problems with 'first impressions' (Spool, 1978) or 'halo effects' (Landy and Sigall, 1974; Kaplan, 1978). A 'halo effect' occurs when a trait (characteristic of a person) has an influence on other traits or characteristics of that person. For instance, research has shown that people considered to be 'attractive' are thought to be more successful in their working and social lives (Thorndike, 1920; Dion and et al, 1972; Landy and Sigall, 1974; Kaplan, 1978), while other work by Martell et al (1995) suggests that work-related memory of behaviour may be exaggerated by performance expectations, such that an individual's appraiser may identify behaviour as either better or worse without that behaviour even having occurred. Work by Latham and Mann (2006) adds further caution to the process by suggesting that age, race, sex and ethnicity may all have an impact on appraisal processes.
- Feedback, together with the establishment of new stretching targets to be achieved, are core parts of all appraisal systems. However, it is unusual for people to work on their own in the sector. This raises questions about whether both individuals as well as their team should be reviewed, as it is likely that skills and knowledge exist at a team level rather than just in a single individual. However, the rating of a team increases the level of complexity compared to the rating of individuals alone, and if a team rating was to be undertaken, different performance achievements than those used for individuals are likely to be needed (Chen et al, 2005). Finally, a decision must be made regarding rewards, provision of training/ongoing development or whether the individual should be retained in employment by the organisation. Munro (2011) highlights that social work performance should be considered within a context of professional expertise and the opportunities in work to exercise this expertise. As a result, these opportunities would extend to organisational culture, social support systems, organisational tools and systems and management culture and systems. As a result, a factor in undertaking an individual performance appraisal is the use of documentation to both assess and appraise the performance of an individual by their manager. Earlier in this chapter we identified that for many organisations this approach might be a focus on outcomes or goal achievement, but while at face level this seems relatively simple, this approach is also disputed. For instance, the performance goals/outcomes that are

being sought by the organisation may be outside of the direct control of the individual being appraised, with some measures even depending directly on the manger for their attainment. An example of this dynamic might be where the individual or team aims to achieve their performance goals 'at all costs', resulting in knock-on consequences for the rest of the workplace, teamwork or interprofessionally based relationships. We can see that while at one level the evaluation process may seem relatively simple, it also has considerable potential for interpersonal conflict, especially where individuals feel they are being evaluated on the wrong performance goals/targets. The by-product of this so-called rational process can result in a process that can cause substantial demotivation rather than motivation for the individual.

Operational recruitment

We began this chapter with an exploration of the appraisal of individual staff, but the process naturally commences with recruitment of the staff member into the organisation. Recruitment is therefore often linked to selection, but the former involves the use of HRM techniques to ensure the widest possible range of applicants is available to support the selection process. Recruitment of staff is therefore an important consideration, especially in light of the wider challenges of workforce sector changes, key staff shortages, socioeconomic conditions and the costs of attracting appropriate staff. This difficult task relates directly to the debates raised in Chapter Four in considering the strategic nature of workforce management. For organisations at an operational level, there is a need to decide who they should recruit, where to recruit these people, the channels used to undertake the recruitment (that is, web, job fairs, secondment training), when the recruitment should be undertaken and finally, the messages that need to be communicated to support the process (Breaugh and Stark, 2000). This requires consideration of the organisation's overall strategic aims, how these will be achieved and the HR needed to accomplish this. While recruitment and retention within the sector is often conflated, the challenges and responses for both may differ significantly. Staff shortages within the UK social sector extend beyond large population centres such as London and high-profile services such as childcare (Balloch, 2005), and many of these difficulties include recruiting and retaining qualified staff, staff sickness rates and reduced numbers being attracted into social work training (Harlow, 2004). All of these are influenced by high occupational stress levels, considerable workloads and a lack of resources (Houston and Knox, 2004; Evans et al, 2006). These challenges continue despite considerable workforce management literature identifying that job satisfaction as well as a high level of work-related pressures increase the likelihood of staff leaving (Forsythe and Polzer-Debruyne, 2007) or feeling undervalued (Huxley et al, 2005). Marsh and Triseliotis (1996) highlighted that most newly qualified social worker (NQSWs) did not receive any organised induction, and later work by Bradley (2006) also found diminutive evidence of formalised induction. In recent years efforts have been made to encourage the recruitment and retention of workers, supporting the development of practice competence (GSCC, 2008) using national strategies such as the NQSW scheme to support social workers in the first year of employment following qualification. This has now been superseded by ASYE (Skills for Care, 2012). Moriarty et al (2011) identify that there has been little research on the transition of NQSW into the workplace, and highlight the importance of induction in helping this transition, but caution that it is not a magic potion for difficult working conditions. Relatively small numbers of line managers have used national induction frameworks in social work and social care (Skills for Care, 2010) and CWDC standards, or even knew of their existence (Bates et al, 2010). This is despite extensive evidence that induction contributes towards improving retention as well as helping to support and motivate staff (Maher et al, 2003; NSWQB, 2004; Bradley, 2008). However, these studies are contradicted by the *Adult, children and young people: Local authority social care workforce survey* (LAWIG, 2005) that identified over 80 per cent of local authorities as using the national induction standards. This discrepancy and contradiction between the work undertaken by the National Social Work Qualifications Board (NSWQB) (2004), Bradley (2008) and the Local Authority Workforce Intelligence Group (LAWIG) survey raises questions about whether the LAWIG survey results were an example of respondents achieving national performance targets by answering the questions positively and thereby meeting their target requirements. You may remember the earlier discussions and debates on potential adverse impacts of performance management on organisational and staff responses and practice, and this discrepancy, rather than clarifying practice, raises further questions.

Caring for staff in the organisation

The challenges of operational workforce management in social work and social care agencies include factors already highlighted such as high workloads, inadequate resources and elevated levels of occupational stress (Houston and Knox, 2004; Evans et al, 2006) and staff vacancies (Harlow, 2004; LGA, 2009). Evans et al (2006) highlight that among approved social workers (ASWs) (now known as approved mental health practitioners, AMHPs) there are higher stress levels and burnout. The complexity of employment in the sector is underlined by findings from Curtis et al (2010) which suggest that the working life of a social worker is approximately 8 years, a social care worker 13 years, compared to 28 years for pharmacists. This level of turnover is expensive in both replacement and training costs, but also has implications for service quality and continuity. Responses to the recruitment and retention crisis have included overseas recruitment (Engelbrecht, 2006; Bowcott, 2009; Walsh et al, 2010; Pullen-Sansfaçon et al, 2011) and initiatives that have included enhanced pay and benefits, improved working conditions or supported professional development (Evans and Huxley, 2008). In recognition of the need to develop worker-centred approaches, family-centred work practices have been encouraged by many organisations (Guest, 2002) to support staff achieving a greater work–life balance. Work undertaken by Doherty (2004) on work–life initiatives suggests that a stronger equal opportunities approach directed to support women may also result in drawing attention to differences between men and women and the perceived need for special treatment to be given. Rather, it is suggested that stronger rights are needed to protect all members of the workforce, especially where the voice of trade unions is weak, and that male managers should be engaged to humanise the workplace to benefit both men and women to improve their work–life balance (Doherty, 2004). In this regard it is important for us to consider examples beyond the UK, to recognise that Western European models of work engagement have differed from the UK in respect of work hours (reduced work hours in France) and support for parental leave in Nordic employment models (Gregory and Milner, 2011). For many employees in the UK, the experience of workers has been one where the arrangement needs to be negotiated individually with managers and could easily be constrained by organisational needs or the needs of operational teams (Gregory and Milner, 2011). As a result, individual choice in respect of work–life balance is often related to the culture of the organisation, gender expectations and labour market prospects (Gregory and Milner, 2009), underlying the importance of corporate approaches to staff care.

Work-related stress

While there is no medically defined condition of occupational stress, it is commonly understood as the process where the individual experiences demands that exceed their resources (Bendelow, 2009). Work-related stress is also correlated with other ill health outcomes such as cardiovascular disease (Kivimäki et al, 2002), musculosketal disorders (Hoogendoorn et al, 2000) and work absence (Houtman et al, 1999; Morris, 2009). Higher levels of stress were correlated with lower work satisfaction and organisational commitment (Elangovan, 2001). Using a comparison of 26 occupational groups according to three factors, namely, physical wellbeing, psychological wellbeing and job satisfaction, social workers were found to have experienced above-average work related stress levels compared to other occupations (Johnson et al, 2005). Within the UK a study in 2008 found that 20 per cent of social workers had been signed off work for 20 consecutive days in the previous five years due to stress and anxiety, and that this was double the rate of teachers' stress-related absence (Asthana, 2008). Brown and Benson (2005) highlight that the lack of career development can cause psychological suffering and higher rates of illness. Time conflicts in trying to achieve a balance between work and home commitments may result in role conflict and distress (DeFrank and Ivancevich, 1998). It is clear, however, that stress levels have an impact on individuals, families, teams and organisations as well as resulting in both their families and work suffering and inadequate work role performance (Cooke and Rousseau, 1984; DeFrank and Ivancevich, 1998; Axtell et al, 2002). In addition, as we shall see later in Chapter Eight, bad working relationships, work overload and unfair pay are also significant stressors in the workplace (Vakola and Nikolaou, 2005). The problems faced by organisations in relation to staff retention, together with the duty of care employers towards their staff for the creation of safe working environments (Bradley, 2008), and adherence to the relevant codes of practice, highlight their importance and priority for organisations. However, these challenges are complex and are often multilayered and multifactorial. Employer support to review job designs, improved communication and work–life balance can assist in motivation, retention and reducing ill health in the sector. We continue these themes in Chapter Six by exploring support mechanisms that managers can offer to support staff in order to reduce these concerns.

Leading development and learning

The focus placed within organisational management literature on aligning organisational strategy and effectiveness has resulted in an emphasis on professional training and continuous professional development (CPD). This is underlined by the requirement for CPD in order for registered professions such as social work and occupational therapy (OT) to retain their professional registration. A further substantial influence has been organisations undertaking strategic and workforce reconfiguration, regulation, developing new roles and empowering users of services. These changes have influenced the organisational strategic direction as well as the type of skills and nature of competences, all of which are considered important in the sector. For example, training and education has sought to blur the edges between professional roles – AMHP (DH, 2008) and best interest assessor (DH, 2009) roles do not require the work to be undertaken by qualified social workers as other professions can also undertake this role after appropriate training. New leadership roles also have been seen as key to service improvements, particularly those within a participatory and distributary model. Policies promoting accountability, partnership, commissioning, efficiency and community engagement (I&DeA, 2008) have all had a substantial influence in this process. HR development and professionals consider 'development' in four key ways (Lee, 1997, 2001). The first is in the context of a series of stages through which individuals, groups and organisations could be understood and developed, along a course of pre-determined stages and through a progression-based learning approach. The second is the notion of 'development' as a process of shaping, which involves staff being shaped to fit into the organisation. The third category comprises those who view 'development' as a voyage where the individual undertakes a personal journey in which they construct their own reality (in or outside of an organisation). Thus, the individual is seen as the motivating force behind identifying their own needs and the meeting of them. The final group is emergent, with development of the development of the organisational group viewed as a social system being disorderly and lacking a single leader (Lee, 2001). While Lee identified that individuals mostly speak of 'development' within a context of a voyage of learning, growth and discovery, senior managers most commonly view 'development' in the context of a shaping activity (Lee, 2001). Social theorists and HR development professionals encompass perspectives between maturational or emergent, and as a result, Lee (2001) does not view 'development' and HR as 'unitary' concepts. This has important implications for leaders in managing the workforce, both strategically and operationally.

Training and development

To enhance workforce capability, organisations often provide training and development via internal provision, externally commissioned training or possibly by poaching staff already equipped with the 'competencies' needed by the organisation. The latter strategy may be used together with higher pay, the savings being created by the reduced need for the provision of additional training. The use of outsourcing may enable the procurement of external skills without the costs of long-term staff employment. The decisions on whether training and development is provided in-house or procured externally is often influenced by available training skills, capacity as well as governmental, regulatory and sector requirements. Perhaps one of the most published examples of this in the sector is the recruitment by UK sector employers of staff from the so-called 'global south' (Pullen-Sansfaçon et al, 2011). Communication in respect of managing people helps them to have a clear understanding of expectations, ensuring that they feel confident, have the skills and expertise to undertake the task and provide feedback on their achievements. This conversation will naturally vary according to their role, time horizon and their achievements, all of which relate to the workforce management processes explored so far. In particular, we have noted the importance of interdependence within team working, where achievements are often only possible through the combined achievement of all individuals and processes working in concert. Through the successful design of roles and team functions it is possible to ensure teams that are multiskilled, owning the entire process from development, implementation, delivery and evaluation.

Other processes that are often used by organisations to improve productivity include:

- Rationalisation/reorganisation of staff and resources in order to promote synergy. Reductions in staffing and resources through the reduction or denial of expenditure. In a market-based economy this might result in certain services being stopped.
- Redesign of the service or the flow of direction through which people pass in a care system. In the health service this is referred to as the patient pathway in which process-mapping is used to reduce unnecessary use of resources to ensure the service is as efficient and focused on service users as possible.
- Critical reflection of individuals and team performance, to review if and where improvements can be made.

The strategies of reorganisation and cuts might only result in one-off savings, and unless well considered can sometimes result in cost increases elsewhere in the system, that is, reductions in preventative services can result later in more severe and expensive problems that need to be addressed or will have unintended consequences.

Managing change

We have already explored the stressful and emotional nature of work within the sector; these, together with the complexity of decisions, ethical dilemmas, negotiating with various stakeholder partners and a changing sociopolitical and economic climate, can result in a complex and stressful work environment. In addition, managers, leaders and professionals are constantly seeking to achieve equilibrium in their responsibilities, supporting relationships within and external to the organisation and attempts to improve productivity. Managers in the for-profit and non-profit sectors increasingly need to also manage improved market share and profitability, maximising resource allocation and social policy changes. As a result change seems to be a constant companion of managers, leaders and staff. In managing this change a variety of tools and models exist with one popular approach being Kotter's model (Kotter, 1996; Kotter and Cohen, 2002). Kotter's (1995) model provides an eight-point action plan for the effective leadership of change that is summarised as follows:

- *Stage 1:* Ascertain the urgency of the change.
- *Stage 2:* Establish a group of people who could work as a team to successfully undertake the change needed.
- *Stage 3:* Create a vision that can help to focus the proposed change, together with strategies that when implemented will help to achieve the vision.
- *Stage 4:* Communicate the vision and strategies, together with modelling any new behaviour that you are wishing to implement.
- *Stage 5:* Give power to those involved in the change so that they can act, by removing obstacles and changing systems and supporting risk-taking.
- *Stage 6:* Plan and support short-term wins, recognising the efforts and any success in this undertaking.
- *Stage 7:* Consolidate changes and improvements as well as undertaking further changes to processes that don't support the vision that has been set out.
- *Stage 8:* Institutionalise the new approaches that have been adopted to ensure they are ingrained in the organisation's fabric, support career succession planning and highlight the links between the new changes and organisational success.

Within Kotter's (1995) model the process of creating the change occurs in the first four stages, the process of enacting change in stages 5-7, and the steps made to achieving sustainability the final stage 8. After considering Kotter's model you may also be thinking that there are other questions that change leaders would also need to consider, such as:

- the size of change required, what the change involves, for example, by asking whether this is at a team or service level
- the optimal speed and level of change
- how visible the change leader should be or
- whether they should work via change champions and
- what level of sustainability needs to be included.

All of these questions require consideration by leaders and organisations, together with a review of available tools and techniques to decide on how to undertake the change. Change leaders will almost always have their own perceptions of change that might be influenced by factors such as professional training, values and personality, but also by the sociopolitical and economic environment. As a result, Bolman and Deal (2008) suggest four dimensions to change that change leaders will need to consider: cultural, human, structural and political. Their model suggests that it is possible for leaders to reframe change processes by changing the emphasis from cultural change to structural change if there is too much emphasis on this former aspect (Bolman and Deal, 2008)

Learning from error

Chapter Two introduced the theory of organisational culture and, given its importance to organisations and the workforce, this chapter returns to exploring alternative discourses in more detail. Social work and social care contexts and organisational intercession are important in helping to establish and promote environments that improve service outcomes, the wel-being of staff and service users an, quality Glisson and Green, 2006; Glisson et al, 2006). High-risk economic sectors such as aviation, nuclear power and health (Edmondson, 2004) have all invested heavily in seeking to reduce the risk of failure, either by mistakes due to human error or problems as a result of organisational/systems impediments. Munro and Hubbard (2011) highlight that children's social care has some similarities to these high-risk sectors, but also a history of attributing errors to individuals with efforts in the sector. To reduce these errors being undertaken through higher levels of workforce control, detailed procedure manuals and closer scrutiny of practice to judge an organisation's ability to learn, it is important to observe how it manages failures (large or small) and not just those that are highly visible (Edmondson, 2004). Within these organisational failures, individual actions should be seen within the context of highly managed organisations that have undertaken reform and whether these reforms may have unintentionally resulted in serious consequences (Munro, 2005; Seddon, 2008). This highlights the need for the sector to develop a focus that is broader than the individual being at the centre of the systems failure, and that recognises the systemic factors and interactions, including the relationships and roles of individuals within these systems (Dekker, 2007)

This has been recognised in high-risk sectors such as aviation and nuclear power that have introduced organisational processes and cultures of "no blame" reporting, with an emphasis on improvement through the redesign of systems, the workforce and tasks that are at risk of failure (Berwick, 2003). These "no blame" cultures recognise the reasons underlying errors and create a "blame-free" environment for the reporting of near-misses or errors. This form of organisational intervention within the work environment supports the early identification of error causation rather than attributing blame to individuals. It recognises that reporting is unlikely in a climate of fear among staff groups or caregivers (Weick et al, 1999; Walton, 2004., The underlying assumption and commitment of these changes being that error understanding should extend to organisational and psychological issues and not individual factors alone, that is. lack of expertise, poor communication during changing staff shifts, and in doing so raise questions about culture, work flow and work design (Walton, 2004). Systems improvement requires effective regulators, resources and tools to assist organisations to identify poor working practices or conditions that workers may ignore, have learned to tolerate or are afraid to deal with (Reason, 1997). This is not to suggest that in understanding error it should either be viewed as an individual or system failure. However, we need to recognise the complexity in organisations, which would include the interface and interaction between individuals, teams and systems. While individuals need to ensure that they remain professionally competent, and accountable for their actions, we also need to appreciate the importance of organisational factors in errors and predicaments. The majority of error studies have often been undertaken from the perspective of the professional or organisation involved, but recent research has found that communication influences service users' perceptions of adverse events, that users identified emotional consequences and that they supported these events being disclosed (Massó Guijarro et al, 2010). This is often problematical for organisations concerned about the legal, reputational and financial damage that such an error may cause for the organisation

Efforts to understand the learning from serious incidents within social work and social care have often been the subject of serious case reviews (Ofsted, 2010). These are defined as "... local enquiries into the death or serious injury of a child where abuse or neglect is known or suspected to be a factor. They are carried out by Local Safeguarding Children Boards so that lessons can be learned" (Ofsted, 2012). Sidebotham et al (2010, p 3) highlight that many case reviews identify similar areas of difficulty which include; "... Professional "blindness" to more deep seated systemic failings"; difficulty of turning findings into realisable goals; failures to follow up on recommendations; and delays which have an impact on the speed that lessons can be learned. The Munro (2011, p 9) report highlights that problems with serious case review methodology is o-going, and recommends that regular review should become customary and that approaches used in the health sector should also be adopted. The Welsh Government (2011) has consulted on replacing the current review system in favour of one that recognises multi-agency and inter-professional perspectives, focuses on accountability and not just culpability, and makes managers more accountable for the context and culture in which staff work together with speeding up learning. These issues are the subject of detailed examination in Chapter Seven.

Organisational culture

As we saw in Chapter Two, the study of organisational culture includes a range of frameworks developed in order to facilitate understanding. This diversity in frameworks is probably a reflection of the range of views on the definition of organisational culture and the processes of organisational change (Alvesson and Sveningsson, 2008). It is therefore likely that organisational culture may be connected to both organisational structure and strategy. In relation to this chapter, we can often see organisational culture the clearest in the first month of starting a new job – we observe and experience organisational behaviours and values that we later come to accept and that become less obvious. Any cultural change therefore requires change at both the observable and unobservable levels through understanding the unwritten rules of behaviour and attempting to change them, modelling attitudes and behaviours that everyone should adopt, supporting positive sub-cultures and encouraging teamworking and professionalism. These challenges extend beyond simplistic efforts of implementing new statements of values, policies and procedures, and require inspired and dedicated leadership that engages the workforce and stakeholders in its developments.

Summary

This chapter has critically reviewed many key areas that challenge leaders, managers and professionals within their day-to-day operation of care provision. These workforce and organisational obstacles are complex and multifaceted, and while there are always work-related pressures, broader society anxiety and a need to constantly improve care processes, there is always a temptation to seek easy, quick and affordable responses. However, as we have explored in this chapter, there are important influences and interrelated complexities that need to be reviewed, and it is therefore important to stop and reflect whether we fully understand the individual and the system in which they work, and the interrelationship between the two before making changes that may exacerbate problems or lead to unintended consequences. The system and process of care provision is challenging, fraught with multiple agendas and the need to provide responsible, ethical and appropriate services, it is important that leaders fully understand and respect this complexity in order to implement effective change

In recognising the needs of all stakeholders – service users, policy-makers, citizens, professionals, managers and other agencies – we need to seek frameworks, language and systems that understand the complexity, experience, practicality, inherent contradictions and dilemmas of practice. Very often there is a plethora of literature that purports to portray solutions and change in simplistic positivist terms, but our care systems are multifarious, human and challenging. Managing and leading these challenges, the human resources within organisations, making change and ensuring safety, effectiveness and efficiency are often harder than initially anticipated, and plans take longer to achieve. As leaders we owe stakeholders a moral and ethical responsibility to undertake our roles and any changes with empathy, understanding, consideration and an ethical approach.

SIX

Providing formal and informal support to staff, service users and carers

Introduction

Having explored the strategic and operational context that support care, we now return to focus on the core of leadership practice. As traditional relationships between recipients of care services and professionals change, so must ideas about how services can support staff, service users and carers. In Chapter Two we considered systems theory as a particularly useful paradigm for thinking about the interdependency of organisations through its alliances and partnerships. In this chapter, a systems perspective has also been adopted to help examine how organisations can ensure appropriate support to staff, service users and carers, as these relationships are transformed by neoliberal ideas and policies through more inclusive approaches, including inclusive leadership, as new ways of relating become established.

A systemic view of formal and informal support

Organisations that commission or provide care services operate within complex systems, which, when examined closer, are comprised of sub-systems populated by service users and carers, managers, professionals and support staff. In England, for example, local councils are part of a national government system. Each local council has a children's services department, where social work is organised and carried out by social workers in 'looked-after children's teams', 'duty and assessment teams', and so on. Social workers routinely interact with other systems (for example, other government departments) and sub-systems (local police stations, hospitals, and so on). In some cases care provider organisations may be joined together in formal partnerships, or they may have joint working arrangements. In England, in common with other European and UK countries, some care and health organisations have merged to become fully integrated services, and increasingly more services are being delivered by voluntary organisations or social enterprises. Social workers can therefore be found working alongside a variety of other professionals in a variety of systems. These systems provide a 'context' for social work practice.

There is much evidence in the literature of managers and leaders developing new ways of thinking about, and providing organisational support to, staff, service users and carers, within and across a variety of organisational settings. In the

London Borough of Hackney's Children and Young People's Services, for example, a more targeted service was developed, supported by integrated teamworking, and a change programme was evaluated (Cross et al, 2010). The change programme addressed the challenges posed when working with risk, which goes beyond financial consequences into the area of what Cross et al (2010) refer to as 'human tragedy' (Cross et al, 2010). The change programme was called 'Reclaiming Social Work' and required professionals to work in new ways. The evaluation focused on the impact of the changes that were being introduced into the organisation, including changes to the organisational culture, social work processes and outcomes. Reclaiming Social Work resulted in professionals organising themselves into small units, thereby bringing together a range of expertise and perspectives, to enable better assessments and interventions. The evaluation asserted that organising professionals into work units led to improvements in the quality of the service as professionals focused on providing early support and engaged in direct work with families, which increased the protective factors necessary to keep children safe. Cross et al (2010) concluded that the Reclaiming Social Work programme led to positive outcomes for service users and carers.

The link made between an organisation and the formal support the organisation offers to service users and carers is important. In a recent report by an English inspection agency (CQC, 2011c), one local authority was praised for designing services that targeted support to families with children with special needs. The report highlighted that this particular service was an exemplar of good practice. The inspectors noted the good take-up of early services and the use of respite care by 'parents who are experiencing isolation, stress and anxiety to prevent family breakdown and the need for children with special needs to enter the care system' (CQC, 2011c, p 8). Care systems are, however, large and complex, and service users may need to access more than one service or professional to get their needs met. It is therefore highly possible that workers across any care system, employed by different organisations, may have different priorities or even conflicting goals when they meet with service users and carers. The Care Quality Commission (CQC, 2011c) inspection report also recommended that the same local authority needed to work with general practitioners (GPs) to ensure that they were more proactive in child protection work. This work takes places across sub-systems and this recommendation was designed to ensure that GPs supported other professionals across child protection services in the city. In this way, while formal support and intervention can be designed 'into a system' (through procedures and protocols), it is staff, service users and carers, supported by managers and leaders, who must make the system work. While the context in many countries may differ from the examples provided here, which are about the English care system, issues of organisational form and culture discussed in Chapter Two, and the role that service users, professionals and other workers play, are all relevant. These remain universal factors that can be found in any care system, and it is within this context that the support that is on offer must be understood.

Systems, support and protection issues

Munro (2011) highlights how difficult it can be for managers and professionals to provide support to service users and carers when responding to child protection issues. In addition, the motivation to engage with social workers and the child protection system is a challenge for many families who may reject support, even when they really need it, because they fear that their child (or children) will be taken into care. The Family Rights Group cited in Munro's report (2011) summarised the obstacles that families faced when engaging with the social care system in these circumstances. This included a lack of clarity about the concerns that social workers and other agencies had, anger, upset, fear and confusion about the process that could affect the family's capacity to get advice, as well as feelings of being overwhelmed by the process, which could make it hard to trust social workers. As a result, the Family Rights Group said that '... the system doesn't support families to take responsibility; instead parents often feel decisions and actions are done "to" rather than "with" them, thus encouraging a sense of dependency and resentment' (quoted in Munro, 2011, p 44). The voice of families and carers, even when there are potential protection issues, has largely been ignored in the past. The challenge of providing formal support to children and families in child protection work, has, however, led to some new practice developments emerging in recent years, although it is widely recognised by professionals and managers that this is a challenging area of practice. Legal duties and responsibilities, as well as rights and system developments, are informing how managers and social workers implement policy developments to promote greater partnership between organisations, workers, service users and carers. Healy and Darlington (2009), for example, suggest that promoting service user rights in child protection decision-making is highly complex work that requires sensitive social work practice. There is a tension between working with a family where there are child protection concerns that require social workers, with the support of their managers, to exercise power, sometimes against the wishes of the service user, in order to keep children safe. The active participation of families even in such circumstances reflects a raised awareness by social work organisations of people's human rights to participate in the decisions affecting them, the commitment to self-determinism that is central to social work, and participatory practice, which is increasingly linked to better outcomes (Healy and Darlington, 2009). Social work interventions, including child protection interventions, require the use of evidence-informed approaches, and evidence of what works is not always available to social workers and managers.

Healy and Darlington (2009) have developed participatory approaches in decision-making with service users and carers in child protection work, and suggest that social workers need to adopt three principles of participation. First, social workers need to show respect for all family members, their differences, and seek to find ways to work with all members of the family, to find solutions. Second, social workers need to understand the issues relating to the appropriateness of service user participation in the process; and third, social workers need to ensure transparency of purpose in the process. They suggest that: 'Without the development of practice principles and strategies addressing these tensions, the capacity of child protection services to deliver on the promise of participation will be constrained and rightly viewed cynically by service users and the broader community' (Healy and Darlington, 2009, p 420). These developments can be very challenging for managers who work in systems that have become defensive, risk-averse and controlling, in response to the pressures placed on social workers and managers, when mistakes have been made and individual workers have been blamed (Munro, 2011). However, Munro (2011) argues that it is the quality of the relationship between service users, carers and professionals that has a direct impact on the effectiveness of the help that is given, so managers and leaders need to provide supportive systems for workers, service users and carers to develop these relationships. Inclusive and participatory approaches can support this work.

Participatory approaches within child protection systems are emerging across Europe, as new policies and ways of organising and managing service provision is developed, leading to new challenges for social work practice. In Norway, for example, one service recognised that the support that had been offered to parents who had lost custody of their children was very poor. This led to child protection services offering parents the opportunity to form a group to voice their concerns about the service, and to give and receive support. Slettebo (2013) found that the parent group was mutually beneficial – it provided social workers with useful knowledge that led to organisational developments while service users were able to access the support they needed from other parents in a similar position. However, the group experience did not lead to any changes in the individual cases, suggesting that these groups largely benefited organisations, providing an opportunity for organisational learning. For participants the key life-changing decisions had already been made (their children were permanently removed from their care), and participants were aware that this situation would not change as a result of participation in the group.

As we saw in the discussion about learning organisations in Chapter Two, the link between formal systems of support and organisational learning is an interesting area to examine. Munro (2011) suggests that child protection systems need to learn in order to improve, and managers and professionals can do this through the use of feedback loops. She suggests that the services that support children and families need to monitor the impact of interventions by collecting feedback from children and families to see how these interventions are contributing to children's safety and wellbeing, particularly if they are having a negative impact. In this context, attention has been drawn to frontline managers as leaders. Schorr (1997) also links the achievement of effective child protection outcomes with managers displaying a range of leadership skills: willingness to experiment, to take risks and learn by mistakes; ability to cope with ambiguity; ability to gain the trust of key stakeholders including frontline staff; ability to establish evidence of results; ability to collaborate with other staff; and capacity to provide staff with discretion at the front lines of practice. Thus, system innovations and social work interventions that have a negative impact on children and families, she suggests, need to be identified and adjustments made (Munro, 2011). This requires different types of learning to take place, which Beeby and Booth (2000) identify as 'organisational learning' (the process of learning within organisations), as well as learning that takes place across a system, as already discussed in relation to the concept of 'the learning organisation'. An example of this is exemplified in a management model developed in a child protection practice context by Wilson (2007), where the design of the service provided a conceptual link between child protection outcomes, service activities and management activities, and consolidated a range of skills and strategies that supported frontline managers to proactively manage for these outcomes. In this model, the service outcomes of improved child safety, child wellbeing and family functioning became the central focus of statutory child protection service delivery. Practitioners contribute to these outcomes through service activities that have been strongly linked with them: building relationships with children, young people, their families, carers and significant others; participative planning with children, young people, their families, carers and significant others; collaborative practices with other agencies; and tenacious casework. Managers in turn proactively manage for outcomes by using management strategies to develop an office environment that strongly supports direct service staff to undertake these service activities, creating a change process that enables an increase in the capacity of direct service staff to undertake effective service activities (Wilson, 2007).

As care services are increasingly shaped by marketisation and its new organisational forms and policies, this in turn reflects a changed relationship between the citizen and the state in which learning at an individual and systems level becomes a more challenging activity. This is particularly concerning given the role that new workers may play in protecting vulnerable people, many of whom are not qualified professionals, such as social workers. Given the management and leadership challenges this situation generates, and building on the more generic discussion in the preceding chapters on workforce development and people management, there is a need to consider what specific support is being offered to these new workers.

Policy changes and changing worker roles

As we saw in Chapter One when we explored the concept of leadership in its context, frequent changes across welfare systems have included the development of new 'support' functions to enable people to access services in new, and potentially more empowering, ways. These new worker roles are emerging across many countries, and in England these workers have role titles that include advocates, personal assistants and brokers. Managers and leaders designing care services continue to use social workers to deliver specialist services, but they are also providing a wider range of services, which are being delivered by new worker roles.

These developments, however, have been raising concern among some people, including service users, who say that some service user groups such as in adult services in England, for example, hardly ever see a social worker despite placing a high value on what they do (Beresford, 2007). As outlined in both Chapters Three and Five, these changes require leaders to understand the demands of the system in which they work, and to adopt proactive strategies to develop appropriate forms of support infrastructure to meet the different needs of workers and service users, within the context of seemingly contradictory policy messages. Care workers need to balance empowerment and support, as highlighted by the Commission of Social Care Inspectorate (CSCI, 2008, p 30). This is based on the principle that vulnerable people are at greater risk of abuse if they receive inadequate support in their lives. However, support should not be geared purely towards protection as this can lead to restrictions on people's freedom to make choices and to take considered risks. One of the risks inherent in these new developments, therefore, is failing to provide the right support; critics suggest that these developments do not genuinely take into account proper consideration of the needs of vulnerable adults and how they will be supported and protected (Lymbery and Postle, 2010).

Personalisation and personal budgets have led to the development of new worker roles in social care, including those associated with the brokerage role. But it is unclear what this role involves and who should be doing it. Support brokerage, as a term, has been used in some social care services over the last 20 years or so. In the context of self-directed support, it has become fairly commonly used to describe a range of help for people with a personal budget. As self-directed support develops, an understanding of the assistance that people need is continuing to emerge. A definition of brokerage needs to be seen in this context (Advocacy Resource Exchange, 2011). In his review of the concept of brokerage (and a range of other similar titles, as already highlighted) Scourfield (2010) suggests that this has replaced some aspects of the social work role. He makes a number of useful observations. First, he found that 'brokerage' had featured strongly in the discourse of both the independent living and disability rights movement for three decades, but had been largely ignored within social work literature. He makes the case for how the discourse associated with these roles has emerged separately to developments within social work. Second, he suggests that some of the functions of support brokerage are already to be found in social work roles, but unlike social work, 'brokers' do not belong to a professional body and brokers are unregulated. While this may be desirable for some service users, Scourfield (2010) suggests that there is a lack of accountability, which is concerning. In addition, non-professionally qualified roles may leave service users, and indeed workers, vulnerable to exploitation. The insertion of new worker roles into the care system is a pragmatic development to expand the range and scope of services to deliver policy promises in England, but these new roles challenge us to consider the interface with social work, and this activity is not confined to England. In Denmark, the introduction of new hybrid roles to deliver 'activation policies' (a popular neoliberal solution to welfare issues in Europe) has led to frontline workers who are not qualified in social work relying to varying degrees on their own experiences, routines and intuitions, despite the fact that workers encounter often very vulnerable citizens (van Berkel et al, 2010). The impact on worker practices varies, but some workers adopt rigid practices that enforce rules and regulations, while others are more protective of clients. With the most vulnerable clients, some workers argue that they did not have the knowledge and skills to deliver specialist services, and so refer the person to another agency (van Berkel et al, 2010). The research concludes by suggesting that this situation can pose a risk to clients because the service is unpredictable and lacks transparency. These frontline workers are described as 'professionals without a profession'. In England, Scourfield (2010) has similar concerns about the emerging new roles, as he suggests that there is little clarity about how these new roles might develop, or indeed be developed. Protection work, in whatever country social workers work in, will increasingly bring together social workers and these new roles, and therefore an overriding system challenge will be to ensure role clarity as well as accountability. In addition, managers and leaders will need to develop and deliver support strategies for service users, carers and workers, within the context of individual, organisational and systems-level learning.

Lymbery (2010) views the policies driving these developments as problematic. He argues that there are inadequate resources allocated for social care despite the increase in demand for services. This is a problem that is not just confined to the care sector in England, but is a problem in any country where the demand for services cannot be met within resource allocations, and is leading to rationing decisions. As highlighted in Chapter Three, system responses to policy initiatives are being informed by rationing or targeting of resources to those most in need, but inevitably, rationing decisions are also taken at practice as well as a systems level. Klein, Day and Redmayne (1996) identified six forms of rationing that can take place, all of which are summarised below and can be found across social care systems:

- First, organisations set thresholds for services that will *exclude* some people. Setting thresholds is very problematic. The public sector trade union, Unison, found that while most local authority organisations had established clearer thresholds for services, 'there is evidence that thresholds are still not well understood by referring agencies and thresholds are sometimes raised by local authority children's services in response to workload pressures, staffing shortages and financial resources' (Unison, 2008, p 3).
- Second, Klein et al (1996) identified rationing by *selection*, which occurs when some individuals are given access to a service by a professional because of a perceived benefit to them or because of their status and influence. This is reflected in any assessment process where one person's needs are selected over another.
- Third, rationing can occur when the service *deflects* the service user away from a service to another one, thereby avoiding responsibility for care.

- Fourth, people may be *deterred* from accessing a service, for example, where the telephone is hardly ever answered, or there are long waiting times, and so on.
- Fifth, Klein et al (1996) identified *dilution* of services as a form of rationing, for example, where service users can access a service for only three days a week rather than five.
- Sixth, *termination* of a service so needs are no longer met, for example, local authorities often support services that are provided by charities or voluntary agencies, which are terminated when budgets are cut.

These forms of rationing may be supported by resource allocation strategies but they also have an impact on what support is offered to workers, which in turn can affect what support is available to service users and carers. One social worker from Wales said that cutting funding could lead to cost containment strategies that include 'replacing a social worker when they leave. She argues that this leads to social workers not being supported and suggest that this is a dangerous practice. The lack of resources also impacts on the preventative services that can be offered to children in need to keep them safe' (quoted in Unison, 2008).

Other critics take the view that new policies that focus on independence and choice neglect the reality of some service users' lives. Lymbery (2010) argues, for example, that there is a lack of consideration for those people who are either unable or may struggle to exercise choice or control. He draws from work by Oldham (2003) who suggested that older people negotiate their lives between dependence, independence and interdependence to accommodate the realities of daily living as they become older. As such, any policies that focus on independence simplify these realities, and are more likely to assess needs and support in a fairly simplistic and potentially negative way – for example, an older person may be perceived as 'inadequate' rather than 'frail'. Tanner (2007, p 125) also endorses this point when she highlights a question posed by Jordon, 'Why then does the government emphasise independence and choice as central to well-being of these (service user) groups, when it is obvious that interdependence is the reality for them, even more that for the rest of us....' Tanner (2007) suggests that this discourse is at odds with the meaning and perspectives of older people.

Netten et al (2011, p 16) undertook research to assess the impact of personal budgets, which have been introduced across many care systems to enable people who are eligible for public funds to have more control over the way in which resources are used to provide care and support. This research found that some groups, such as young disabled service users, fared better than others such as older service users, but 'to achieve these benefits, social workers and other professionals may need to adopt a variety of approaches to supporting people in the process of planning and management, particularly older people' (Netten et al, 2011, p 15). Older people, who are the largest group of service users nationally, appeared to find personal budgets a problem; indeed Netten et al (2011) suggest that personal budgets had a negative impact on the psychological wellbeing of older people as a result of the way in which the new arrangement was introduced and implemented.

Older people did not in fact feel more in control with personal budgets, and this feeling only reduced slightly when they used proxies (usually a relative). These policies are relatively new and ongoing evaluation research is needed to review the impact over time.

Consideration of the different skills, knowledge and practices that are needed by workers in these new service areas, to provide safe and effective services, requires managers and leaders to think critically about these emerging roles to ensure that the system they design is appropriate to meet the desired goals and objectives of individuals as well as the system. As outlined in Chapter Three, vulnerable service users need appropriate support to 'empower them' (and clearly more work is needed to examine what this support might be for different user groups), and systems need to be put in place to ensure that participation is a safe experience. Workers as 'leaders' was explored in Chapter Three, and is relevant to considering the different ways in which the diversity of service user needs can be met. Tactical strategies involve training staff who work directly with service users to understand the barriers that service users and carers face, and how staff can enable service users and carers to participate. These developments need to run alongside training and system developments that support service users and carers to use the power that these new policies give them. Therefore, in order to be able to provide support, social workers, and other care workers, will need to deal with some of the challenges these developments are generating for them in their work. These challenges can arise anywhere within or across systems, and managers and leaders need to think about what support mechanisms they have in place. In addition, managers and leaders need to think about, and ensure, that in their own interactions with staff, they are also providing the kind of support that professionals need.

Social work support: networks, groups and teams, and supervision

Working across and within complex systems to support carers and vulnerable service users requires an effective system of support for workers. This support is shaped by the structure of the organisation, its boundaries and the organisational processes. As we saw in Chapter Two, systems theory is concerned with both these elements (structure and process), and with feedback loops to reinvigorate the organisation to prevent entropy. Social workers and the new care workers are located within often-complex organisational settings and/or contracted services, and therefore professional support may be accessed in many ways, from within or outside the employing organisation. Managers and leaders of social workers are concerned that even in times of transformational change, systems of support are provided to ensure people continuously adapt to change without losing their professional identities or becoming distressed.

There are many ways that organisations can support social workers, which includes effective management support, although there is evidence in England that social workers may feel less supported today by their manager than in the past (Dustin, 2007). This lack of support can translate into high staff turnover rates, which are to be found not only in England but throughout the world, where there are high levels of worker absence as a result of sickness and stress (Webb and Carpenter, 2011). Burnout is a recognised problem in social work (Coulshed and Mullender, 2001). The importance of effective support therefore cannot be underestimated. While child protection work may look to the casual observer like an information-gathering exercise, it is in fact an emotionally charged process, which is both complex and demanding for the social workers and families involved. The work requires high levels of scrutiny, which is made more challenging by organisational cultures that seek to blame social workers if they make the wrong decision (Munro, 2011). Effective leaders and managers need to provide opportunities for social workers to process their experiences (and feelings) when they are engaged in such demanding work, and a supportive system must also provide workers with the time to undertake this emotional labour.

One of the ways in which social workers and other professionals are supported is through networks. Tafvelin et al (2012) also refer to the importance of co-worker support, the extent to which employees can count on their colleagues to help and support them when needed. Co-worker support may be hampered by organisational change, as it needs connectedness to develop, which is hindered if work groups are frequently reorganised. It includes caring, tangible aid and information, and may increase employees' comfort within the organisation by fulfilling needs for esteem, approval and affiliation (Stinglhamber and Vandenberghe, 2003; Liao et al, 2004). This can enhance commitment through an emotionally satisfying work experience, which, over time, translates into an emotional attachment to their employing organisation (Rousseau and Aube, 2010). Empirical studies also confirm the positive relationship between co-worker support and commitment (Ng and Sorensen, 2008; Rousseau and Aube, 2010), as well as shielding individuals from the worst aspects of role ambiguity (Tafvelin et al, 2012).

In a child protection network across one city in England, professionals and managers proactively sought to address problems and better solutions (while avoiding bureaucracy) across child protection services (CQC, 2011c). While informal networks can and do emerge spontaneously, formal organisations are increasingly supporting professionals and managers to network across systems. Some of the reasons why individual workers and organisations might support these developments are summarised here:

1. Networked groups bring together professionals who can share information, so that if support or protection is needed, everyone is well informed of any issues when decisions are made.
2. The relationship that develops between professionals when working in this way can transcend individual organisational constraints, which may try to impose

a cultural, financial or narrow focus on a situation. This enables professionals to provide creative solutions to presenting issues.

3. Professionals can provide emotional and psychological support to each other as well as develop knowledge and skills to help them navigate unfamiliar systems and expertise.
4. Networked relationships can enable flexible and responsive services to emerge as professionals take responsibility for enabling support and protection to be provided across a system.
5. Networks can also provide psychological and emotional support, which is important when working with service users and carers experiencing distress.

Networks represent a form of 'open system' whereby the processing of inputs to achieve desired outputs is enhanced by worker experiences and interactions that enable equilibrium across networks. Such networks can enable three key aspects to come together: the need for human support (emotional/psychological), support to undertake procedural and professional work (management and professional) and the support that is needed to engage in change and learning (development and learning). Operating in a network can provide opportunities to get these support needs met, but this requires workers to develop a good understanding of each other's perspectives and needs (acknowledging and accepting diversity), effective leadership (which is cooperative and democratic), as well as a willingness to work outside professional comfort zones and to engage in critical thinking and learning with each other. Networks can be designed across a number of organisations, or they can emerge informally.

Within organisations, social workers have traditionally received support from working with others in teams or groups. Indeed such support has been ranked as more important than formal supervision or support from professional associations and unions (Gibson et al, 1989). A recent report by the regulator of children's services in the UK, Ofsted (2012), highlighted how teams can support workers by providing practical, emotional and intellectual support. The report noted that 'The key distinguishing features are mutuality, "all for one and one for all" and "we know we need each other" and reciprocity, "we've got each other's backs [covered] all the time"' (Ofsted, 2012, p 28). The report (2012) highlighted how managers (as leaders) provided a pivotal role in setting cultures of high support, but also created a safe space for workers to engage in reflective learning through creating a culture of collaboration rather than competition, which can support professional challenge and high-level critical thinking. Also of note in the report is the way in which social workers 'helped each other to manage their emotions, in particular providing immediate support and a safe opportunity to "vent" their feelings before processing them. One local authority was taking steps to formalize the support the more experienced staff provided for newer colleagues' (Ofsted, 2012, p 28).

Germain and Gitterman's (1996) work on the life course model of social work highlights the interdependent nature of people and environments, and this is relevant here. As social workers move through their own life course they will experience life stressors, transition events and other events that can challenge the fit with the environment. In these situations staff need support to be able to identify the stressor or event to judge how serious the disturbance is. They may then need support to look at the measures needed to take to cope with their environments, and how colleagues and managers can provide feedback with how they are coping. In the past the team leader role was important in this regard. Team leaders were focused on interpreting policy (staying abreast of what was coming into the system) and maintaining morale (providing support to ensure equilibrium) by mediating for staff, ensuring sufficient resources for staff development, facilitating communication between people, defining work priorities for the team and liaising with other organisations as needed (Smith, 1984). However, some managers today may be distracted by performance and budgetary concerns, which inevitably squeezes out time for discussion on how people are feeling and for important support activities. They may be less interested in staff development for their team as they struggle to manage caseloads and high turnover, and they may be less able to protect workers and teams from work overload. The Ofsted (2012) report, however, highlighted evidence of effective and supportive teams, and they linked this to good outcomes for service users and carers. Where teams had introduced buddying arrangements, for example, crisis and transitions for service users and carers were better managed, particularly when staff were unwell, or when a family needed the support of more than one social worker. This attention to the task as well as the group and individual needs is an important aspect of the leadership role (Adair, 1973).

As more and more social workers find themselves working within multiprofessional or integrated teams, as senior managers design structures around the needs of service users and carers, leaving social workers to access support within this context. This can provide an excellent opportunity for meeting a wide range of the support needs of individuals (Anning et al, 2010). However, the research also suggests that these teams can be difficult places for all professionals. Melin Emilsson (2011, p 116) reported that cross-professional teamwork was very challenging for participants, particularly in relation to understanding and accepting each others' roles. The research suggested that the professionals who stayed in these teams were able to adjust their role to the new context, while others preferred to leave. Trust was seen as a key ingredient to the decisions that people made regarding staying or leaving, as trust-building was closely linked to interpersonal relationships, and teambuilding processes.

The previous chapter also referred specifically to the importance of leaders in supporting workforce management approaches to enabling the psychological contract, especially as most staff identify leaders and value them in the overall context of the organisation climate. We saw how breaches of the psychological contract can have serious negative consequences (Robinson and Morrison, 2000), with lower workforce commitment, reduced job satisfaction and increased workforce turnover (Conway and Briner, 2005). In recent years, some have argued that the workplace appears to have become a less supportive environment for social workers, as workers report bullying and low morale (Jones, 2001), high levels of dissatisfaction with the management of the organisation, limited career opportunities, poor rates of pay and very little recognition for good work (Coffrey et al, 2004). Some of the empirical evidence in relation to these issues was discussed in Chapter Five. We also look further at the concept of bullying in our discussion of abdicated leadership in the following chapter. Critics blame management (Jones, 2001; Ferguson, 2008), and indeed there is evidence that workers today are managed in some parts of social care as if care services were 'factories', where workers are required to 'get in, get out and move on to the next one' (Dustin, 2007, p 67). Workers reported that they did not have the time to build professional relationships with service users and carers, even though they were aware that this was central to good social work practice, which is a relationship-based activity. Dustin (2007) argued that the overly rational and simplistic approach used by some social work managers was leaving social workers, users of services and their carers, unsupported. Lambley (2010), however, argues that the view of managers being to blame is in itself overly simplistic, as there is evidence of supportive and collaborative relationships between managers and professionals, and so the picture is mixed. What we do know from research into worker–manager relationships is that management and leadership practice really matters, 'Positive actions by management promote worker attachment to leaders and the organization and are crucial in sustaining work values that diminish the likelihood of turnover' (Taplin and Winterton, 2007, p 5). Some managers may find that the work itself leads them into working in ways that avoids the messy business of people's lives, but it not without a cost to service users, carers and workers. Ruch (2011, p 4) suggests that it may seem easier for managers to limit their understanding and engagement with practice issues because this makes the job more bearable, but this is more likely to lead to ineffective interventions, and, 'The challenge for managers is to take responsibility for simultaneously implementing both structural and cultural changes that acknowledge the complexity of practice and to avoid a polarized "either"–or response.'

From a systems perspective, poor management and leadership is likely to infect relationships between workers and managers, and therefore managers and leaders need to develop insight into their own behaviours to reflect the leadership outlined in earlier chapters in this book, and which is needed in social work. Evans and Kearney (1996) identify seven key principles of a systems approach that can inform social work practice, but these principles are also applicable to management and leadership (see Table 6.1).

First, managers and leaders need to be consistent in their practice. This doesn't mean always doing things the same way, but rather means adopting consistent approaches, for example, where social work has a common code of practice and ethics are designed to provide principles that can ensure practice guidance on any situation or circumstance. We discuss these in more detail in the following chapter, specifically in relation to potential value conflicts (Postle, 2007) when

Table 6.1: Seven key principles of a systems approach

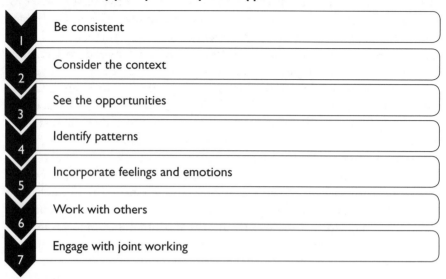

1 Be consistent

2 Consider the context

3 See the opportunities

4 Identify patterns

5 Incorporate feelings and emotions

6 Work with others

7 Engage with joint working

Source: Adapted from Evans and Kearney (1996)

working in challenging organisational cultures, and which form part and parcel of the landscape in which social work takes place. Therefore, and second, the systems view requires workers (and managers and leaders) to think about the context for practice. Understanding the context can enable a manager/leader to connect their work to relevant parts of the system, to build a sense of events, to inform developments that support and enable people and environments to stay connected. Third, a systems approach can support managers and leaders to stay positive, particularly in times of system changes, when loss of old ways of doing things can be replaced by new opportunities that can lead to improvements. Fourth, being able to identify patterns of behaviour to identify the changes that are needed can improve the experiences and relationships of self and others. Fifth, the focus on process can help managers and leaders to look beyond the structure, to incorporate relationships and feelings as well as content and outcomes. Working with others and joint working are the sixth and seventh principles, which together provide a context for practice that is rich, dynamic (can be open to feedback that can transform services) and can thereby provide much learning. This approach is consistent with leadership approaches outlined in Chapter Three.

Checkland (1981) developed 'rich pictures' as part of a soft systems methodology to enable individuals to gather information about complex situations, and to engage in creative problem-solving. Leaders and managers can use 'rich pictures' to tackle messy real-life situations by presenting the situation in a drawing. The picture that is created can identify difficult relationships between groups of people (parts of a system) that may highlight barriers to effective working, as well as areas (or groups of people) where things work well. By presenting the 'picture', it is possible to take action to improve the situation. However, this methodology needs to be used carefully, according to Berg, Pooley and Queenan (2011), as the process can be hijacked by 'group think', 'unethical behaviour' and 'inappropriate use of facilitator power'. They suggest that the use of soft systems methodology is therefore a moral activity, and that ethical considerations need to be built into its process. It would be possible to use this approach when working with service users as it can bring together different views of a service, and could be used to identify the support needed by all participants and how this need can be met. One of the particular strengths of the systems approach is that it is possible to use other theoretical approaches within this approach. This is best illustrated by the way in which supervisors can draw on psychosocial and other approaches to inform supervision, which is a formal means of providing workers with support.

Social work supervision

For social workers, supervision has traditionally supported three functions – education, administration and personal support (Kadushin, 1992) – although Morrison and Wonnacott (2010) added 'mediation' as a fourth function. The characteristics of each of these functions are highlighted in Table 6.2.

Table 6.2: Four functions of supervision

Support	Characteristics
Education	A focus on reflective practice and learning
Administration	A focus on meeting goals and planned outcomes
Support	A focus on emotional support and trust
Mediation	A focus on areas of difficulties in relationships and tasks

From a systems perspective, these functions connect the worker, the organisation and service users and carers 'in an interactional' process (Tsui and Ho, 1998) designed to deliver specific outcomes for individual service users. Supervisors are focused on organisational as well as professional concerns, while workers are focused on professional work with the service user and carer(s), and working together in a process that is challenging, supportive, informative and engaging, supervision support is provided to ensure continuous learning and change. Models of social work supervision nearly always include the first three support characteristics, although it is possible to strip out administration in some supervision models, so that clinical supervision (often used interchangeably with education) is separate and distinct (Tsui, 2005), or indeed in some agencies the model of supervision may be one framed by management, professional or clinical knowledge or any combination (Lambley and Marrable, 2012).

Empirical research on supervision tends to focus largely on the supervisor/ supervisee relationship that is an over-simplification of what is happening in the interactions within supervision (Tsui and Ho, 1998). The empirical evidence base for supervision in social work and social care is weak, and 'most of the evidence is correlational and derives from child welfare services in the US' (Carpenter, et al, 2012). The strength of evidence, therefore, according to Goldman (2013), is not strong, that is, 'there was little reported qualitative evidence focusing on intervention mechanisms', and as such, 'it is difficult to attribute positive outcomes to specific intervention components'. Importantly there is little or no strong evidence that links supervision to positive outcomes for people who use services or workers. However, Mor Barak et al's (2009) meta-analysis highlighted the importance of a combination of emotional and social support, task assistance and interpersonal interaction, which generated beneficial worker outcomes. They also found that supervision appeared to improve short-term effectiveness, and in the long term, could enhance worker knowledge, skills and experience (Kadushin and Harkness, 2002), which in turn may improve outcomes for service users (Glisson and Hemmelgarn, 1998). However, research into the relationship between supervision and good outcomes for service users and carers remains under-developed (Collins-Camargo and Millar, 2010). Lambley and Marrable's (2012) practice enquiry highlighted the views of workers who said that supervision helped them to help service users, and the research provided examples. In addition, supervision supported both practice and service innovations. People using services said that they wanted supervision to be a place where their concerns were heard and where they could feed back examples of good and bad worker practices. They suggested that supervision didn't seem to lead to the changes they would like and wondered why this was the case; for example, why did workers continue to work in unacceptable ways despite supervision? Service users also wondered why input into supervision was at the discretion of workers when the supervision was focused on them.

These questions challenge the current supervision paradigm and raise questions as to the role that service users can play in leadership practice, which is more inclusive. Currently at the heart of the supervision process is a relationship between the supervisor and the supervisee, and the supervisee is tasked with bringing the service users' concerns and issues into the supervision process. Work by Simmonds (2010, p 215) suggests that the process of 'relating' in supervision can result in 'the social worker feeling understood and supported, and improve the quality of social worker's practice ... (or) may also result in the opposite.' The supervisor and supervisee relationship is key. Simmonds (2010) introduces a two-dimensional framework, developed by Heard and Lake (1997), which identifies two categories of human relating. The first dimension is supportive/companionable, which is characterised by 'a protective, explanatory and exploratory form of relating' (Heard and Lake, 1997, p 217), while the other is domineering/submissive and is characterised by a form of relating that 'forces others to follow the decision of a controlling leader' (Heard and Lake, 1997, p 218). The model provides a framework against which managers and social workers can begin to understand what happened in a supervision session where both people wished to support and be supported, but instead the discussion (and thereby mean of relating) became domineering and dismissive. Simmonds (2010, p 223) suggests that 'lifelong experiences of supportive companionable mental models also aids supervision', as it provides a 'counter-balance' to 'the evolution of the organisational setting of practice that is a context that is essentially non-mentalising and this has resulted in the imposition of a dominant-submissive form.' What is interesting about Simmonds' (2010) work is that it reveals the interconnected world of the service user, worker and manager at a most personal and intimate level within the supervision process. The worker and manager is engaged in constructing a narrative to make sense of events, which is built on events and feelings and explored within the supervisory relationship, which adds another dimension to practice.

Time to reflect is a precious and arguably expensive requirement for good social work interventions. Holmes, Munro and Soper (2010, p 26) undertook research to identify the cost of providing supervision in England. They found that 'the unit cost of a supervision session lasting one and a half hours is £86.90 per frontline social worker.' However, if fortnightly supervision sessions were carried out, then the costs could increase to £1,216, which 'For a referral and intake team with five social workers and three family support workers ... would be an additional annual cost of £9,407.72' (Holmes et al, 2010, p 26). Given these costs, as a method of support, supervision needs to be effective. A group of academics from Belgium, Croatia, Slovenia, Germany, Spain, Sweden and the Netherlands came together to explore supervision as a teaching method for practical training and professional development across participating European countries. They identified some of the key themes, which have been collated in Table 6.3.

In terms of experience, some countries required supervisors to be licensed, whereas in other countries this was not the case. In terms of how supervision was

Table 6.3: Learning and teaching themes within supervision

Issues	Key messages
1) Experiences	Supervision is a licensed activity for some, and occurs in all countries
2) Organisation	Supervisors differ from field teachers, is one-to-one and in groups, regular and requires critical reflection on self
3) Understanding	A place for free speech, reflection, learning and personal development and growth
4) Content	Challenging questions, live problems and issues, theory, practice and methods, and research-informed
5) Challenges	Role conflicts, ethical dilemmas, lack of supervision theory, empirical data, unclear links to education
6) Cultural aspects	Transferability to other countries, role of culture and history in supervision experiences, and learning
7) Therapy?	War has brought therapy and supervision closer together for some, and social work attracts people with psychological issues
8) Research	Lack of research on what supervisors do in practice, lack of information on outcomes, and we need a theory
9) Competence	Does the knowledge and skills underpin supervision as countries differ?

Source: Adapted from van Hees (2007)

organised and delivered, there was a range of organising models, but a common feature was critical reflection on self and practice. This chimes well with how supervision is conceptualised and delivered in England. The content, and challenges raised, reflected the nature of the social work tasks, requiring evidence-informed interventions, and this also mirrors developments in England. The cultural context for supervision practice reflects social and historical differences between countries, and it is interesting to reflect on how these differences are manifested in the different types of support (more need for therapeutic interventions in some countries in response to the impact of recent wars). In terms of research there is a clear focus on developing a theory and evidence to underpin supervision practice. This European work is useful because it helps us to think about how social workers are supported by supervision in other countries where there may be some similarities in relation to policy developments but the context for practice will be different, and yet social work practice needs particular types of support, which is provided by supervision.

In the UK supervision is offered to workers to deliver improved outcomes (for the individual worker as well as the service users they are working with). It is commonly understood that supervision is a necessary means of support for social workers. Coulshed and Mullender (2001, p 187) suggest that 'It is not healthy to the individual or to their employing organisation to expect them to suppress their own emotions, avoid facing their own anxieties, or deny their own stress levels.' In other European countries research by the Rutgers University Center for International Social Work (2008, p xiii) found that 'There is an overwhelming recognition that social work supervision contributes to quality of services, yet supervision, as practiced in the region, is primarily administrative. Models in Romania, Bosnia & Herzegovina, Croatia and St Petersburg, Russia need increased visibility.' BASW (2011) undertook research into supervision in England and from 143 responses they built the following picture:

1. The majority of respondents received supervision once a month.
2. Over 50 per cent of respondents were happy with the frequency of supervision.
3. Just over half the respondents said that supervision was either fair or poor, while just over 40 per cent said supervision was good or excellent.
4. Nearly 70 per cent of respondents said that supervision covered emotional issues that arose from practice.
5. Sixty-two per cent said that supervision did not adequately cover personal development and training.
6. Forty-four per cent reported that supervision adequately covered management accountability issues.

Carpenter and Webb (Carpenter et al, 2012, p 1) undertook a more comprehensive overview of the evidence concerning the value of supervision in supporting the practice of social care and social work. They looked at different models of supervision and outcomes for workers, employers, service users and carers. They considered evidence on the costs of supervision and provided the following key messages:

- Research has demonstrated that good supervision is associated with job satisfaction, commitment to the organisation and retention.
- Supervision appears to help reduce staff turnover and is significantly linked to employees' perception of the support they receive from the organisation.
- Good supervision is correlated with perceived worker effectiveness. There is some evidence that group supervision can increase critical thinking.
- Supervision works best when it pays attention to task assistance, social and emotional support and when workers have a positive relationship with supervisors.
- The emotionally charged nature of the work can place particular demands on people in the field. It is important to provide opportunities for reflective supervision.
- In an interprofessional context, workers relate job satisfaction and professional development to their supervisors' expert knowledge, regardless of whether respondents shared the same professional background.
- The impact of supervision on outcomes for service users and carers has rarely been investigated. Anecdotal evidence suggests that supervision may promote empowerment, fewer complaints and more positive feedback.
- Overall the empirical basis for supervision in social work and social care in the UK is weak. Most of the evidence is correlational and derives from child welfare services in the US.

There is clearly a need for leaders and managers to take advantage by increasing their understanding, knowledge, skills and capacity to engage with supervision. These findings suggest that there is room for improvement in supervision practices given the important supportive role that supervision is expected to play.

Summary

There are many ways that workers, service users and carers can access both formal and informal support, but these need to be appropriate and properly understood, so that people using or working in emotionally demanding services can be nurtured and 'replenished' by appropriate means of support. In order for service users and carers to get their care needs met, there is therefore a need for effective formal organisational arrangements that reflect and support the choices that service users make. Leaders and managers need to ensure that when they are designing support systems that they do this with support in mind, and in an informed way. Previous chapters have highlighted how engagement strategies with service users can be developed, and these need to be fully used to ensure the best possible support to the variety of people who use social work services. Traditionally, organisations have provided support for workers through 'rational, formal and highly prescriptive' methods, but this has only served to expose tensions between achieving performance targets while ignoring the often hidden emotional labour involved, which can have an impact on the quality of service provided, but also on the health and wellbeing of the worker. The challenge for social work managers and leaders will therefore be to ensure that support mechanisms are in place that actually meet worker and service user needs. These challenges, most interestingly, are not country-specific, and therefore there is much to be gained in sharing our understanding of how to most effectively deliver effective support to staff, service users and carers.

SEVEN

When leadership fails: examining 'dignity' through an institutional case study

> If staff do not recognise dignity, if they feel taken for granted, if their self-esteem is dented, then it becomes more difficult for them to deliver dignified care. (Tadd et al, 2011)

Introduction

So far we have referred to culture in a number of different ways. This chapter focuses on a relatively neglected topic in social work and social care, that of 'dignity' within the context of organisational culture. Despite dignity being widely used in UK current policy and practice documents (see, for example, DH, 2010; Commission on Dignity in Care for Older People, 2012), it remains a difficult term to define and even more difficult to operationalise. This chapter begins by presenting various definitions of this term and discusses some of the complexities that exist between the direct professional relationships social workers have with service users and the organisations in which social workers are employed. In arguing for the usefulness of the concept, Jacobson (2007) has drawn a distinction between the discussion of 'social dignity', or dignity as defined in social situations such as health or social care, and intrinsic 'human dignity', or the 'intrinsic dignity of human beings' (SCIE, 2012). Whatever its theoretical manifestations, this notion of dignity has a meaning for the way in which relationships are conducted at an organisational level and for users and carers.

As well as discussing the literature where some of these concepts are defined, this chapter also explores where problems have emerged within the working practices of organisations, using, as an example of where things have gone wrong, one recent serious case review based in the UK affecting residential care. This was the scandal at Winterbourne View Hospital. We recognise that there will always be new situations in terms of serious case reviews and enquiries into the failures of care, but reflective analysis of cases offers great potential for transferrable learning, in this case, on the failure of leadership to ensure a dignified culture of care. By way of background, this private hospital was a short-stay assessment facility for adults with learning disabilities and autism, and the NHS commissioned beds at the hospital. Many statutory organisations had ongoing contact with the hospital since it opened in 2006, and some had specific responsibilities for safeguarding adults, including the Healthcare Commission and the Mental

Health Act Commission (until April 2009), the CQC (from April 2009), Avon and Somerset Police, South Gloucestershire Council Adult Safeguarding, NHS South Gloucestershire Primary Care Trust (in a coordinating role), the First Tier Tribunal Mental Health and the Health and Safety Executive (Flynn, 2012). Despite a number of different attempts by various staff at Winterbourne View to whistleblow to the CQC and the local authority (BBC 2011, 2011a, 2012), and despite clear procedures within these organisations about their monitoring and safeguarding obligations in such circumstances, the level of abuse was not picked up until after a documentary aired on English national television by the popular Panorama programme. This is a common theme highlighted in many serious case reviews (Stanley and Manthorpe, 2004; Munro, 2011). Many other issues are raised in the serious case review about the poor response of Castlebeck Holdings Ltd. (the owner of Winterbourne View) to concerns raised by regulators, and to poor practice in commissioning by the NHS. Again, like so many other serious case reviews, it was not until all the information from different agencies was collated that an accurate picture emerged about the care practices at Winterbourne View. What is different about this scandal from many others is the shocking graphic visual evidence of the behaviour of the staff working in the home towards the patients who lived there.

This chapter returns to and further explores in more depth the concept of organisational culture discussed in Chapter Two and how it manifests itself, by drawing on systems and psychoanalytic theory and in particular the concept of organisational 'defensive anxiety'. We link these to the case of Winterbourne View in order to explore these concepts more meaningfully. Chapters Four and Five introduced us to some of the positive imperatives in relation to workforce management. Throughout this chapter, however, we make significant links to some of those imperatives that arise from poor workforce management, specifically, bullying, supervision and workplace stress-related illness. These may lead to difficulties in staff retention, staff turnover and absenteeism. Finally, the role of managerialist cultures in care organisations is also further explored in the light of the UK-based Munro report (2011), offering a critique of the defensive process of risk management frequently observed in many social care organisations.

A definition of dignity

We have already discussed the importance of culture within organisations in Chapter Two, and it is against this backdrop that we now turn to the concept of dignity. Dignity is a term used ever more frequently in political discussions, most often when referring to the care of vulnerable people. The concept has its links to philosophy and religion, and while there is considerable debate about what the term actually means, most definitions signify somewhere that each human has an innate right to respect and ethical treatment. Kant (1988) says:

> In the realm of ends everything either has a price or a dignity. Whatever has a price can be replaced by something else as its equivalent; on the other hand, whatever is above all price, and therefore admits of no equivalence, has a dignity.

The meaning of dignity used by SCIE (2010) is based on a standard dictionary definition:

> A state, quality or manner worthy of esteem or respect; and (by extension) self-respect. Dignity in care, therefore, means the kind of care, in any setting, which supports and promotes, and does not undermine, a person's self-respect regardless of any difference. Or, as one person receiving care put it more briefly, "Being treated like I was somebody". (Policy Research Institute on Ageing and Ethnicity/Help the Aged, 2001)

Across the breadth of research that has been carried out, there is some agreement concerning a number of key principles that should be included in any understanding of dignity from a service user's perspective. These are: respect; privacy; self-esteem, identity, a sense of self and self-worth; freedom from unnecessary pain, including chronic pain; recognition that pain is avoidable and treatable at all ages; and autonomy (SCIE, 2010). SCIE (2010) has identified eight factors synonymous with dignity, called 'the dignity factors':

- Choice and control
- Communication
- Eating and nutritional care
- Pain management
- Personal hygiene
- Practical assistance
- Privacy
- Social inclusion

There has also been considerable interest in this term within medical ethics and in healthcare generally. Haddock (1996) thought that dignity was dependent on an interaction between internal and external factors as relevant to an individual, comprising a sense of identity and self-esteem (internal), and the respect with which a person is treated by others (external). Jacelon et al's (2004) work included focus groups with older people, and they found that dignity was a reciprocal concept: those who behave with dignity are more likely to be treated with dignity. Discussions about dignity within policy papers relate to how service users are treated when receiving health or social care services. Often it is a term used where there are concerns about the treatment of people. To this end, within the UK, a National Dignity Partnership Board was established in 2007 by the Department of

Health. The Department of Health also launched a Dignity Campaign, including a Dignity Champions register. The Dignity in Care network is now hosted by SCIE (www.dignityincare.org.uk).

So how relevant are these definitions and understandings of dignity and culture for the experiences and practice of staff in the workplace? As can be seen from some of the more recent serious case reviews that have been undertaken when there have been significant failures in service provision, there is a difference between the intention of the organisation when discussing dignity as a key principle underpinning practice and the experience of the service user or patient in practice. In the same way there can also be a difference in the public profile of an organisation compared to the culture experienced by the workers. It is these differences in perception and experience that are now explored.

Culture in the care environment

According to Payne, 'management in social work involves a clash between control by an organisation and freedom of professional action' (2009, p 143). In Chapter One, we referred to the professionalisation of social work, the development of professional autonomy and the necessity of leadership development for social work. Here, we focus more on the role of the 'employer' and organisation as a provider of care services. Both perspectives recognise the centrality of the service user perspective as a key stakeholder in the development of care services. This triangle, represented diagrammatically in Figure 7.1, depicts the interconnectedness between these three stakeholders. The way in which organisations approach the management of these relationships, including the resulting tensions, will have a significant effect on the staff working in the organisation, and may greatly affect the culture of that organisation. While this may sound obvious, there is potential for these values to conflict (Postle, 2007). They are part and parcel of the landscape in which social work takes place, and have been commented on by other social work academics (Hugman, 2005; Banks, 2006).

Hugman (2007) uses the term 'moral fluency' to describe the necessity of social workers of being able to navigate between these conflicting value positions. Internationally, social work has asserted that one of its main activities is working with people to solve problems and to affect social change. For example, the IFSW definition of social work is:

> The social work profession promotes social change, problem solving in human relationships and the empowerment and liberation of people to enhance well-being. Utilising theories of human behaviour and social systems, social work intervenes at the points where people interact with their environments. Principles of human rights and social justice are fundamental to social work. (IFSW/IASSW, 2000)

Figure 7.1: The interconnected relationship between values and culture of the social work profession, the service user and the employer

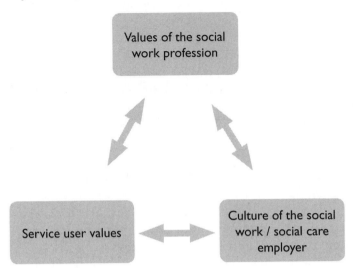

While in the UK the social work role is largely influenced by its relationship to its statutory function, it stands to reason that social workers develop skills and expertise in resolving conflict and working with differing values within that context, as according to Jordan (1978, p 25), social work is all about, 'learning to live with the inevitable, uncertainty, confusion and doubt'. Parton and O'Byrne (2000) talk about social work as a 'practical/moral' rather than a 'rational/technical' activity, and like many other social work academics, note the rise of 'managerialism, systems of audit, procedures, legalism and an emphasis on outcomes and evidence based practice' (Parton and O'Byrne, 2000, p 30) within social work organisations. They are of the view that:

> ... uncertainty, confusion and doubt are key elements in characterising the nature of social work. Rather than be embarrassed by this and try to define them out via increasingly scientised and rationalised approaches, it is our view that we should recognise they are at the core of what it is to do social work and are significant factors in what makes it distinctive. They should form an essential part of any theoretical approaches which are serious about being usable in practice.

This leads us to pose questions as to how one then manages effectively in organisations where social workers are undertaking that kind of work. Are social workers able to identify and equipped to problem-solve when conflicts occur in the organisations in which they work, given that this is the area in which they supposedly have expertise? Overriding critique of social work organisations in relation to the rise of managerialism and rational/technical leadership inevitably points to tensions and potential problems in this arena. Again, Parton and O'Byrne comment, 'while the proliferation of procedures and so on in most areas of social work aim to make practice more accountable and transparent, they render the social work process and the tacit assumptions upon which "thinking as usual" takes place in practice immune from analysis' (Parton and O'Byrne, 2000, p 31).

Organisational processes and cultures are complex phenomenon and social workers are just as vulnerable to working in unhealthy organisations as in every other sector. This can be indicated by conflict and tensions between the three points of the triangle in Figure 7.1. Postle (2007, pp 253-6) identifies three potential value conflicts for social workers:

- Practitioners' own values conflicting with the context in which they work – trying to cope with high workloads and reduced resources:

  > ... ignoring, or at least not examining, clashes of value inherent in routinising and stereotyping becomes, in effect, a survival mechanism for some staff and, indeed, part of some teams' and organisations' cultures. (Postle, 2007, p 254)

- Practitioners' own values conflicting with those of the organisation for which they work – bureaucratic or economic goals are on a collision course with professional values (Hugman, 2007); practice equates to surveillance, monitoring and control, and antagonism and mistrust displacing empowerment (Braye and Preston-Shoot, 1995):

  > A real danger here is that "groupthink" (Irving, 1972) occurs where, typically, agencies and teams within them will not consider alternative ways of working, fail to be critical of actions taken, fail to seek expert opinion (such as legal advice) and rationalise their behaviour. (Postle, 2007, p 255)

- Practitioners' own values conflicting with those of the family with whom they are working. Postle (2007) suggests this can occur in three main ways: when the values of a service user differ considerably to those core to social work; where conflict exists regarding the interface between rights, risk, autonomy and protection; and social workers' own value base clashing with their professional obligations. She notes Shardlow's (2009) view that in such specific circumstances, generalised professional codes of ethics have limited use.

These ideas are further expanded on by Obholzer and Zagier Roberts (1994), who investigate and name many of the unconscious processes occurring that add further layers of meaning and complexity to much of the work undertaken in the caring professions. These perspectives can be used to expand our understanding of these conflicts and to the potential resolution of some of the tensions that exist in the workplace. We return to these ideas later on in this chapter.

Dignity in the workplace

The term 'dignity at work' most often refers to bullying and harassment policies that organisations have in place to protect staff, but dignity is much more than that (Bolton, 2007; Sayer, 2007). First, the constant referencing to bullying and harassment narrows and reduces the meaning of dignity to the extent that it then becomes something that is associated with problems and negativity. Second, as a result of this, the term 'dignity' is associated with some of the 'rights'-based discourses, and that fundamental rights are coming under pressure (Bolton, 2007). An example of this is the high-profile 'dignity at work' campaigns run by Amicus and Unite unions and the Andrea Adams Trust. The Unite union's pamphlet states,

> Everyone deserves to work in an environment free from bullying. Bullying can have devastating effects on the individual targets and on colleagues who have to witness it. It is bad for morale and leads to increased sickness absence and high staff turnover. That is why Unite is campaigning, through its DIGNITY AT WORK project, to eradicate bullying in the "not for profit" sector and wants to ensure that every workplace has effective policies and procedures for dealing with bullying. (www.unitetheunion.org)

Bolton's view is that this narrow focus on dignity misses many other factors that are associated with dignity. She locates this narrow focus within a 'bad work' or 'mismanagement' directive, and in an attempt to broaden the focus she contrasts this with discussion about 'good work', alongside the International Labour Organization's belief in 'decent work', emphasising equality of access, employee voice and just reward (Bolton, 2007).

Hodson defines dignity as 'the ability to establish a sense of self-worth and self-respect and to appreciate the respect of others' (2001, p 3). He argues that there are four workplace 'denials of dignity' (2001, p 19): mismanagement and abuse; overwork; constraints on autonomy; and contradictions of the employee. As a response to these 'denials of dignity', employees have developed four means of safeguarding dignity: resistance; organisational citizenship; pursuing meaning at work; and social relations at work.

Dignity is not a static concept, and in this regard, how it is understood within organisations is also subjective. Using a simplistic model that recognises dignity on a spectrum that extends from normative, proactive and reactive to unhealthy practices can help organisations develop their work. The key for organisations is being able to recognise its multidimensional nature in practice. The concept of dignity is important in leading effective care services. In examining the dignity of nurses in the workplace, Lawless and Moss (2007) comment that the little attention this has received may lie partly 'in approaches that privilege patient dignity over nurse dignity and which rely on the altruism and self-sacrifice of nurses to sustain patient care in environments dominated by cost-control agendas' (2007, p 225). They suggest that 'worker dignity' may be a critical factor in sustaining development of healthy workplaces and healthy workforces.

Just as with nursing, many social workers are attracted into the profession for altruistic reasons. This notion of altruism is not fully recognised within the neoliberal approach that relies heavily on close regulatory practices, managerialism and the consequent deprofessionalisation of care management. However, there is legitimacy to a career in nursing because of its status as an 'allied health profession' that does not exist with social work. Nurses offer a universal service when people are sick, whereas social workers deal with many hidden and often unpopular social problems, such as child abuse and protection, and this invisibility places a different kind of strain on the psyche of social workers.

Bullying

Van Heugten (2010) reminds us that although much has been written about bullying in the workplace, very little has been written that specifically examines this issue in relation to social work. Most of the literature associated with bullying in the workplace focuses on the delinquent or deviant behaviour of individuals or groups; however, bullying in the workplace should be frequently understood in terms of the dynamics of individual power. Remedies are often sought, including systems or procedures aimed at reporting, investigating and sanction rather than focusing on issues of coercion that are linked to functions of control and the paradigms concerned with order and efficiency. However, van Heugten suggests that, 'relying on data derived from research with other professions can lead to untested assumptions about causes and about appropriate interventions' (2010, p 638). Van Heugten's research comprised a qualitative study using grounded theory to analyse data collected from 17 social workers in New Zealand. Her analysis identified bullying,

> in the context of stressful changing workplaces in which professional people experience status uncertainty, and compete for job control and respect. Conversely, prevention and intervention require the adoption of health-promoting organisational policies that foster supportive working environments and relationships. (2010, p 638)

Although this study is based on a small sample, van Heugten's findings are worthy of note. She found that experienced social workers were potentially vulnerable during work reorganisations and transitions due to a lack of job control, professional competition and isolation which were contributing factors to a social worker feeling bullied. She also found that organisations that proactively addressed these factors had a 'health-enhancing' culture within the workplace, and had clear equality policies that 'offer the best chance of a way forward' (2010, p 653).

Organisational perspectives on supervision

In the previous chapter we were reminded of the integral nature of supervision to effective social work. Considerable literature exists about supervision from the social work manager and practitioner perspective (see, for example, Browne and Bourne, 1996; Knapman and Morrison, 1998; Hawkins and Shohet, 2000; Morrison, 2009; Hafford-Letchfield et al, 2011a). However, less attention has been given to the organisational commitment to supervisory practice and the association between quality supervision and the association statistically, with the decision of the employee to stay with the organisation (Renner et al, 2009). The degree to which employees feel supported by their supervisor affects their emotional satisfaction with the job and contributes to the appraisal of how the organisation values and cares about them (Carpenter et al, 2012). Professional development through supervisory practice is also associated with workers' attachment and sense of belonging in the organisation. According to Kim and Lee (2011), where frontline workers feel able to communicate their opinions and feelings to management, this can have an effect on stress or burnout. Hafford-Letchfield et al, (2011a) suggest that frontline managers in the UK have a key role in mediating organisational culture. Their small-scale qualitative study of recordings and transcripts of trainee managers' supervisory sessions indicates that supervisors frequently use humour, somewhat ironic apologies or other tactics for diffusing conflict and aggravation or for gaining compliance with the implementation of otherwise unwelcome procedural changes. The authors conclude that the supervisory relationship has an important mediation function: it is a channel through which organisational culture is conveyed to supervisees as well as providing an opportunity for staff to convey information upwards to the organisation. Indeed, Phillipson suggests that despite the enormous changes made to social work over the past 30-40 years, the practice of social work supervision has changed very little (Phillipson, 2009).

Particular interest in frontline supervision following the publication of the Munro review (2010, 2010a, 2011) and the creation of the SWRB after the publication of the Social Work Taskforce implementation report (DCSF et al, 2010) both emphasised the importance and essential contribution of skilled and confident frontline managers to practice. The need for better access to training and development support in professional supervision was recognised by SWRB, and this improvement occurred alongside the introduction of the NQSW scheme, which has now been replaced by ASYE for newly qualified social workers (Baginsky et al, 2010). An organisation is only ever as 'good' or 'effective' as the quality of its frontline managers, as it is these managers who are the organisation's eyes and ears, and ultimately they are the gatekeepers of practice standards and quality. Because of this criticality, this lowest tier level of management can also be the site of conflict and strain within the organisation. Dimmock (2003) comments that 'the boundary between practice/service delivery and management is often the point at which [such] tensions are played out, and the role of the front line manager is often the key to handing this tension successfully' (2003, p 40).

In addition to the summary of the systematic review of supervision by Carpenter et al (2012) and the study by BASW (2009) summarised in the previous chapter, Tepper (2007) provides a useful summary of the behaviours and characteristics associated with effective supervision relevant to sustaining a positive climate and culture. These include high motivation, high individual and group performance, favourable attitudes toward the job, the organisation and the leader of the organisation (2007, p 261). Tepper's work also includes a literature review and examination of what is termed 'abusive supervision', including physical violence, non-physical intimidation and hostility as well as sexual harassment, and a discussion of the consequences of abusive supervision on staff. Tepper highlights work-related attitudes, resistance behaviour, anti-social and deviant behaviour, performance consequences (including in-role performance contributions and extra-role or citizenship performance), psychological wellbeing and family wellbeing (2007, p 274). This list indicates a potentially widespread 'knock-on' effect for workers on the receiving end of abusive supervision, as well as for the organisation. Sparr and Sonnentag (2008) examine employees' sense of their own personal control and feelings of helplessness at work as partial mediators of the way in which feedback is given to and received by the employee, and they consider the impact this then has on the relationship between the supervisor–employee environment and wellbeing at work. Constructive feedback is an important part of this process and has wider benefits for the organisation. They comment that, 'making aware the importance of feedback and constructive dealing with feedback could therefore contribute to both the employees' and organisation's wellbeing' (Sparr and Sonnentag 2008, p 410).

Workplace stress-related illness

This area was considered in Chapters Four and Five; in particular the costs to businesses of the loss of productivity, turnover of staff and absenteeism is enormous. Spell and Arnold consider that the different ways in which mental health has been constructed and measured in the workplace has made it difficult to understand and assess the antecedents and outcomes of mental ill health (2007, p 724). Depression and anxiety are two central components of wellbeing they examine, and their research suggests the importance of collective perceptions of organisational justice in the formation of individual employees' mental health.

> Managers should be aware of perceptions that develop and are shared in a work group ... a consistently held group judgement of low distributive justice with low procedural justice would likely have a horrible effect on the mental health of individual group members. (Spell and Arnold, 2007, p 748)

At a micro level, this may get played out in terms of fairness of case allocations. At a surface level, the existence of policies detailing processes to ensure adequate support and equity of treatment to staff are important. However, while such policies set out general intentions and expectations, sometimes individual factors also need to be taken into consideration. Tehrani et al (2007) explore the concept of wellbeing across individuals, employees and organisations. They acknowledge the subjective nature of wellbeing, the importance of the relationship an employee has with their immediate line manager as a way of managing employee welfare, and highlight the importance of organisation strategy being one of managing employee health rather than employee sickness. There are a number of positive benefits that programmes for managing stress in the workplace can bring to employees and organisations. However, it is important to remember that stress is another subjective concept. The National Institute of Clinical Excellence (NICE) (2009) defines it as, 'the adverse reaction people have to excessive pressure or other types of demand placed on them.' Workplace stress would fall into this definition.

There are a number of significant cases that have set a legal precedent in terms of what employers should take into consideration where employees face work-related stress. One of these is a case involving a social worker (*Walker v Northumberland County Council* [1995]).

> Walker was a social worker who suffered a nervous breakdown as a result of his excessive workload. He suffered another breakdown and was in due course dismissed on the grounds of permanent ill health. The High Court found that the council was not liable for the first breakdown as it was not reasonably foreseeable to the employer. But once he had returned to work, the employer was on notice of the possibility of another breakdown if the employee was exposed to the same workload without adequate support. Walker was awarded £175,000 in damages. (McMullen, 2011, pp 4-5)

McMullen (2011, p 5) also discusses *Southerland v Hatton* [2002] EWCA Civ 76. The Court of Appeal gave a landmark judgment that set out overall principles and guidance on employers' common law obligations towards an employee's stress-related illnesses. These are:

- Was the stress-related illness reasonably foreseeable in the individual?
- Are there characteristics particular to the employee?
- Are there unusual demands based on the employee by the employer?

Several factors are relevant in relation to 'foresee ability':

- Is there an abnormal level of sickness absence?
- Are other employees doing the same job experiencing unacceptable levels of stress?
- Are there warning signs from employees?

Employers need to be vigilant but are not expected to be clairvoyant. The court specifically said that an employer who offers confidential help (for example, counselling) to employees suffering stress is unlikely to be found in breach of the duty. This should be treated with caution, however (see *Intel Corporation (UK) v Daw* [2007] EWCA Civ 70).

Ultimately, managers need to be able to manage staff and the work of an organisation appropriately, and this is not an easy or straightforward task. Payne states that 'management is a practice, just as social work is a practice' (2009, p 156), so skills in effective management can be learned. Attention to issues of stress and support are part of a supportive culture that indicates the value that staff have for the organisation (Orme, 2009). However, not all stress is negative as it is also a part of everyday work, and resilience can be supported, and once recognised, developed to enable staff to cope with the appropriate stresses and pressures of social work.

Unhealthy and unsafe institutional cultures: a case study from Winterbourne View

Organisational cultural norms have a significant impact on the behaviour of staff, both individually and as a group. Winterbourne View was a purpose-designed privately owned acute hospital unit near Bristol, offering assessment, intervention and support for people with complex needs and difficult behaviour. Castlebeck Holdings Limited was the owner of the facility and shut down the home following the screening of a BBC Panorama documentary shown in the UK on 31 May 2011, titled, 'Undercover care: the abuse exposed' about systemic abuse in the hospital (BBC, 2011a). Terry Bryan, a senior nurse who was formerly employed at Winterbourne View, was concerned about the behaviour of some of the support workers caring for the residents and had attempted to report his concerns to managers at Winterbourne View and to the CQC, the government regulator, on more than one occasion. Managers at Winterbourne View did not investigate his complaint, despite the existence of whistleblowing policies and the multiple reporting of abuse by Terry Bryan to Castlebeck and the CQC.

The events at Winterbourne View offer an opportunity to consider the links between abuse, management, organisational culture, actions and supervision of staff and the dignity of service users and staff members, and it is an extreme example of where the care of vulnerable people went horribly wrong. As discussed earlier, there is a spectrum of practice in relation to dignity and safeguarding. The ADASS, in their guidance on safeguarding adults, say, 'All organisations who have responsibilities in relationship to safeguarding adults should share a common value base that ensures people are treated with dignity and respect, safeguarding from harm and their support and care is person centred' (ADASS, 2011, p 8. This shared value base was not present at Winterbourne View.

In England since the 1970s there have been a number of public inquiries, inspections and serious case reviews following serious cases of neglect and abuse regarding children and families, people with mental ill health, people who have learning disabilities and older adults (for an overview, see Stanley and Manthorpe, 2004). The aim of such inquiries is to ensure that 'lessons can be learned'. Unfortunately, however, tragedies at an individual and organisational level continue to occur, indicating that we are either not sufficiently adept at 'learning the lessons' or our approach to understanding what continues to go wrong is rather too simplistic. The value of such inquiries is hotly debated (Stanley and Manthorpe, 2004). A public inquiry serves a number of different purposes, but in the eyes of the public such an inquiry can highlight who or what is to blame for an incident occurring (Dent and Cocker, 2005), and that is a powerful, albeit worrying, rationale. It is this 'collision of the horrific with the "innocent" or "ordinary" status of the victim [that] provides high emotional responses from the public' (Stanley and Manthorpe, 2004, p 5). Stanley and Manthorpe think there are occasions where inquiries can be useful: 'we believe that abuse on a large scale by those formally entrusted with the care of vulnerable people does require a full-scale independent inquiry' (2004, p 13).

While the Winterbourne View scandal was not the subject of an independent public inquiry, we have used it here as an example to illustrate the effects of culture and values within an organisation working in an unhealthy way. Winterbourne View was not a social care institution, but a private hospital where service users were referred and placed by NHS commissioners. However, many of the points made about organisational culture are transferrable to a social care context, and there have been a number of public inquiries into social care organisations over the years (see, for example, Utting, 1997; Waterhouse, 2000; Francis, 2013). Winterbourne View is not and will not be the only institution where patients have been systematically mistreated by the staff entrusted to care for them. But it is rare to have such graphic portrayals of the abuse experienced by service users available publicly – the images showing how these vulnerable people were cared for were shocking. However, it is not the abuse itself that we want to discuss here, but rather how the dignity of the service users was able to be so completely disregarded as it was by the employees of the organisation.

Margaret Flynn (2012) was commissioned to undertake the serious case review about Winterbourne View. Her report highlights practices within the organisation that were far from satisfactory. She reports:

> Before Castlebeck Ltd received a letter from the BBC alerting them to the "systematic mistreatment of patients by staff," it was business as usual at Winterbourne View Hospital. Patients' distress, anger, violence and efforts to get out may be perceived as eloquent replies to the violence of others – including that of staff – rather than solely as behaviour which challenged others and confirmed the necessity of their detention. Winterbourne View Hospital patients were chronically under-protected. (2012, p v)

Since the publication of Flynn's serious case review there have been a plethora of other government documents damning practice within Winterbourne View and the regulatory bodies for overseeing the quality of practice (CQC, 2011); DH, 2012a 2012a; LGA, 2013). So what causes an organisation to 'turn a blind eye' to the kinds of abusive behaviours seen in this television programme? What stopped other staff coming forward when they witnessed service users being systematically ill-treated by staff, and what stopped the member of staff who did whistleblow being heard by senior managers?

Another example of poor practice on a much larger scale occurred at the Mid Staffordshire NHS Foundation Trust Hospital from 2005-08. In February 2013 Robert Francis QC published a public inquiry report into the abysmal care that patients received at this hospital:

> ... the story it tells is first and foremost of appalling suffering of many patients. This was primarily caused by a serious failure on the part of a provider Trust Board. It did not listen sufficiently to its patients and staff or ensure the correction of deficiencies brought to the Trust's attention. Above all, it failed to tackle an insidious negative culture involving a tolerance of poor standards and a disengagement from managerial and leadership responsibilities. This failure was in part the consequence of allowing a focus on reaching national access targets, achieving financial balance and seeking foundation trust status to be at the cost of delivering acceptable standards of care. (Francis, 2013, p 3)

The precise circumstances surrounding the Mid Staffordshire case might well be different than for Winterbourne View, but what are similar are the instances of poor professional practice that went unchecked for too long by the organisations themselves and the staff working in them, and many external agencies, such as the CQC, who had regulatory responsibilities. We will not be looking at the Mid Staffordshire Hospital case in any detail in this chapter as it has been the subject of an independent inquiry and a public inquiry, the latter of which cost £13 million, and the recommendations make salutary, yet sobering reading. However, this inquiry also raised issues of dignity in caring practices, and discussed the influence and effect that organisational cultures can have for the staff working in them. Francis described this culture as having the potential to spread like a cancer if left unchecked (Triggle, 2013).

Leadership failure: surface and depth discourses

Surface cultural discourses: structure and organisational issues

At a surface level, as discussed already, it is expected that a variety of policies and procedures will be in place in an organisation such as Winterbourne View, including whistleblowing, dignity at work and supervision policies, policies for safeguarding vulnerable adults investigations, working with challenging behaviour from residents and also upholding the dignity, privacy and confidentiality of residents, among others. It should not be forgotten that residents were living at Winterbourne View. In addition to this, a formal inspection and review function exists in the role of the CQC, and in this instance the media reports indicate that the CQC had inspected Winterbourne View on a number of occasions previous to these incidents being recorded, and not found anything of concern. This raises issues about the effectiveness of the inspection process, and the public confidence in the CQC, but more importantly it shows the difficulties in using a surface-level approach to pick up on unhealthy working practices and organisational cultural issues that were far more deeply embedded within the organisation. The Concordat (DH, 2012a) has picked up on some of these issues, and the LGA's Joint Improvement Programme (LGA, 2013) should go some way to shaping strategy across sectors, but will this translate into improved quality of care for service users?

Depth cultural discourses: attitudes, values and emotional competence

Joe Casey, the Panorama undercover reporter who filmed the abuse, said,

> 'On a near-daily basis, I watched as some of the very people entrusted with the care of society's most vulnerable targeted patients – often, it seemed, for their own amusement. They are scenes of torment that are not easily forgotten.... These are all people's sons, daughters, parents, aunties, uncles. These are all people who have got families … the families themselves do not know what goes on there.'

In considering how individual workers' attitudes and values can change within different work environments, it is important to think about how workers respond to conflict at this deeper level. 'It becomes very hard for practitioners who are trying to operate according to their value base to swim against the tide and challenge inappropriate policies and practices or work in ways that do not compromise social work's value base' (Postle, 2007, p 255). Flynn comments that at Winterbourne View, 'fundamental principles of healthcare ethics such as respect for autonomy, beneficence and justice were absent' (2012, p ii). This paints a damning picture.

Psychodynamic and systemic ideas offer alternative or useful insights to processes at work within caring organisations, with the work of Obholzer and Zagier Roberts (1994) and Huffington et al (2004) being particularly useful here. The power dynamics operating help us to understand, inform and influence both macro and micro social processes within care environments. We have already discussed Sparr and Sonnentag's ideas (2008) in respect of how processes and functions of subtle coercive workplace relationships and procedures affect how paradigms of thought and meaning are constructed before being used to inform these processes.

Obholzer's approach to managing social anxieties also acknowledges the role of emotion and group processes. He comments:

> Management, structure and organisation are not unimportant – in fact, they are vital. Nor is the emphasis on money inappropriate: financial constraint is a reality. In my experience of consulting to institutions, however, I regularly find that no attention whatsoever is paid to social, group and psychological phenomena. Consequently, by neglect, the factors that should be an integral part of good management become the very factors that undermine the venture. (1994, p 169)

Halton (1994) highlights a number of unconscious aspects of organisational life that are useful to consider in light of the Winterbourne View scandal:

- *The unconscious:* referring to the hidden aspects of a person's mental life that influence conscious processes. These hidden aspects also apply to group processes.
- *The avoidance of pain:* institutions also develop defences to protect themselves against pain and difficult emotions. Halton suggests that 'they may arise from the nature of the work and the particular client group ... some defences are healthy ... some institutional defences, like individual defences, can obstruct contact with reality and in this way damage the staff and hinder the organisation in fulfilling its task' (1994, p 12).
- *The contribution of Melanie Klein:* she identified 'splitting' and 'projection' as two concepts that children use to cope with difficult feelings and emotions. 'By splitting emotions, children gain relief from internal conflicts ... projection involves locating feelings in others rather than in oneself' (1994, p 13).
- *The paranoid schizoid position:* 'in an institution the client group can be regarded as the originator of the projections, with the staff group as the recipients ... schizoid splitting is normally associated with the splitting off and projecting outwards of parts of the self-perceived as bad, thereby creating external figures who are both hated and feared. In the helping professions there is a tendency to deny feelings of hatred or rejection towards clients' (Halton, 1994, p 14).
- *Envy.*
- *Projective identification* (an unconscious interpersonal interaction in which the recipients of a projection react to it in such a way that their own feelings are affected: the unconsciously identify with the projected feelings) and *counter-transference* (the state of mind where other people's feelings are experienced as one's own) are both psychoanalytic terms (Halton, 1994, p 16). Halton suggests that it is through this mechanism of projective identification that one group on behalf of another group can serve as a kind of 'sponge' for all the anger and negative feelings in a staff group. When considering the actions within the Winterbourne View staff team observed in the Panorama documentary, this concept of projective identification seems particularly useful.

- *The depressive position:* when a group functions in a depressive position, 'the group will be more able to encompass the emotional complexity of the work in which they all share' (1994, p 18).

Stokes' descriptions of Bion's three basic assumptions about groups is also useful:

> According to Bion, much of the irrational and apparently chaotic behaviour we see in groups can be viewed as springing from basic assumptions common to all their members ... each giving rise to a particular complex of feelings, thoughts and behaviour. (Stokes, 1994, p 21)

The three basic assumptions are: basic assumption dependency (baD); basic assumption fight–flight (baF); and basic assumption pairing (baP) (Stokes, 1994, p 21). In terms of the members of staff from Winterbourne View, they displayed some of the characteristics from baD. In this position, 'the group will behave as if its primary task is solely to provide for the satisfaction of the needs and wishes of its members ... the leader serves as a focus for a pathological form of dependency which inhibits growth and dependency' (1994, p 21).

Obholzer's (1994) comments about the use of defensive structures in public sector organisations are helpful in understanding how organisations can avail themselves of the external and psychic reality in which they operate. Even though he was writing in 1994, his comment below about managerialism in the public sector is insightful:

> The new style of management is to give managers more power and to eliminate consultation as "inefficient". It has become a top-down model with dialogue and co-operation between the different sectors seen as old fashioned, and care staff increasingly excluded from policy – and decision-making. This style of management could be described as "paranoid-schizoid by choice", fragmenting and splitting up systems instead of promoting collaboration. The splitting up of functions makes it easier for managers to make decisions. (Obholzer, 1994, p 173)

These challenges remain for current managers, given that the preferred culture of management continues as Obholzer describes. Halton comments that, 'within organisations it is often easier to ascribe a staff member's behaviour to personal problems than it is to discover the link with institutional dynamics' (1994, p 16). It is this focus on attitudes, values and emotions that has the potential to bring a different understanding to organisational cultural issues, including some of the other unconscious processes at play in this organisation that resulted in this behaviour from a number of staff within it. While the individual staff members remain ultimately responsible for their behaviour, which was criminal in nature, were the actions of these staff members the result of a few 'rotten apples' within the organisation or were there other unconscious organisational dynamics at play? The Concordat (DH, 2012a) and LGA Improvement Plan (LGA, 2013) will have a role to play in addressing these issues and in creating working environments that are healthy and safe for the service user and for the workforce. As we can observe from the Francis inquiry (2013), meeting the performance indicators established by the sector or set by government does not in itself guarantee quality of care.

Managerialism as a feature of a serious case review

We have already referred extensively to managerialism throughout this book given that it has become a popular critical discourse within the analysis of what is not working in social work and social care. In relation to those features of managerialism (Pollitt, 1990, pp 2-3; White and Harris, 2007, p 243), we have reiterated these in relation to summarising some of the ways in which social care management has changed in the last two decades:

- 'management' is a separate and distinct organisational function;
- progress is seen in terms of increasing productivity;
- increased productivity comes from the application of information and organisational technologies;
- there must be a shift from a focus on inputs and processes to outputs and outcomes;
- measurement and quantification need to increase;
- markets or market-type mechanisms should be used to deliver services;
- contractual relationships should be introduced;
- customer orientation should be central;
- the boundaries between the public, private and voluntary sectors should be blurred.

While previous chapters have reflected the negative implications of these features, one could argue the moral position that asserts an obligation to spend public money without waste. Langan (2000) is of the view that the rise in managerialism within social care occurred as a result of the sector being seen as failing. A large number of public inquiries in the 1980s and 1990s have brought to the public's attention some of the situations in which tragedy occurred (Stanley and Manthorpe, 2004). While these have continued to occur in various guises, Lees et al (2013) argue that prescriptive and tightly defined risk and performance management techniques have developed within the child protection system in an attempt to defend against the uncertainties of cases, fears of making the wrong decision and of public criticism. Additionally in the 1990s, political pressure for economy, efficiency and effectiveness in public sector services was marshalled in such approaches as CCT (compulsory competitive tendering), and 'Best Value' reviews, while the 2000s has ushered in new jargon by way of 'mixed economies of care', and no doubt such managerial practices will continue to change and develop. Critique of the 'unintended consequences' of two decades of managerialist approaches to welfare (see, for example, Langan, 2000; Payne, 2009; Munro, 2010a, 2011, 2011a) have highlighted changes giving rise to distortions that have resulted in practice from a defensive process of risk management. Both Munro (2011) and Lees et al (2013, p 542) recommend that practice would be better managed within organisational cultures that acknowledge the emotional dimensions of child protection and support them through skilled supervision, training and access to research.

As stated earlier, Munro draws heavily on systems theory in her work. She believes that 'the increase in rules and guidance governing child and family social work activity over the past two decades has had a number of unintended consequences on the health of the profession and outcomes for vulnerable children and young people' (Munro 2011, p 136). This prescriptive practice and resulting unintended consequences also applies to adult services, albeit through a different journey. Munro argued for less prescription and bureaucracy, the development of social work skills and expertise to raise the quality of provision offered to children and families, creating a learning system within organisations, promoting the exercise of professional judgement, and using a systems model for reviewing serious incidents or cases of abuse. Her stress on the need for emotional literacy within organisations should be taken seriously. While Lees et al (2013) go on to highlight the similarities between Munro's review and the work of Menzies Lyth's (1988) exposition of primary and secondary anxieties within the nursing profession, there is evidence presented in this chapter that shows the importance of public sector organisations taking into account emotional and psychological issues when considering the health of the culture of respective organisations. By moving away from dignity for staff being solely attributed to the presence or absence of a policy document about bullying and harassment, organisations can demonstrate a level of complexity in their management and support to staff that mirrors the practice experience of staff delivering services, and the complexities of the relationships that staff have with many service users and carers.

Summary

This chapter has examined the concept of dignity within the context of organisational culture, and explored ideas about what dignity means within social work/social care organisations. Organisational culture has a powerful influence on the way in which our public and voluntary sector organisations function, and surface and depth discourses indicate the breadth and profundity of this cultural power. There are a myriad of challenges for social workers and for managers in the current work climate, yet social work always seems to find itself in the midst of a crisis of some sort or another. We have used the events at Winterbourne View to explore 'dignity at work', and have raised a number of points about organisational practice when things go wrong. Unfortunately Winterbourne View will not be the last institutional inquiry to be undertaken where issues of staff abusing and mistreating clients goes unreported, or is reported, but no response or a poor response is forthcoming from the institution itself or other significant organisations. The publication of the public inquiry exploring the care at the Mid Staffordshire NHS Hospital between 2005–08 is a case in point (Francis, 2010; Francis, 2013). Flynn (2012) comments:

> On paper, the policy, procedures, operational practices and clinical governance of Castlebeck Ltd were impressive. However, Winterbourne View Hospital's failings in terms of self-reporting, attending to the mental and physical health needs of patients, physically restraining patients, assessing and treating patients, dealing with their complaints, recruiting and retaining staff, leading, managing and disciplining its workforce, providing credible and competency based training and clinical governance, resulted in the arbitrary violence and abuses exposed by an undercover reporter. (p x)

At one level it is difficult to understand how such a situation could ever occur. At another, there are some powerful messages in the Winterbourne View serious case review (Flynn, 2012), the responses from the government (DH, 2013), as well as the resulting programmes of action, including the Concordat (DH, 2012a), the LGA's Joint Improvement Programme (LGA, 2013) and the Winterbourne Review's good practice examples (DH, 2012b) which talk about the kinds of organisational practices we should be advocating for in our places of work. Staff value being part of a learning, reflexive organisation; good management and leadership practice is also valued. In order that the social work profession can meet such challenges and continue to adapt and change, social work leadership and management approaches have to rise to the challenge of applying knowledge to practice, to ensure that the emotional aspects of organisational culture are acknowledged and embedded firmly in the working practices of the sector. If that happens then we stand a good chance of practising and managing ourselves and our work with a depth of dignity that we, and the users of our services, expect and deserve.

EIGHT

Advancing leadership and management skills for effective practice

So far in this book we have talked a great deal about support, but what about the support needed by leaders and managers themselves, and their own needs for support and development? As outlined in previous chapters, within the UK, messages from both major reviews of social work and serious case reviews (Scottish Executive, 2006; DH, 2010; DfE, 2010; Centre for Workforce Intelligence, 2011) have highlighted working conditions on the front line of services in which poor communication and antagonistic relations between staff and managers have served to work against the capacity of managers to lead and to manage services. There is evidence relating to the experience of managers in relation to unmanageable workloads, and a significant issue is managers' own expressed unmet needs for adequate support and CPD. A more coherent approach to leadership and management development merits further attention. In England, the Munro review of child protection (Munro, 2011) and the SWRB (Social Work Taskforce, 2009) both emphasised the particular importance of s) both emphasised the particular importance of skilled and confident frontline managers in terms of their essential contribution to practice. A range of approaches to supporting and developing aspiring, new-in-post and experienced team managers has emerged and given particular emphasis to access to training and to development in professional supervision (DCSF, DH and BIS in partnership with the Social Work Reform Board, 2010; Bourn and Hafford-Letchfield, 2011). The National Skills Academy for Social Care (2009), the Leadership Group for the Children's Workforce (Hartle et al, 2009), the NHS Leadership Academy (a single, comprehensive home for leadership) and the Scottish Leadership Foundation provide just a few examples of the public bodies charged with consulting on proposals designed to bring greater coherence to the development of middle management across an increasingly integrated workforce.

Within health, a report commissioned by The King's Fund (2011) conveyed a clear message that the NHS will not be able to rise to the financial and quality challenges it is faced with unless the contribution of managers is recognised and valued 'from the board to the ward' (p 2). More generically, it is also essential that the number of managers and expenditure on management should be based on a thorough assessment of the future needs of services, and supported by continuing investment in leadership development at all levels. Central to any development initiatives is the recognition of the increasing importance of leadership across *systems* of care as well as within individual organisations. This systems approach has been one we have taken in most chapters so far. This also has implications for the type of approach taken to staff development, the logistics in workforce development and associated costs of any development programmes. Some of these issues have already been discussed in more detail in Chapters Four and Five in relation to the workforce, and so this chapter now turns specifically to the professional development of managers and leader-managers.

Whatever strategic architecture is developed, employers need to take local action to develop and support a wider culture of learning and development that enables managers at different levels to achieve both confidence and competence to make improvements and to engage in CPD. In the professional areas outlined above, there are already detailed national occupation standards, specialist standards and requirements for education and training in leadership and management (GSCC, 2005; Skill for Care, 2008, 2008a), but how we actually measure management skill and its associated knowledge and values remains a relatively under-researched and under-documented area. More systematic evaluation of what constitutes effective management and leadership development has not yet been established. Management, for example, is essentially a practical activity, and managers use a range of knowledge and skills within their practice. This integrative task involves achieving synergy, balance and perspective. Most management activity is undertaken through complex webs of social and political interaction involving a continuous process of adaptation to changing pressures and opportunities (Hafford-Letchfield, 2009). The development of management skills and the acquisition of insight into self, others and the process of critical reflection on one's own learning relies on a number of sub-systems working together to support such practice. Some approaches to management learning have been criticised for overemphasising its technical aspects and for the oversimplification of the social work management agenda through vocationalism (Hafford-Letchfield and Lawler, 2010). Aspirations towards more humanist or existential management (Lawler, 2005) might lead us to discover alternative orientations and to return to the values embedded in the 10 underpinning social work management principles that reflect its professional orientation (see GSCC, 2007). Internationally, there have been a number of attempts to define core management standards and principles in social care through various national networks of social work managers such as in the US (Wimpfheimer, 2004), New Zealand (Webster and Tofi, 2007) and Canada (van Zwanenberg, 2010a). At the time of writing, however, there are no explicit international agreements or consensus on what should be in the curriculum, or developmental programmes specific to social work and social care managers. Cross-comparison of work done so far demonstrates that it is important to achieve an appropriate balance between what is often referred to as 'hard' and 'soft' areas (Beinecke, 2010). Given the suggestion (Raelin, 2004) that worldwide, some US$50 billion is now spent on leadership development, of which expenditure within social work and social care is a mere drop in this vast ocean, the question still arises as to how effective this spending is. Organisations aiming to develop their leadership potential will want to be clear about what they need to do to achieve the best results possible for users and carers (Tourish and Pinnington, 2010).

The different perspectives and complex requirements on how to carry out the varied tasks of managing and leading in an organisation have implications for management education and its curriculum, particularly if we are to avoid accusations of 'leaderism', as discussed in Chapter One (see O'Reilly and Reed, 2010). Here we consider some of the more practical issues and contexts for leadership and management development. We focus mainly on 'management' given that the majority of the ground covered in this book so far has been concerned mainly with leadership. Following on from the previous discussions in other chapters, we also return to the concept of establishing a learning environment within which a climate for management learning can be fostered, as the impact of organisational climate on social work services has been said to be a more powerful issue than commonly appreciated (Gould, 2000). We have seen that the generic literature on learning cultures and climates is rich and is expected to continue as a focus of academic theorising, empirical investigation and methodology development as well as practice development. This area is still developing within the social care workforce literature in relation to leadership and management (Gould, 2000; Hafford-Letchfield, 2007; Hafford-Letchfield and Harper, 2013). More relevant, contemporary and urgent for social work and social care is the issue of management learning transfer, particularly in relation to how this occurs across sectoral partnerships, and the extent to which application of learning is able to influence radical reform to public services. As we have seen so far, fundamental to this is how the context and purpose for leadership and management development shapes subsequent learning strategies, processes and positive outcomes for practice. This has already been picked up in relation to the discussion on organisational culture, workforce development, providing support and, in the last chapter, the potential for learning from mistakes and challenges. Like other areas of social work and social care, improvement in management skills should ultimately remain focused on improving the quality of services and sustainable outcomes for users and carers.

This chapter also reviews some of the pedagogies and methods underpinning a democratic approach to learning how to be an effective manager. Some attention is given to the different issues competing for attention within leadership and management development, the ethics and values essential to retain the professional nature of the work and the tensions inherent in management and social work practice. Lambley (2011) makes this explicit in her analysis of the blame that managers take in the downgrading of social work, the contradictory positions that need to reconciled, and the importance of keeping in touch with the welfare ideals of social work. Developments in management education and learning that have promoted more collaborative practices through inclusion of arts-based methods and pedagogies are reviewed in relation to some of the key findings from these initiatives.

Developing a leadership and management development framework

Throughout this book we have made frequent reference to the different contexts for leadership and management development, from which we have derived key messages about the conditions that mean successful leadership is likely to emerge and flourish. We have referred frequently to increasing neoliberalism during the 1990s and rapid reform of the public sector during periods of economic austerity in the 21st century towards more individualised support based on explicit commitment to the market and competition, which have rapidly changed the world in which social work and social care management operates and the skills and knowledge it requires. In terms of *how* managers will need to manage in the future, Martin (2011) suggests that they will need to be: 'flexible, agile, and capable of adjusting quickly to environmental changes and willing to reallocate resources to take advantage of new opportunities' (not paged). In short, they will have to not only know and understand what their organisation's core capabilities are, but be able to recognise and take advantage of the core capabilities of their collaborative partners. Relationships between the public and business sector, according to Makaros (2011), should emphasise the principles of reciprocity and win-win relations, and be seen as a mutual relationship in which each party has something to give and something to gain. Within the management development process, any knowledge and skills taught in this area should recognise that establishing collaborative relationships with business can provide an opportunity to establish a powerful and influential lobby for planning social policy and human rights as well as help learners deal with the threats and dilemmas associated with such relationships (Makaros, 2011). Social work managers need to be sufficiently assertive about professional matters, and it is therefore important to develop appropriate training programmes where they can acquire theoretical and practical knowledge about the advantages and strengths of collaborative work, particularly in the interorganisational sphere.

Coulshed and Mullender (2001) assert that 'all social workers *are* managers' (p 2; emphasis added) as the core skills required for managing themselves, others and the systems they work in are integral to social work practice. How far social work education has grappled with providing graduates with leadership and management skills remains unknown, but the *Professional capabilities framework for social workers in England* (DfE, 2011), illustrated in Figure 8.1, gives a clear message about the integration of professional leadership and organisational studies within its revised curriculum.

Figure 8.1: The professional capabilities framework for social work

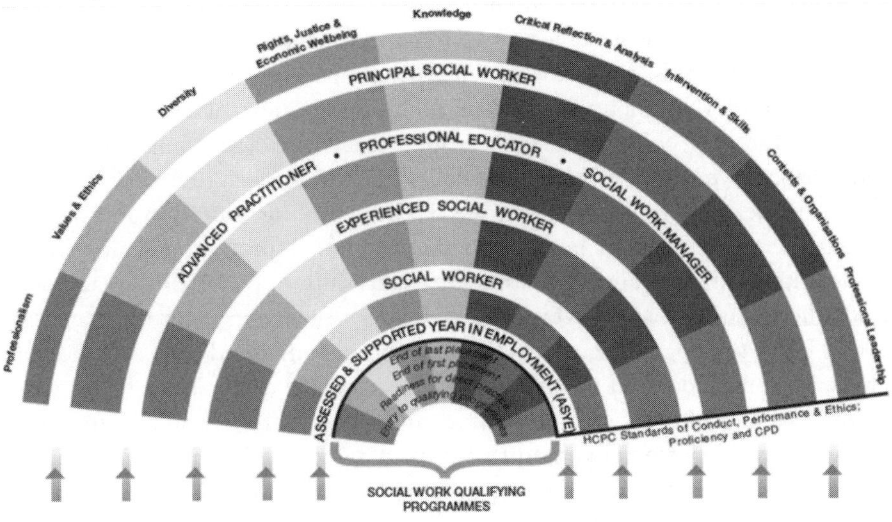

Reproduced with kind permission of The College of Social Work

Types of knowledge and skills needed by social work and social care managers

There has been an emphasis on the development of a range of concrete knowledge and skills in relation to entrepreneurship and business, where competition and conditions that increase efficiency have certainly become more prevalent in social work and social care management. These have permeated debates about which type of qualifications are most relevant to social work managers. The type of relevant programmes, for example, the Master's in Business Administration (MBA) and mainstream public sector management development programmes, have been in direct competition with emerging tailored programmes for social work where one is often working with smaller cohorts and in local partnerships with sponsoring organisations. Ongoing development has also been challenging in conditions where funding is unstable and unpredictable. This scenario may reflect the status of social work management as a discrete discipline. There may also be stigma associated with practitioners moving into management roles. Social workers and other professional practitioners managing in social care who move into management are not likely to have had any formal training, at least until they are already well into the role. The lack of opportunities to reflect on their role within a clear framework may ill equip novice managers to work with the technical skills required as well as being able to work constructively with the inevitable conflicts confronted with the everyday experiences faced when working within their local community and workplace. These roles require sophisticated analysis and sound ethical practice, particularly to minimise any erosion of shared obligations within a new globalised context (Beck and Beck-Gernsheim, 2002).

There are also some development issues for those educators developing and delivering management development, and the empirical evidence and knowledge base about what constitutes effectiveness in management practice (Hafford-Letchfield, 2010). It is argued that specific attention to social work leadership and management development has become even more important as complex social, cultural, economic, political and demographic factors are demanding rapid change and collaborative work with other providers and professionals to find new ways to design and deliver services. As mentioned earlier, enabling leadership and effective management also needs to be developed at all levels – professional and practice leadership, political leadership, strategic leadership, operational management, academic leadership and citizen (user and carer) leadership (Scottish Executive, 2006). From the beginning of this book we have emphasised how management of social work and social care needs to reflect people's aspirations to be active citizens, to be in control of the services and support they need and to ensure that services are personalised and that human rights are safeguarded. Managers therefore need a sophisticated range of interpersonal skills to build relationships and empower people, as individuals – in their families and in communities, often working indirectly through those they manage determined by legislative and policy frameworks – the 'softer' areas of management development.

An extensive review by Beinecke and Spencer (2007) of training programmes in eight English-speaking countries identified in each a range of leadership and management models and competencies on which they were based. From these, they then identified five comprehensive but key areas of leadership competency as follows:

1. Personal skills and knowledge (emotional intelligence, self-awareness, values and beliefs and ethical behaviours).
2. Interpersonal (people) skills (communication, teamwork, coaching, enabling others, negotiating and facilitating, working with other cultures, stakeholders and empowering others).
3. Transactional skills (execution, business management).
4. Transformational skills (visioning and strategic planning, catalysing change, innovation and goal-setting).
5. Policy and programme knowledge (policy, legislation and discipline expertise).

These core leadership and management competencies offer flexibility when applied to different levels of management such as with senior executives or aspiring practice managers as well as in different environments including the statutory or third sector. All of these may confront learners with a wide variation in priorities and needs. Some areas, for example, could be given emphasis at any given point in a manager's career or specific role. Finally, management development needs to be framed in relation to achieving the competencies and capabilities that 'includes a performance component, an ethical component, a component that emphasizes reflective practice in action and the capability to effectively implement evidence-based interventions and a responsibility for lifelong learning' (Beinecke, 2010, p 171). The design of learning programmes and activities should be able to describe these competencies and capabilities in sufficient detail to facilitate thorough assessment and evaluation of the learning achieved and its transferability to practice.

Wimpfheimer (2004) notes that recognising and defining the competencies needed by managers is a first step towards improving service delivery as well as being clear about how these might be used and accredited. She lists a number of desirable competencies specific to social work managers:

- Knowledge of contemporary social policy through being well informed and ensuring that staff and service users benefit from their expert knowledge or act as a spokesperson within their network.
- The integral nature of advocacy, which represents both individuals and issues. Advocacy involves inspiring people as well as telling the right story to the right people.
- Thinking about community and marketing relations within an ethical framework and acknowledging the unique context for marketing and promoting services that she sees as significantly unique in relation to other sectors.
- Understanding how an agency is 'governed', which is an essential skill of an effective manager, and being clear about the appropriate roles and responsibilities of people as well as being able to communicate them with clarity and diplomacy.
- Being good at planning by taking the lead and achieving a balance between the day-to-day operational needs and being able to see the bigger picture – strategic planning.
- Being able to lead and commit to change and take people with them and to develop a programme of work to support this.
- Financial and fiscal development and being able to manage these.
- Recognising the importance of evaluation and how to frame important questions and use the outcomes of evaluation to bring about service improvement. Wimpfheimer does not insist that managers necessarily have the skills of evaluation but should know how to use people and data, to make judgements about the quality of services and act on them.
- HRM that involves the softer skills and balancing individual needs with the wellbeing of the organisation and its effectiveness. Managing people can be very challenging, and managers need to be sensitive with good personal skills.
- Knowledge of staff development, an area frequently overlooked, including skills in resourcing this and selecting the right opportunities for staff to acquire the skills they need for the job.

Alongside these areas of competency, Wimpfheimer (2004, p 56) also notes the informal areas managers need to address in their day-to-day jobs. She asserts that they need to understand their *roles as managers* in organisations, not only what the specific tasks are, but also what the organisation expects of its managers.

Understanding the *organisation's style of operation* is also crucial, for example, whether professionals are expected to operate relatively independently or whether they are expected to rely heavily on the direction of their supervisors. This has been the subject of much debate in a more recent review of social work in the UK (Munro, 2011) and is dependent on the climate of the organisation and how relaxed or formal it is. Wimpfheimer refers to how managers understand their organisation in its *interagency environment* and whether the style is collegial or competitive. She also comments on the need to understand the *values and priorities* of the agency and how far this is 'results'- or 'process'-oriented: who or what comes first in the priorities of the agency? The fiscal *condition* of the agency and whether it is relatively stable financially. Finally, an understanding of the *informal structure* of the agency and how well its elements work well together and whether they act independently or in competition with itself. Some of these issues around knowledge transfer and the nature and challenges of learning and knowledge management through fostering a culture and climate for learning, and particularly in relation to collaborative approaches within the public sector, have already been discussed in Chapter Two.

Learning that includes followership

As we have seen in many of the case studies examined throughout this book, the role that leaders play in follower engagement at work suggests that engagement is best enhanced when employees feel they are supported, recognised and developed by their managers (Harter et al, 2002). These further highlight that leadership development needs to be based on practice experience, and support critical reflection on that practice as well as recognise the role of managers in developing leadership at all levels in the organisation.

The role of followers is relatively neglected in leadership development, and the critical role played by followers that is often vaguely described as background roles relative to the leader's foreground role (see Blake and Mouton, 1978). Leadership development tends to overemphasise the leader's responsibility for achieving the task and reduces the responsibility of followers. Learners can be encouraged to think about leaders and followers as interdependent actors who share responsibility for group process and outcomes (Sronce and Arendt, 2009). Harper and Hafford-Letchfield (2013) advocate the use of experiential methods to influence leadership – followership relationships – and have utilised literary works in their pedagogic practice to facilitate students' examination of moral issues and responsibilities within leadership towards those who follow. Further, Hackman and Wageman (2007, p 43) described the tendency to put the responsibility for group performance on the leader as the 'leader attribution error'. They suggest that the 'invisibility of structural or contextual factors' leads to this type of incorrect assessment. If they are correct, then drawing attention to the factors involved in a group's success or failure, including especially the follower role, may reduce leadership attribution error that requires attention in any learning process. The leader and follower relationship is a complex one based on influence (Bennis, 2007). If followers believe in a goal, then it seems appropriate to expect that they will share responsibility in helping achieve this goal. Developing 'effective followers' may be a better way to support achievements towards an organisation's goal. We looked at methods used within AI in Chapter Two that attempt to capitalise on this. As we saw, systemic approaches like AI have gained increased popularity in social care (Cooperrider, 1998). After all, even leaders in senior positions within social work and social care must act as followers if they are really to fulfil their responsibilities. Followers too require critical thinking ability, and the ability to independently assess what is required from them and the others and to participate in the process of developing and implementing ideas about how to get there. Van de Luitgaarden (2009) compares the debates on rational decision-making theory with evidence-based practice, and suggests that a more naturalistic decision-making process is required to recognise that 'decision making in a real-life setting is fraught with ill-structured problems in dynamic environments, characterized by rival goals, feedback loops, time constraints and high stakes' (p 253). He links support to followers to retention of expertise in an organisation and, as we saw in Chapter Five, studies within various national contexts show that staff turnover in social work contexts remains high. Uncritical thinkers may be disengaged. They do not offer ideas or evaluate plans, instead choosing dependence on the leader. Given that the task of leadership in social work and social care is often expressed as being able to motivate people to achieve outcomes that benefit the individual, the team and the organisation, a balance between all of these is needed (Hafford-Letchfield et al, 2008).

Evaluations of different leadership development programmes have suggested that the features supporting successful leadership development include models that support distributed leadership such as the utilisation of networks and the use of action learning sets or communities fostered and supported for a sustained period of time (Gray et al, 2010; McAllen and MacRae, 2010). Potential leaders therefore need constructive opportunities within their development programmes to critically reflect on how they actually lead, facilitate and promote more effective engagement of those with a direct stake in such changes and how they might embed this in their day-to-day work. Programmes should support leadership of those responsible for developing responses to new policy initiatives or who are going through periods of intensive change. They require knowledge of how to effectively promote learning in their organisations and within the different partnerships involved. As public services often have to pick up the pieces when initiatives or systems fail, building resilience to stress alongside social networks is also crucial to learning about leadership in the sector. The legitimacy of the local state in the UK is highly dependent on relationships with civil society, including informal networks with the community, patients, service users and minority groups as well as formal partnerships at both strategic and operational levels (Birney et al, 2010). As we saw in Chapters Four and Five, given the difficult history of recruitment and retention in social work and social care, employing and retaining the best talent depends equally on training and supporting the knowledge, skills and associated morale of aspirant leaders to reduce turnover.

Leadership development in practice

Any leadership and management training should give attention to facilitating the functioning of the interrelationships between the internal and external aspects of the organisation and its sub-systems. These include psychological and social relationships in the workplace, knowledge of the formal structure of the organisation and technological factors, the constraints or limitations on the organisation and the reciprocal relationships across its external and internal partnerships (Glisson et al, 2006). Blumenthal (2003) emphasises the critical relationship between managerial capacity and organisational capacity. He identifies capacity-building tools such as research, planning, implementation and monitoring and evaluating the impact of the capacity-building process on the organisation itself. Blumenthal outlines four components that shape the design of a management training programme that seeks to expand organisational capacity: (1) making explicit the organisational capacity-building goals; (2) creating a supportive practice environment within the training programme and in the agency; (3) training approaches that include multiple approaches to learning, for example, didactic, experiential, reflective, self-assessing and lifelong learning; and (4) the use of different training tools such as self-assessment, blended learning and observational methods.

While management and leadership development in social work and social care share a lot of common approaches with other disciplines, particularly in the public sector, Tourish and Pinnington (2010) have attempted to conceptualise seven main forms of leadership and management development based on their experiences of running tailored programmes in Scotland. Their headings have been utilised to discuss development initiatives below:

Formal credited programmes and courses: these may be externally or internally provided and entail staff attending formally organised learning, 'off-the-job'. They may vary in quality, duration, location, credibility and impact, and usually attract accreditation or recognition through certificates, awards and qualifications. Recent attempts to undertake a more systematic evaluation of the outcomes of social work education in the UK (Burgess and Carpenter, 2010) made some progress in identifying, developing and adapting measures of the impact of formally credited education. Outcome measures for leadership and management education requires further work before they can meet the exacting standards of reliability and validity expected in pedagogical research and, more relevant, the impact on services and ultimately service users' experiences and quality of care. One of the key questions debated among those designing and running programmes should be the methods used and the need for more comparative research. At the time of writing, there are no comparative methods including whether leadership and management in social work and social care should be taught uni- or interprofessional.

Multisource feedback: this describes a variety of methods used to obtain, reflect and build on feedback obtained from individuals within a manager's circle of direct influence, and readily lends itself to blending business know-how with social work values (Richardson, 2010). A typical model is illustrated in Figure 8.2 where each source of feedback provides opportunities to build a more collaborative culture that is participatory in nature. It also has the potential to utilise feedback from users, carers and relevant members of the multidisciplinary team to achieve more holistic and inclusive assessment. This approach encourages a shared understanding about the management skills and competencies being seen as desirable, and therefore makes a statement about what people can expect from their leader-manager.

Figure 8.2: Using a multisource feedback process

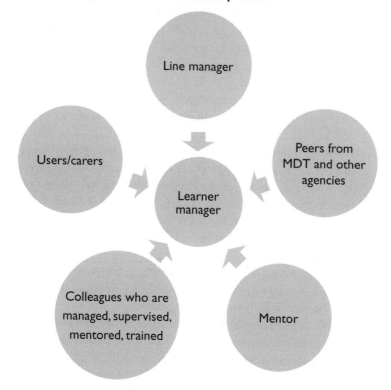

Managers seeking feedback and being willing to assess and evaluate their progress through this method go one step more towards including different stakeholders, including those they manage or deliver services to, equal partners in a management development strategy. It also increases capacity for change (Skinner et al, 2004). Analysis and responding to the feedback can relate directly to the learning opportunities available in the workplace, and any development plan can then seek to align skills with practice realities. The use of multisource feedback systems has become more widespread in management development, and they work best when integrated into other sources of evaluation. A further advantage is how they help learner-managers direct their own learning alongside the work they are doing.

Hafford-Letchfield and Bourn (2011a) based their own multisource feedback tool on national social work standards and key principles for management (Skills for Care, 2008), and used this for enhancing management skills on a postgraduate qualification. While some of the national standards might be perceived as being quite behaviourist (Hafford-Letchfield et al, 2008), consideration of the learner-managers' own competence against these served to raise awareness about the political dimensions and processes implied in meeting them, including scrutinising the language that managers used, how they positioned themselves in relation to others and what events were perceived to be within or out of their control. An evaluation undertaken by Hafford-Letchfield and Bourn (2011a) suggested that the process needed careful preparation, and transparent guidance should be given so that those giving the feedback should understand its purposes and how it might be used. Learner-managers were advised to be mindful of whom they approached for feedback, with the purpose of ensuring that it would be constructive and useful in their subsequent development. Being proactive in seeking feedback builds on the premise that one can have more control, both in acquiring feedback and putting oneself in a position of being able to respond to it positively. Managers are, in effect, demonstrating how they are willing to give up control by allowing others to have a voice and, in turn, by being willing to respond. It also illustrated the complexity involved in determining the ideal structure for defining and measuring outcomes of management skill development. Organisational complexity, size, changing employee roles and multilayered structures make simplistic evaluation impossible, and a tailor-made approach would appear to work best to stimulate motivation. Likewise, Richardson (2010), in his discussion of using 360-degree feedback in a social work setting, recommends that training and support is given to raters, and that the process is facilitated to ensure that follow-up is encouraged. He notes that this type of management development can be tailored for smaller organisations or individuals, and can provide a cost-effective method that is linked to the performance, job satisfaction and the business plan.

There are of course some costs associated with developing these types of feedback mechanisms, even if these are developed 'in house'. Besides the resources required to support the process, Whitaker et al (2007) also refer to self-presentation costs and ego costs that have been shown to affect the extent to which one actively seeks feedback. Effort costs are also present, which describes the amount of effort one must expend when seeking feedback.

Coaching and mentoring is now a very common method of learning in most management development, and the emphasis is generally on improving the individual's performance and has both a practical and goal-focused role, is ongoing and generally one-to-one. Mentoring is said to promote both psychosocial and career functions. It is one means by which learners are facilitated to acquire new knowledge and personal growth within their own organisational structure. The notion underpinning mentoring is that the 'mentee' or 'learner' is the world expert on themselves, and the role of mentor is to help them maximise their potential to achieve from what is available and from the learner's own inner resources. With no prescribed objectives, the learner establishes their own specific objectives and outcomes and agrees these with the mentor, perhaps using a contract. Essentially, mentoring is based on establishing a voluntary relationship of equality, openness and trust that involves building rapport and achieving clarity of role or purpose. Coaching is perhaps more directive and can be facilitated and supported through observations, shadowing and assessment of skills being developed.

Gallop and Hafford-Letchfield (2012) suggest that there is a different dynamic at work when acting as a mentor compared to other types of support meetings such as supervision. When we engage in mentoring we 'park' accountability (unless something untoward comes up, in which case the mentoring session will need to move into a different sort of conversation), and focus on development and learning. This can provide a very different environment for managers who may work in quite directive cultures.

There is also, of course, an organisational context for mentoring such as in succession planning (Hafford-Letchfield and Chick, 2006), or where this is being used to promote interprofessional management learning (Hafford-Letchfield and Chick, 2006a). Mentoring and coaching can also complement formal learning while managers follow an accredited programme. The mentoring role in social work and social care, for example, may also be accompanied by assessment, and is nearly always time-bounded, examples being practice assessors/educators in social work qualification, supervisor-mentors for NQSWs, mentor-assessors in post-qualifying programmes, and the arrangements for induction in social care. These are thus often 'hybrid' models, and carry little in their remit about general career development or providing openings for mentees into promotional opportunities, activities that are often discussed in mentoring literature, particularly books based on US models. Critiques of mentoring are clear that it is not the panacea for orientation, training, skills development and retention as it generally provides just one aspect of learning. Nor is it an option for tackling wider and deeper institutional or cultural issues within an organisation. Where mentoring and coaching is used it is recommended that there is a structural training programme for mentors and coaches as well as those utilising their skills and knowledge (Hafford-Letchfield and Chick, 2006; 2006a).

Networking seeks to break down barriers between functional areas of management development to foster wider individual networks, create a greater business literacy and more in-depth organisational knowledge (Tourish and Pinnington, 2010). We saw some of the potential of networking for staff in the previous chapter. Within management development, this will enhance any interprofessional management development where networking helps to operate effectively within multi-agency and interprofessional settings, particularly around service development and quality issues. Barr (2010) talks about the permeable boundaries of interprofessional learning in these settings which may change in response to changes in policy or practice, or learners' needs and expectations, as well as being valued and protected, for example, in the face of budgetary cuts when interactive learning in small groups may seem too costly.

Communities of practice are based on concepts of networking, and this is a relatively underdeveloped theory on learning (Gray et al, 2010). Communities of practice are groups of people who share a concern or a passion for something they do and learn how to do it better as they interact regularly, where practice provides 'ways of ameliorating institutionally generated conflicts' (Wenger, 1998, p 46). Gray et al (2010) assert that whilst professional and managerial cultures have to be accommodated, these should be complemented by the development of a more communal and humanistic culture if the emotional nature of the work and the impact of society and community on the self and learning is to be recognised. As seen in previous chapters, particularly the last, democratic learning cultures are essential for social care to maintain awareness and to engage with the power differentials that disempower users and carers.

Gray et al (2010) argue that participation, values and direction-setting at all levels, alongside a management approach that trusts the wisdom of practitioners and 'works for those practitioners' creates a knowledge-enabling environment that nurtures communities, encourages and legitimises learning. Developed teams require minimalist facilitation and individuals take responsibility for their work, reporting back to the team leader, keeping them briefed on progress or consulting on significant problems – but otherwise working independently. Gray et al (2010) argue that community of practice initiatives in social care could mirror the knowledge management initiatives being taken in the most competitive of private sector organisations with, it could be argued, the greater possibility of success, as social care practitioners are motivated by a strong value base that means they seek to empower others and should have a developed self-awareness and awareness of others from their training in social work methods and their everyday practice.

Job or project management assignments: these provide managers with a challenge in which they have the opportunity to develop their leadership skills by taking up new roles, tasks and responsibilities alongside opportunities to develop specific technical skills and knowledge specific to the project they are working on. Pressure and motivation to learn, often generated by a degree of dissonance between the desired knowledge or skill and their current state, is sufficient to prompt motivation to achieve it, perhaps identified through multisource feedback mechanisms.

Action learning: this assumes that managers learn most by getting things done and working on real problems. An action learning set normally consists of a group of people with different or similar backgrounds, positions in the organisation and work experience. Its purpose is through use of reflective questioning techniques – the holder of the problem can create and implement innovative solutions to complex problems. The development goal for participants is to reflect and learn from both their own actions and those of others. Action learning is particularly suitable for interprofessional management development where exchange of experience can be valuable as well as drawing on knowledge of cross-partnerships to find solutions to operational problems. It also provides opportunities to explore differences as well as similarities in values, skills and knowledge, roles and responsibilities.

All of the above-described methods of learning and development activities are by no means exhaustible but serve to give a flavour of how learning and development activities can take place within a framework aligned with organisational goals and objectives. They can also be utilised to facilitate innovative responses to working through the 'wicked issues' (McAllan and McCrae, 2010). A blended approach enables self-directed and autonomous learning although the latter poses challenges, as managers may need to explore whether their perceived learning needs and desired outcomes are in harmony, and whether their preferred approaches to learning coincide (Barr, 2010). Mismatches may lead to negotiation and provide excellent opportunities for collaborative learning. Lived professional experiences, and their influence on professional attitudes and behaviour, also provide a good basis for interprofessional learning where participants can compare perspectives and experience and sometimes challenge each other.

Overall, methods used need to engage with active and relevant pedagogies that can be transferred easily into practice and are relevant to the manager individually as well as instigated in response to the perceived needs of the team, the organisation, the professions or the overall service delivery system (Barr, 2010). This may only occur if previously held attitudes and beliefs are open to challenge in a safe, supportive and cooperative learning environment.

The importance of a learner's developing autonomy has been at the heart of adult education theory, more particularly in relation to self-directed learning. Eneau (2008) notes the paradoxes in the concept that he suggests stems from a fundamental ambiguity as much about the nature of autonomy as about the value assigned to it in the learning process. This could be the final outcome of learning or as the preferred method of adult education. He clarifies this in relation to the confusion between an autonomous learner and a learner who could become autonomous; between fundamental, psychological and methodological autonomy; between autonomous learning and autonomy of the learner; and even, in a more general sense, between self-directed learning and self-directed education (Eneau, 2008, p 230). Looking at the role of personal relationships the learner has with others allows attention to the autonomy of the adult learner and has significance in a larger sense. The practical implications are positive construction of the learner's autonomy through reciprocal exchanges in learning communities and the social aspects of learning. Eneau goes as far as to suggest that even if it remains the final objective of any form of education, individual autonomy can only be established:

> ... in a dialectic between individual liberty and external constraints, in an intermediary state (a process of balance, to use the constructivist terminology) that depends on the situation and the context. In this way, learning, like the individual, can only ever be qualified as relatively autonomous. (2008, p 231)

Autonomy is not merely the ability to direct one's own learning; it takes into account emotional, intellectual and moral dimensions. It reveals itself as much through the adult's conception of him- or herself as an autonomous learner as through his or her aptitude to manage his or her own learning. It is as much through an ability to make informed judgements in the framework of the individual's situation as through the ability to use appropriate strategies to learn.

Learning about management critically

Critical management studies are most often associated with critical theory, postmodern and poststructuralist ideas where relevant central themes of critical theory provide a critique of contemporary society, the capitalist system, commodification processes and managerialist ideologies. Programmes that facilitate critical management education may focus on identifying structural and economic inequalities, systems of power relations and modes of domination, with a view to offering more democratic, humanistic, emancipatory and socially responsible forms of managing organisations (Cunliffe and Linstead, 2009). Postmodern and poststructuralist approaches encompass a broad range of work covering postmodernism as a cultural logic – a society characterised by fragmentation and simulation – to a more philosophically oriented poststructuralist critique of representation, addressing the nature of reality, agency and knowledge. Critical pedagogy should open up new ways of thinking and acting by addressing the ideological and political processes (including the politics of race, gender and ethnicity) present within social and institutional life. According to Cunliffe and Linstead (2009), it is pedagogy of resistance, social justice and social transformation, drawing on work developed in both education and management.

Critical approaches within social work and social care, if not embedded in practice realities, may be viewed as being overtly theoretical, focusing on abstract systems, structures and language, often ignoring the practicalities of managing and changing organisations. Furthermore, when critical approaches do take a practical focus on the empirical circumstances of organisational change, they often concentrate on the generation of evidence of resistance to managerial control initiatives, and inadvertently distance themselves from managers themselves – who may of course not necessarily be managerialist in their approach to their task. However, it is important to consider the different ways that the 'critical manager' can and does exist, and explore various approaches to developing as such. For aspiring managers or those already embedded within the very ideologies and systems of power under critique, they might not initially be predisposed to changing prevailing ways of acting. Critique that takes a distanced and oppositional view will only make the task of engagement harder (Cunliffe and Linstead, 2009). Ruch (2011) considers the contribution of psychodynamic theoretical perspectives to developing a critical model of management that can hold in creative tension both the reflective and relationship-based dimensions of management and the positive aspects of managerialism. In reference to safeguarding, she refers to the 'risk-ridden, uncertain and anxiety-provoking context of child-care social work' (p 1), and acknowledges that such an approach requires facilitation within reflective organisational contexts embracing diverse knowledge sources, promoting relationship-based skills and that are underpinned by reflective values.

In her own examples of a local management development programme, Ruch refers to learner-managers' resistance to embracing reflective approaches through their requests for increased teaching that draws on specific technical management tools. Ruch stresses the importance of juxtaposing these latter approaches alongside opportunities to develop reflective management practice. How management is conceptualised by those following a management development programme perhaps reflects the organisational context in which managers are located. Managerial approaches to learning may subsequently afford less importance to the interpersonal components or development. Ruch examines concepts familiar in systems approaches to learning such as the primary task, work group, mirroring, splitting and projection. She highlights the common characteristics that connect them in relation to the frequent adoption of defensive behaviours in the face of complex and emotionally charged situations, and the need for individuals to face and tolerate reality, however complex and fractured this may be (Ruch, 2011, p 16). Ruch asserts that the common thread linking the knowledge, skills and values of management practice is the significant role played by the emotions and feelings that permeate relationships requiring much greater attention to softer skills and knowledge, such as affective understanding and intuition.

Gender and sexuality in management development

Mainstream research, education and practice in management and organisations in social work have also not been strong on gender and sexuality, and any specific analysis is far from being explicit and well established, despite the fact that gender and sexuality issues remain defining features in most social care organisations, for example, in gendered patterns of hierarchy, occupational segregation, the predominance of heterosexuality, harassment and discrimination and in the questioning of work–life balance, particularly in relation to family responsibilities. These are in turn defined by and instrumental in reproducing social relations of age, class, disability, culture and ethnicity. Hafford-Letchfield (2011) has examined some of the issues in relation to the gendered division of labour within the management of social care, and suggests that these divisions are clearly illustrated when looking at both exclusions of women and their exclusion as a group. Broadbridge and Hearn, (2008, p 541) illustrate these through the specialisation of women's role in social care for example the particular forms of formal and informal labour undertaken and the vertical and horizontal divisions in organisations and management around gender roles.

A growing body of research has promulgated theories on how heterosexuality is seen as the primary means by which both people and organisations are gendered, and as a mechanism through which power is exercised within the organisational context (Gutek 1989; Hicks 2008). By exploring aspects of communication, career development, self-presentation and relationships within organisations, a heterosexualised version of sexuality inflects organisational life at all levels with gendered consequences. Most organisations and managements reproduce dominant heterosexual norms, ideology and practices, one of the consequences of which is to render gay and lesbian issues 'problematic' where gay men and lesbian women are forced to 'manage' their sexuality in organisations, choosing whether to come out and how to manage this 'out' identity (which is more than a one-off event) or commonly, to hide their identity. Research commissioned by Stonewall (Miles, not dated) revealed the tensions and contradictions that exist for lesbian women at work. It suggested that lesbian women often think their gender is more of a barrier to success at work than their sexual orientation. Therefore, if they can hide the fact that they're gay, some feel it best to do just that. As one participant said, 'putting your hand up twice' can be difficult (Miles, not dated, p 2). Participants felt that role models and openly gay women made a crucial difference to the confidence and profile of lesbians and bisexual women in the workplace, and wanted to see organisations involve them more in the development and its initiatives.

Discourses about women managers in social care organisations construct women within a subordination relationship that automatically devalues everything that can be attributed to women (Gherardi, 1994). On the other hand, women who 'reach the top' of an organisation's hierarchy are then often desexualised or seen as 'career women'. The woman who adopts a masculine style and behaviour is perceived as having been incorporated and is criticised for assuming the status of an honorary man, while the woman who retains caring or service orientation risks being criticised for failing to conform to the models expected of a manager (Foster, 1999).

Therefore, women's relational style can both help and hinder their effectiveness as leaders and has implications for management development programmes in social work and social care. A study of how women 'learn' to become managers undertaken by Bryans and Mavin (2003, p 129) demonstrated that this involves a complex combination of factors. They refer to the perception of women's personalities, their value systems, their experiences and the culture and interventions of the organisations within which they worked. Learning to 'become' a manager for participants in Bryans and Mavins' study revealed a story of change where a key issue centred on the woman's decision to change herself or to change the management practice in her organisation. Reflecting on this (untypical) research within the management literature, and particularly in the social work management literature, it appears that encouraging the narratives of women opens up more space for contestation and resistance. Greater insights are needed to provide more fluid definitions of different relationships at work whereby women can mobilise power to construct *themselves* within organisations, rather than be constructed by them.

It may be that the managerial ideologies and organisational mechanisms to enhance efficiency, accountability and competition that have dominated and transformed the landscape for organising and delivering social care have actually reinforced some issues around inequality (White, 2006; Ferguson, 2007). Despite a number of aspirational system-wide standards for avoiding discrimination, promoting dignity and person-centred, individualised care within public policy relating to care, policy in relation to gender and sexuality issues is rarely made explicit, or has a tendency to be cast as neutral and uncontentious (Harlow, 2004; Cocker and Hafford-Letchfield, 2010). A few studies (Maddock, 1999; Aronson and Smith, 2009) have focused on managers and how particularly women managers might distance themselves from managerialist practices or develop resistance to find more participatory opportunities for staff and service users. In a qualitative study of Canadian women managers, Aronson and Smith (2009) discerned two broad strategies deployed by women to develop the critical consciousness of those they managed. These included efforts to expand entitlements to service users increasingly excluded from public support, efforts to politicise and expand the scope of practice in their organisations by sustaining advocacy in their work and embedding sophisticated knowledge of institutional politics and enormous skill in using language to expand, deepen practice and develop the critical consciousness of those they managed:

> 'We're able to mediate everybody coming together mostly on that "this would be helpful for women" ... as long as you'd speak about "policy development", "planning". I mean who could say no to that right?... I mean municipalities and certainly policy people in the government will always say; oh yes we need to "coordinate" you know? So we played up to that stuff.' (quoted in Aronson and Smith, 2009, p 14)

The above quote illustrates the internalisation of gendered divisions of authority in management, both formal and informal, and the way in which women and men may be valued differentially in terms of both formal authority, by virtue of their post and positions and informal authority from their status and standing in the organisation.

Gendered leadership

Leadership is also a gendered concept, and as suggested earlier, is applied within a social context that is itself gendered (Yoder, 2001). Critical markers for evaluating the gender congeniality of the social context in which leadership is embedded include group composition, the gender-typing of the task, valuing task performance over all other outcomes and power emphases (Yoder, 2001). Yoder proposes a gender-sensitive model where exploring and developing leader effectiveness recognises both the gender of the leader and the gender congeniality of the context in which the leader operates. The leadership literature is highly masculinised by drawing on stereotypical skills evaluated for goal attainment within a hierarchical organisation where power bases operate. Models of transformation and charismatic leadership emphasise influence rather than power and empowerment of self and others such as concepts of distributed leadership largely equated with teamwork and collaboration (Hafford-Letchfield et al, 2008). Highlighting the gendered stereotyping of leaders, Eagly and Carli (2007) likewise give examples of everyday descriptions used to describe leaders as 'competitive', 'political', 'ambitious', 'driven', 'social', 'tough', 'task-focused', 'instrumental', 'passionate' and 'committed'. These are seen as positive attributes for men but as negative for women. Mavin (2009) distinguishes communal behaviours that are more helpful, sympathetic, empathetic and compassionate and highly valued in traditional social work practice with more argentic behaviours, such as 'assertive', 'controlled', 'determined', 'self-reliant', 'independent' and 'individualistic'. The latter argentic behaviours are automatically assumed as effective leadership whereas communal behaviours are not (Eagly and Carli, 2007). This is despite the fact that women who display argentic behaviours are likely to jolt assumptions about how they should behave, and highlights the different expectations of how men and women can vent emotions. For example, traditional gendered emotion behaviours include mothering, nurturing and caring roles, supporting and developing others and resolving conflict. A woman's success as a leader therefore depends on how well or how poorly she navigates her way through her sexual stereotype and her work competence and how men and women judge that balancing act (Mavin, 2009).

In summary, any critical analysis of management development will need to look beyond and deconstruct the obvious, and the dominant taken-for-granted perspectives by which organisations are constructed and analysed. In this chapter we have looked specifically at gender and sexuality, but this is relevant to any managers from groups subject to the dominant norms. In doing so, one is shifting to the sub-texts of organisations and the manifest forms of processes around these. According to Halford and Leonard (2001, p 26), in reviewing theoretical perspectives, the key to achieving a more integrated understanding of the relations between these hierarchies of subjectivity within organisations lies in focusing attention on the question of 'power' as the lynchpin on which power is seen to flourish. The systematisation of power relations between members in an organisation enables organisational power to strengthen its position around issues such as race, disability, gender and sexuality and vice versa, so that these then come to characterise some forms of organisational power. This is a complex landscape that has to be viewed within its historical, social, economic and political context. While wave metaphors are not always useful when talking about political movements that have affected care and its environments, we have moved on a long way from an historical era during which different movements around feminism, racism and heterosexism had a mass base and influence. Similarly, the removal of legal barriers and new public policies within the area of diversity and equality have since offered important opportunities for management to engage more directly in learning and development to ensure the achievement of equality in succession planning and to combat the glass ceiling (Hafford-Letchfield and Chick, 2006). Conceptualising organisational positioning within these critical perspectives can broaden debate about anti-oppressive practice in the over-deterministic framing of services and frontline social work. The central question is how current discursive practice in relation to diversity and equality within the organisation might be deconstructed and challenged in relation to the role that leadership and management plays. The idea that identity is simply a construct of language, discourse and cultural practices is not sufficient. The goal is to dismantle these fictions and thereby to undermine hegemonic regimes of discourse (Hafford-Letchfield, 2011). Some of the features of Foucault's analysis (1984), particularly his focus on subjection, 'othering' and how some marginalised groups within management might internalise oppressions, could be helpful here. New surveillance and control methodologies used in performance management and assessment have taken us away from giving enough attention to achieving equality in social work practice. There are some glimpses of possibilities in developing a more equitable or co-productive relationship with service users. The move towards personalised services offers opportunities to examine issues of gender and sexuality but also requires an appreciation of the values, connections and desires that bind these social networks together so that there is parallel commissioning and service developments, and away from fixed identities (Cocker and Hafford-Letchfield, 2010).

It requires a very skilled analysis of puzzles, and in the work by Mavin (2009), she referred specifically to the gendered assumptions that make up the maze and how these change the closer you get to the centre of the labyrinth:

> The labyrinth gives me the opportunity to see different pictures of women's perceived behaviours and women's experiences in management, particularly as they hit the walls of the maze, have to regroup and think, where do I go from here? (Mavin, 2009, p 83)

There are limitations of a modernist approach to resolving some of the issues discussed in relation to these issues. In relation to women managers, Millen (1997) argues that through a range of feminist approaches it may be possible to get the best out of both worlds by using postmodern insights to continually critique the role of feminist research and the gendered aspects of mainstream research in social work and social care, but using postmodernist ideas to advance feminism's political agenda. Lawler and Bilson (2010) suggest taking a more relative pluralist approach to enable the incorporation of the voices of both men and women in management and leadership positions and those who aspire to such positions to include their interpretations of gender and its influence and importance in social work organisations.

Using the creative arts in management development

Examples of evidence submitted to the Munro review in the UK (Munro, 2010) included initiatives where creative approaches to service development are promoted alongside the satisfaction of performance requirements from central government. The inclusion of personal and strong democratic elements within management and leadership education is therefore essential to retain the professional nature of the work and the values inherent in social work and healthcare practice. A substantial body of literature is emerging (Gould, 1996; Simmons and Hicks, 2006; Burgess and Laurance, 2007; Hafford–Letchfield et al, 2008a; Warne and McAndrew, 2010) to demonstrate that use of the arts within social work and healthcare practice and education promotes creativity and critical reflection, particularly in the context of more rigid or bureaucratic organisational environments. The arts may offer relevant insights into the diversity of human behaviour, personality and relationships, emotions and feelings, life events and culture, to mention but a few. Critical theory, critical reflection and personal accountability are all cited as key aspects of professional identity and essential to the facilitation of professional learning and development (GSCC, 2005; NMC, 2008; Watson, 2008). According to Burgess and Laurance (2007, p 2), drawing on the arts in education and practice can therefore facilitate 'looking outside the box, seeing things from a different perspective or experiencing oneself differently, than effectively doing and promoting these in others are essential for good practice'. Likewise, the use of interactive drama has been found to increase internalisation of students' understanding of both issues and processes as well as in developing flexibility and thinking on their feet (Kerr, 1995; Hafford–Letchfield et al, 2010). For example, some management development programmes have incorporated music into the curriculum that provides a particular metaphor within teaching with the potential to offer richer insights (Leonard et al, 2013). Its use has been evaluated within different educational settings. Fairfield and London (2003) found that introducing music into their teaching enhanced the discipline of 'deep listening' in relation to different voices of the students in the team and their reactions to its members. They developed a diagnostic instrument for looking at the impact of musical experience using six principal dimensions that offer potential insights into team functioning. Moore and Ryan (2006) introduced drumming circles into their management education as a source of experiential learning.

The impact of drumming was evaluated and found to provide a resonant and complex alternative to explore themes associated with organisational dynamics and teamwork. Their analysis of learner feedback demonstrated that students were more able to make spontaneous links between aspects of the experience and features of organisation and management theory following the experience. Both these studies referred to the significance of generating emotional depth within individuals through such musical learning experiences. Leonard et al (2013), within an interprofessional learning context, found that the experience of playing Gamelan provided a potential metaphorical frame of reference with which to address some of the above learning needs and to depart from more habitual schemas for describing and thinking about the different attributes of leading change and leading teams. Further, it was a useful tool to engage service users in a co-productive approach, what they termed 'a great leveller' (p x). Such approaches, according to Barrett and Cooperrider (1990), have the potential 'to facilitate the learning of new knowledge, to create new scenarios of future action, and to overcome areas of rigidity' (Barrett and Cooperrider, 1990, p 224).

Rossiter (2011) uses the term 'unsettled practice' in relation to social work, and draws on the work of Emmanuel Levin regarding the practice of ethics defined by conscious and deliberate commitment to working in full view of the tensions and contradictions derived from social work's professional status and knowledge claims. She regards social work as a practice of ethics defined by a conscious and deliberate commitment to working in full view of the tensions and contradictions derived from social work's professional status. This, she posits, accepts the impossibility of resolving the practice dilemma that the 'violence' of social work representations exists in inescapable tension with the need for justice that requires it. Rossiter argues that unsettled practice must take place on the 'razor's edge' of totalising representations of people and the necessity of representation for justice. In this way, critical social work can situate itself in justice-oriented representations, but it can also interpret its chronic discomfort with normative social work as unsettled social work. 'Unsettled' means practice that accepts the impossibility of resolving the practice dilemma that the 'violence' of social work representations exists in inescapable tension with the need for justice that requires it. These types of analysis within arts-based methods are useful in challenging unintended complicity with injustice, or the 'dividing practices' and power relations of those practices that Foucault refers to alongside the many critiques of managerialism within the management and leadership theory.

Summary

As the closing chapter to this book, we have finished by covering a number of issues in relation to leadership and management development and examined the different aspects of developing, implementing and evaluating the conditions and tools required to ensure that support is provided to those leading services in developing the skills, knowledge and behaviours required. We have also used the example of gender and sexuality within management development to illustrate some of the complexity from a critical management perspective. As we have seen, the jury is still out on how to approach and evidence the impact of management development programmes and to develop appropriate, reliable and valid measures that meet the unique needs in social work and social care. We have considered some of pedagogic approaches, including those that are both traditional and creative. We hope that this book has provided some food for thought about the different roles that leadership plays, how you might maximise your effectiveness in your practice and most importantly, take those who are subject to the systems and impact of care services with you in the most participatory way possible. After all, it is all about being a good human being, and striving to be the best human being possible!

Bibliography

Adair, J.E. (1973) *Action-centred leadership*, London: McGraw-Hill.

Adams, R.B. and Ferreira, D. (2007) 'A theory of friendly boards', *The Journal of Finance*, vol 62, no 1, pp 217-50.

ADASS (Association of Directors of Adult Social Services), DH (Department of Health), Skills for Care, BASW (British Association of Social Workers) and Social Care Association (2010) *The future of social work in adult services in England*, London: DH.

ADASS (Association of Directors of Adult Social Services), LGA (Local Government Association) (2011) *Safeguarding Adults* 2011: Advice Note, London: ADASS/LGA

Advocacy Resource Exchange (2011) 'Where does advocacy fit in with brokerage for self-directed support and personal budgets?', Southampton: Advocacy Resource Exchange.

Agashae, Z. and Bratton, J. (2001) 'Leader-follower dynamics: developing a learning environment', *Journal of Workplace Learning*, vol 13, no 3, pp 89-102.

Alimo-Metcalfe, B. and Alban-Metcalfe, J. (2005) 'Leadership: Time for a new direction?' *Leadership*, Vol. 1, No. 1. pp. 51 71, doi:10.1177/1742715005049351

Alvesson, M. and Sveningsson, S. (2008) *Changing organisational culture: Cultural change work in progress*, New York: Routledge.

Anning, A., Cottrell, D., Frost, N., Green, J. and Robinson, M. (2010) *Developing multi-professional teamwork for integrated children's services* (2nd edn), Maidenhead: Open University Press.

Anton, J. (2000) 'The past, present and future of customer access centres', *International Journal of Service Industry Management*, vol 11, no 2, pp 120-30.

Argyris, C. and Schon, D. (1990) *Overcoming organisational defences*, Needham Heights, MA: Alleyn and Bacon.

Armstong, D. (2004) 'Emotions in organisations, disturbance or intelligence?', in C. Huffington (ed) *Working below the surface: The emotional life of contemporary organizations*, London: Karnac Books, pp 11-30.

Arnstein, S.R. (1969) 'A ladder of citizen participation', *Journal of the American Planning Association*, vol 35, no 4, pp 216-24.

Aronson, J. and Smith, K. (2009) 'Managing restructured social services: expanding the social?', *British Journal of Social Work*, vol 40, no 2, pp 530-47.

Aronson, J. and Smith, K. (2011) 'Identity work and critical social service management: Balancing on a tightrope?', *British Journal of Social Work*, vol 41, no 3, pp 432-48.

Arrington, P. (2008) *Stress at work: How do social workers cope?*, NASW Membership Workforce Study, Washington, DC: National Association of Social Workers.

Asthana, A. (2008) 'Social workers buckling under stress burden', *The Guardian*, 15 June (www.guardian.co.uk/society/2008/jun/15/socialcare).

Audit Commission (2008) *Don't stop me now: Preparing for an ageing population*, London: Local Government National Report.

Avolio, B.J., Bass, B.M. and Jung, D.I. (1999) 'Re-examining the components of transformational and transactional leadership using the Multifactor Leadership Questionnaire', *Journal of Occupational and Organizational Psychology*, vol 72, no 4, pp 441-62.

Axtell, C., Wall, T., Stride, C. and Pepper, C. (2002) 'Familiarity breeds content: The impact of exposure to change on employee openness and well-being', *Journal of Occupational & Organizational Psychology*, vol 75, no 2, pp 217-31.

Baginsky, M., Moriarty, J., Manthorpe, J., Stevens, M., MacInnes, T. and Nagendran, T. (2010) *Social workers' workload survey: Messages from the front line. Findings from the 2009 survey and interviews with senior managers*, London: Social Work Task Force/Crown Copyright.

Bailyn, L. and Fletcher, J.K. (2003) 'The equity imperative: Reaching effectiveness through the dual agenda', *Insights,* Boston, MA: Centre for Gender in Organizations, Simmons Graduate School of Management.

Baker, G.R. (2011) *The roles of leaders in high performing healthcare systems*, London: The King's Fund.

Balloch, S. (2005) 'Election 2005: putting social care in the picture. Campaign briefing: workforce', *Community Care*, vol 1564, pp i-xii, 17 March.

Bamberger, P. and Meshoulam, I. (2000) *Human Resource Strategy: Formulation, Implementation and Impact*, Thousand Oaks, CA: Sage.

Bandura, A. (1977) *Social learning theory*, Englewood Cliffs, NJ: Prentice Hall.

Bandura, A. (1986) *Social foundations of thought and action*, Englewood Cliffs, NJ: Prentice Hall.

Banks, S. (2006) *Ethics and values in social work* (3rd edn), Basingstoke: Palgrave.

Barnes, M., Newman, J. and Sullivan, H. (2007) *Power, participation and political renewal: Case studies in public participation*, Bristol: Policy Press.

Barr, H. (2010) 'Interprofessional education as an emerging concept', in H. Barr (ed) *Interprofessional education*, Basingstoke: Palgrave, pp 181-187.

Barrett, F.J. and Cooperrider, D.L. (1990) 'Generative metaphor intervention: A new approach for working with systems divided by conflict and caught in defensive perception', *Journal of Applied Behavioral Sciences*, vol 26, no 2, pp 219-39.

Bartel, A. (2004) 'Human resource management and organizational performance: Evidence from retail banking', *Industrial and Labor Relations Review*, vol 57, no 2, pp 181-203.

Bass, B. (1990) 'From transactional to transformational leadership: Learning to share the vision', *Organizational Dynamics*, vol 18, no 3, pp 19-31.

BASW (British Association of Social Workers) (2012) *Code of ethics*, London: BASW.

BASW/CoSW (College of Social Work) (2011) *England research on supervision in social work, with particular reference to supervision practice in multi disciplinary teams* (http://cdn.basw.co.uk/upload/basw_13955-1.pdf).

Bates, N., Imminsa, T., Parker, J., Keena, S., Rutter, L., Brown, K. and Zsigo, S. (2009) 'Baptism of fire: The first year in the life of a newly qualified social worker', *Social Work Education*, vol 29, no 2, pp 152-70.

Batt, R. and Doellgast, V. (2005) 'Groups, teams and the division of labor', in S. Ackroyd, R. Batt, P. Thompson and P. Tolbert (eds) *The Oxford University Press handbook of work and organisation*, Oxford: Oxford University Press, pp 138-61.

BBC (British Broadcasting Corporation) (2011a) 'Four arrests after patient abuse caught on film', BBC News, 1 June (www.bbc.co.uk/news/uk-1354822).

BBC (2011b) 'Undercover care: the abuse exposed', BBC Panorama documentary [first aired in the UK on 31 May].

BBC (2012) 'Winterbourne View workers raised staff behaviour fears', BBC News Bristol, 28 July (www.bbc.co.uk/news/uk-england-bristol-14316588).

Beck, U. and Beck-Gernsheim, E. (2002) *Individualisation: Institutionalized individualism and its social and political consequences*, London: Sage Publications.

Beeby, M. and Booth, C. (2000) 'Networks and inter-organizational learning: a critical review', *The Learning Organisation*, vol 7, no 2, pp 75-88.

Beer, M., Spector, B., Lawrence, P.R., Mills, D.Q. and Walton, R.E. (1984) *A conceptual view of HRM, Managing human assets*, New York: Free Press.

Begum, N. (2006) *Doing it for themselves: Participation and black and minority ethnic services users*, Participation Report 14, London, Social Care Institute for Excellence and Race Equality Foundation.

Beinecke, R.H. (2010) 'Social work leadership and management development: Comparable approaches', in Z. van Zwanenberg (ed) *Leadership in social care*, London: Jessica Kingsley Publishers, pp 167-67.

Beinecke, R.H. and Spencer, J. (2007) *Leadership training programmes and competencies for mental health, substance use, health and public administration in eight countries*, Auckland: International Initiative for Mental Health Leadership (www.iimhl.com).

Bell, K. and Smerdon, M. (2011) *Deep value: A literature review of effective relationships in public services*, London: Community Links.

Bendelow, G. (2009) *Health, emotion and the body*, Cambridge: Polity Press.

Bennis, W. (2007) 'The challenges of leadership in the modern world', *American Psychologist*, vol 62, no 1, pp 2-5.

Beresford, P. (2000) 'Service users' knowledge and social work theory: conflict or collaboration?', *British Journal of Social Work*, vol 30, no 4, pp 489-503.

Beresford, P. (2003) *'It's our lives': A short theory of knowledge, distance and experience*, London: Citizen Press in association with Shaping Our Lives.

Beresford, P. (2007) *The changing roles and tasks of social work from service users' perspectives: A literature informed discussion*, London: Shaping our Lives National User Network.

Beresford, P., Branfield, F., Taylor, J., Brennan, M., Sartori, A., Lalani, M. and Wise, G. (2006) 'Working together for better social work education', *Social Work Education*, vol 25, no 4, pp 326-31.

Berg, T., Pooley, R. and Queenan, J. (2011) 'Achieving consensus within SSM', *International Journal of Humanities and Social Science*, vol 1, no 4, pp 231-9.

Van Berkel, R., Van der Aa, P., Van Gestel, N. (2010), Professionals without a profession? Redesigning case management in Dutch local welfare agencies, *European journal of social work,* 13(4): 447-63

Berwick, D.M. (2003) 'Improvement, trust and the health care workforce', *Quality and Safety in Health Care*, vol 12, no 1, pp 2-6.

Birney, A., Clarkson, H., Madden, P., Porritt, J. and Tuxworth, B. (2010) *Stepping up: A framework for public sector leadership on sustainability,* Wales: Forum for the Future.

Blair, T. (2010) *A journey* (3rd edn), London: Hutchinson.

Blake, R.R. and Mouton, J.S. (1978) *The new managerial grid*, Houston, TX: Gulf.

Blumenthal, B. (2003) *Investing in capacity building: A guide to high impact approaches*, New York: The Foundation Center.

Blumenthal, B. (2007) *A framework to compare leadership development programs*, New York: Community Resource Exchange.

Boehm, A. and Yoels, N. (2008) 'Effectiveness of welfare organisations: The contribution of leadership styles, staff cohesion, and worker empowerment', *British Journal of Social Work*, vol 39, no 7, pp 1360-80.

Boin, A., McConnel, A. and t' Hart, P. (2008) *Governing after crisis: The politics of investigation, accountability and learning*, Cambridge: Cambridge University Press.

Boin, A., t' Hart, P. and McConnell, A. (2009) 'Towards a theory of crisis exploitation: Political and policy impacts of framing contests and blame-games', *Journal of European Public Policy*, vol 16, no 1, pp 81-106.

Boin, A., t' Hart, P., McConnell, A. and Preston, T. (2010) 'Leadership style, crisis response and blame management: The case of Hurricane Katrina', *Public Administration*, vol 88, no 3, pp 706-23.

Bolman, L.G. and Deal, T.E. (2008) *Reframing organisations: Artistry, choice and leadership*, San Francisco, CA: Jossey-Bass.

Bolton, S. (2007) 'Dignity in and at work: why it matters', in S. Bolton (ed) *Dimensions of dignity at work*, London: Elsevier, pp 3-18.

Bostock, L., Bairstow, S., Fish, S. and Mcleod, F. (2005) *Managing risks and minimising mistakes in services to children and families*, SCIE Report 6, London: Social Care Institute for Excellence.

Bourn, D. and Hafford-Letchfield, T. (2011) 'Professional supervision in conditions of uncertainty', *International Journal of Knowledge, Culture and Change Management,* vol 10, no 9, pp 41-56.

Bowcott, O. (2009) 'Baby P borough takes on social workers from North America', *The Guardian*, Friday, 2 October (www.guardian.co.uk/society/2009/oct/02/haringey-north-america-social-workers).

Bowen, D.E. and Ostroff, C. (2004) 'Understanding HRM-firm performance linkages: The role of the strength of the HRM system', *Academy of Management Review*, vol 29, no 2, pp 203-21.

Boxall, P. (1998) 'Achieving competitive advantage through human resource strategy: towards a theory of industry dynamics', *Human Resource Management Review*, vol 8, no 3, pp 265-88.

Boxall, P. (2003) 'HR strategy and competitive advantage in the service sector', *Human Resource Management Journal*, vol 13, no 3, pp 5-20.

Boxall, P. and Purcell, J. (2000) 'Strategic human resource management: where have we come from and where should we be going?', *International Journal of Management Reviews*, vol 2, no 2, pp 183-203.

Boxall, P. and Purcell, J. (2003) *Strategy and human resource management*, Basingstoke: Palgrave Macmillan.

Boxall, P. and Steeneveld, M. (1999) 'Human resource strategy and competitive advantage: a longitudinal study of engineering consultancies', *Journal of Management Studies*, vol 36, no 4, pp 443-63.

Bradley, G. (2006) 'Using research findings to change agency culture and practice', *Research, Policy and Planning*, vol 24, no 3, pp 135-48.

Bradley, G. (2008) 'The induction of newly appointed social workers: Some implications for social work educators', *Social Work Education*, vol 27, no 4, pp 349-65.

Braithwaite, J. (2011) 'A lasting legacy from Tony Blair? NHS culture change', *Journal of the Royal Society of Medicine*, vol 104, no 2, pp 87-9.

Bratton, J. and Gold, J. (2003) *Human resource management: Theory and practice*, London: Palgrave Macmillan.

Braye, S. and Preston-Shoot, M. (1995) *Empowering practice in social care*, Buckingham: Open University Press.

Braye, S. and Preston-Shoot, M. (1997) *Practicing social work law*, Basingstoke: Macmillan.

Breaugh, J.A. and Starke, M. (2000) 'Research on employee recruitment: So many studies, so many questions', *Journal of Management,* vol 26, no 3, pp 405-34.

Brennan, D. (2005) 'Keeping our staff: the links between job satisfaction and recruitment and retention', *Journal of Nursing Management*, vol 13, no 4, pp 279-85.

Broadbridge, A. and Hearn, J. (2008) 'Gender and management: new directions in research and continuing patterns in practice', *British Journal of Management*, vol 19, no 1, S38-S49.

Brown, M. and Benson, J. (2005) 'Managing to overload? Work overload and performance appraisal processes', *Group & Organization Management*, vol 30, no 1, pp 99-124.

Brown, P. (2002) *Workforce planning for social work supply, demand and provision of newly qualified social workers required 2001/2–2003/4*, Belfast: Northern Ireland Social Care Council.

Browne, A. and Bourne, I. (1996) *The social work supervisor*, Buckingham: Open University Press.

Bryans, P. and Mavin, S. (2003) 'Women learning to become managers: learning to fit in or to play a different game?', *Management Learning*, vol 34, no 1, pp 111-34.

Buono, A.F., Bowditch, J.L. and Lewis, J.W. III (1985) 'When cultures collide: The anatomy of a merger', *Human Relations*, vol 38, no 5, pp 477-500.

Burgess, H. and Carpenter, J. (2010) *The outcomes of social work education: Developing evaluation methods*, Southampton: Higher Education Academy Subject Centre for Social Policy and Social Work, University of Southampton School of Social Sciences.

Burgess, H. and Laurance, J. (2007) *Reflections on creativity in social work and social work education*, A report for the Higher Education Academy's Imaginative Curriculum Project, Southampton: Subject Centre for Social Policy and Social Work, Higher Education Academy, University of Southampton School of Social Sciences.

Bushe, G.R. (2010) 'A comparative case study of appreciative inquiries in one organization: implications for practice', *Review of Research and Social Intervention*, vol 29, pp 1583-3410.

Cameron, D. (2011) Big Society Speech Transcript. Available on Gov.UK from: https://www.gov.uk/government/speeches/pms-speech-on-big-society

Cannon, M. and Edmondson, A. (2001) 'Confronting failure: antecedents and consequences of shared beliefs about failure in organizational work groups', *Journal of Organizational Behavior*, vol 22, no 2, pp 161-77.

Capra, F. (2003) *The hidden connections: Integrating the biological, cognitive, and social dimensions of life into a science of sustainability*, London: Doubleday.

Care Quality Commission (2011) *Review of Compliance: Castlebeck Care (Teesdale Ltd)* Winterbourne View, CQC: Newcastle-upon-Tyne. Accessed on 1.6.13 at www.cqc.org.uk/media/cqc-report-winterbourne-view-confirms-its-owners-failed-protect-people-abuse

Carpenter, J., Webb, C., Bostock, L. and Coomber, C. (2012) *Effective supervision in social work and social care*, SCIE Research Briefing 43, London: Social Care Institute for Excellence.

Carey, M. (2008) 'Everything must go? The privatization of state social work', *British Journal of Social Work*, vol 38, no 5, pp 918-35.

Carr, S. (2007) 'Participation, power, conflict and change: theorizing dynamics of service user participation in the social care system of England and Wales', *Critical Social Policy*, vol 27, no 2, pp 266-76.

Carr, S. (2010) *Personalisation: A rough guide*, London: Social Care Institute for Excellence.

Carr, S. (2010a) 'Remote or related? A mental health service user's perspective on leadership', *International Journal of Leadership in Public Services*, vol 6, no 2, pp 20-4.

Castle, N.G. and Engberg, J. (2005) 'Staff Turnover and Quality of Care in Nursing Homes', *Medical Care*, vol 43, no 6, pp 616–26.

Centre for Workforce Intelligence (2011) *Workforce risks and opportunities:* Adult Social Care. Kings College London. CfWI.

Cernat, L. (2004) 'The emerging European corporate governance model: Anglo-Saxon, Continental, or still the century of diversity?', *Journal of European Public Policy*, vol 11, no 1, pp 147-66.

Chadderton, H. (1995) 'An analysis of the concept of participation within the context of health care planning', *Journal of Nursing Management*, vol 3, no 5, pp 221-8.

Checkland, P. (1981) *Systems thinking, systems practice*, New York: John Wiley & Sons.

Chen, G., Thomas, B. and Wallace, J.C. (2005) 'A multilevel examination of the relationships among training outcomes, mediating regulatory processes and adaptive performance', *Journal of Applied Psychology*, vol 90, no 4, pp 827-41.

Chen, H.C., Chu, C.I., Wang, Y.H. and Lin, L.C. (2008) 'Turnover factors revisited: a longitudinal study of Taiwan-based staff nurses', *International Journal of Nursing Studies*, vol 45, no 2, pp 277-85.

Clarke, J. and Langan, M. (1993) 'Restructuring welfare: the British welfare regime in the 1980s', in A. Cochrane and J. Clarke (eds) *Comparing welfare states: Britain in international context*, London: Sage Publications.

Clarke, J. and Newman, J. (2007) 'What's in a name? New Labour's citizen-consumers and the remaking of public services', *Cultural Studies*, vol 21, no 4-5, pp 738-57.

Cocker, C. and Hafford-Letchfield, T. (2010) 'Critical commentary "out and proud"? Social work's relationship with lesbian and gay equality', *British Journal of Social Work*, vol 40, no 6, pp 1-13.

Coffrey, M., Dudgill, L. and Tattersall, A. (2004) 'Stress in social services: Mental wellbeing, constraints and job satisfaction', *British Journal of Social Work,* vol 34, no 5, pp 735-46.

Coleman, N. (2006) 'Resolve, re-direct or refer: A case study of a social care contract centre', Paper presented to the 24th International Labour Process Conference, Birkbeck College, University of London, 10-12 April.

Coleman, N. and Harris, J. (2008) 'Calling social work', *British Journal of Social Work*, vol 38, no 3, pp 580-99.

Collins, S. (2008) 'Statutory social workers: Stress, job satisfaction, coping, social support and individual differences', *British Journal of Social Work*, vol 38, no 6, pp 1173-93.

Collins-Camargo, C. and Millar, K. (2010) 'The potential for a more clinical approach to child welfare supervision to promote practice and case outcomes: A qualitative study in four states', *The Clinical Supervisor*, vol 29, no 2, pp 164-87.

Commission on Dignity in Care for Older People (2012) *Delivering dignity: Securing dignity in care for older people in hospitals and care homes: A report for consultation*, London: Local Government Association.

Connolly, S., Bevan, G. and Mays, N. (2010) *Funding and performance of healthcare systems in the four countries of the UK before and after devolution*, London: Nuffield Trust.

Conservative Home Blogs (2012) 'Social work training is where the seeds of scandal are sown' (http://conservativehome.blogs.com/localgovernment/2012/11/social-work-training-is-where-the-seeds-of-scandal-are-sowed.html).

Contiandropoulos, D., Denis, J. and Langley, A. (2004) 'Defining the "public" in a public healthcare system', *Human Relations*, vol 57, no 12, pp 1573-96.

Conway, N. and Briner, R. (2005) *Understanding psychological contracts at work*, Oxford: Oxford University Press.

Cooke, R.A. and Rousseau, D.M. (1984) 'Stress and strain from family roles and work-role expectations', *Journal of Applied Psychology*, vol 69, no 2, pp 252-60.

Coomber, B. and Barriball, K.L. (2007) 'Impact of job satisfaction components on intent to leave and turnover for hospital-based nurses: a review of the research literature', *International Journal of Nursing Studies*, vol 44, no 2, pp 297-314.

Cooper, A. (2005) 'Surface and depth in the Victoria Climbié inquiry', *Child & Family Social Work*, vol 19, no 1, pp 1-9

Cooperrider, D.L. (1998) 'What is appreciative inquiry?', in S.A. Hammon and C. Royal (eds) *Lessons from the field: Applying appreciative inquiry*, Plano, TX: Practical Press, .p 3-44.

Cooperrider, D. and Shrivastva, S (1999) 'Appreciative Inquiry in organisational life' in S. Shrivastva and D.L. Cooperrider, *Appreciative management and leadership: Revised Edition*, Euclid, O.H. Lakeshore Communications, pp 483-484.

Coopperrider, D.L. and Whitney, D. (2001) 'A positive revolution in change', in D.L. Cooperrider, P. Sorenson, D. Whitney and T. Yeager (eds) *Appreciative inquiry: An emerging direction for organization development*, Champaign, IL: Stipes, pp 9-29.

Cornes, M., Moriarty, J., Blendi-Mahota, S., Chittleburgh, T., Hussein, S. and Manthorpe, J. (2010) *Working for the agency: The role and significance of temporary employment agencies in the adult social care workforce. Final report, August 2010*, London: Social Care Workforce Research Unit.

Coulshed, V. and Mullender, A. (2001) *Management in social work* (2nd edn), Basingstoke: Palgrave BASW.

CQC (Care Quality Commission) (2009) *Review of the involvement and action taken by health bodies in relation to the case of Baby P*, London: CQC.

CQC (2011) 'CQC calls on Castlebeck to make root and branch improvements' (www.cqc.org.uk/media/cqc-calls-castlebeck-make-root-and-branch-improvements).

CQC (2011a) 'CQC report on Winterbourne View confirms its owners failed to protect people from abuse', London: CQC (www.cqc.org.uk/media/cqc-report-winterbourne-view-confirms-its-owners-failed-protect-people-abuse).

CQC (2011b) *Previous NHS staff surveys*, London: CQC.

CQC (2011c) *Report on the outcome of the integrated inspection of safeguarding and looked after children's services in Brighton and Hove* (www.cqc.org.uk/sites/default/files/media/reports/20110607_Brighton_and_Hove.pdf).

CQC (2011d) 'Review of compliance: Castlebeck Care (Teesdale Ltd), Winterbourne View', Newcastle-upon-Tyne: CQC (www.cqc.org.uk/media/cqc-report-winterbourne-view-confirms-its-owners-failed-protect-people-abuse).

Crisp, C., Anderson, M., Orme, J. and Lister, P.G. (2003) *Learning and teaching assessment skills in social work education*, SCIE Knowledge Review 01, London: Social Care Institute for Excellence.

Cross, S., Hubbard, A. and Munro, E. (2010) *Reclaiming social work, London Borough of Hackney Children and Young People's Services, Parts 1 and 2*, London: Human Reliability Associates and the London School of Economics and Political Science

CSCI (2008) Safeguarding Adults: A study of the effectiveness of arrangements to safeguard adults from abuse, London: CSCI.

Cunliffe, A.L. and Linstead, S.A. (2009) 'Introduction: Teaching from critical perspectives', *Management Learning*, vol 40, no 1, pp 5-9.

Currie, G. and Suhomlinova, O. (2006) 'The impact of institutional forces upon knowledge sharing in the UK NHS: the triumph of professional power and the inconsistency of policy', *Public Administration*, vol 84, no 1, pp 1-30.

Curtis, L., Moriarty, J. and Netten, A. (2010) 'The expected working life of a social worker', *British Journal of Social Work*, vol 40, no 5, pp 1628-43.

CWDC (Children's Workforce Development Council) (2009) *Social workers: Their work with children, young people and their families*, Leeds: CWDC.

CWDC (2012) *Children's views and experiences of their contact with social workers: A focused review of the evidence*, Leeds: CWDC.

Daly, N. (2010) 'Design concepts, methodologies, contexts and their use within service delivery systems', Paper presented to the 12th UK Joint Social Work Education Conference, with the 4th UK Social Work Research Conference, 'Shaping the future of social work: Priorities, challenges, opportunities', University of Hertfordshire, 30 June-2 July.

Daniel, B., Taylor, J. and Scott, J. (2010) 'Recognition of neglect and early response: overview of a systematic review of the literature', *Child & Family Social Work*, vol 15, no 2, pp 248-57.

Day, K., Carreon, D. and Stump, C. (2000) 'The therapeutic design of environments for people with dementia: A review of the empirical research', *The Gerontologist*, vol 40, no 4, pp 397-416.

DCSF (Department for Children, Schools and Families) (2009) *Building a safe, confident future: The final report of the Social Work Task Force*, London: Crown Copyright.

DCSF (2009a) *The protection of children in England, Action plan. The government's response to Lord Laming*, London: The Stationery Office.

DCSF, DH (Department of Health) and BIS (Department for Business, Innovation and Skills) in partnership with the Social Work Reform Board (2010) *Building a safe and confident future: Implementing the recommendations of the Social Work Task Force*, London: HM Government.

DeFrank, R.S. and Ivancevich, J.M. (1998) 'Stress on the job: An executive update', *Academy of Management Executive*, vol 12, no 3, pp 55-66.

Dekker, S. (2007) *Just culture: Balancing safety and accountability*, Aldershot: Ashgate.

Dent, R.J. and Cocker, C. (2005) 'Serious case reviews: Lessons for practice in cases of child neglect', in J. Taylor and B. Daniel (eds) *Child neglect: Practice issues for health and social care*, London: Jessica Kingsley Publishers, pp 147-65.

Design Council and Warwick Business School (2012) 'The Behaviour Design Lab' (www.designcouncil.org.uk/behaviouraldesign).

DfE (Department for Education) (2010) *Building on the learning from serious case reviews: A two-year analysis of child protection database notifications 2007-2009*, London: DfE.

DH (2005) *A national framework to support local workforce strategy development: A guide for HR directors in the NHS and social care*, London: The Stationery Office.

DH (2008) 'Transforming social care', Local Authority Circular, London: DH.

DH (2008a) *Putting People First: Working to make it happen. Adult social care workforce strategy, Interim statement*, London: DH.

DH (2008b) *High quality care for all: NHS next stage review, Final report*, London: DH.

DH (2008c) *Mental Health (Approved Mental Health Professionals) (Approval) (England) Regulations 2008*, London: DH.

DH (2009) *Deprivation of liberty safeguards: Regulations and assessor training*, London: DH.

DH (2010) *A vision for adult social care: Capable communities and active citizens*, London: DH.

DH (2012) *Transforming care: A national response to Winterbourne View Hospital. Department of Health review: Final report*, London: DH.

DH (2012a) *DH Winterbourne View review: Concordat: Programme of action*, London: DH.

DH (2012b) *Winterbourne View review: Good practice examples*, London: DH.

DH (2013) *Patients first and foremost: The initial government response to the report of the Mid Staffordshire NHS Foundation Trust Public Inquiry*, London: DH.

DH (2013a) 'Early warning system to protect against care home failure', Press release, 4 May (www.gov.uk/government/news/early-warning-system-to-protect-against-care-home-failure).

DH and DfES (Department for Education and Skills) (2006) *Options for excellence*, London: Department of Health Publications.

Dickens, J. (2012) 'The definition of social work in the United Kingdom, 2000-2010', *International Journal of Social Welfare*, vol 21, no 1, pp 34-43.

Dimmock, B. (2003) 'Reflections on team and management consultation', in J. Reynolds, J. Henderson, J. Seden, J. Charlesworth and A. Bullman (eds) *The managing care reader*, London: Routledge/Open University Press, pp 35-41.

Dion, K., Berscheid, E. and Walster, E. (1972) 'What is beautiful is good', *Journal of Personality and Social Psychology*, vol 24, no 3, pp 285-90.

Doherty, L. (2004) 'Work-life balance initiatives: implications for women', *Employee Relations*, vol 26, no 4, pp 433-52.

Doorewaard, H. and Meihuizen, H. (2000) 'Strategic performance options in professional service organisations', *Human Resource Management Journal*, vol 10, no 2, pp 39-57.

Drago, R., Colbeck, C.L., Stauffer, K.D., Pirretti, A., Burkum, K., Fazioli, J., Lazzaro, G. and Habasevich, T. (2006) 'The avoidance of bias against caregiving: The case of academic faculty', *American Behavioral Scientist*, vol 49, no 9, pp 1222-47.

Dubnick, M. (2005) 'Accountability and the promise of performance: In search of the mechanisms', *Public Performance & Management Review*, vol 28, no 3, pp 376-417.

Dustin, D. (2007) *The McDonaldization of social work*, Aldershot: Ashgate.

Dyer, L. and Holder, G. (1988) 'A strategic perspective of human resource management', in L. Dyer (ed) *Human resource management: Evolving roles and responsibilities*, Washington, DC: Bureau of National Affairs, pp 1-46.

Eagly, A. and Carli, L. (2007) 'Women and the labyrinth of leadership', *Harvard Business Review*, vol 85, no 9, pp 62-71.

East Sussex Learning Disabilities Partnership Board (2007) *How to involve people with a learning disability in choosing and developing the staff who support them* http://www.eastsussex.gov.uk/nr/rdonlyres/fe267528-be49-429d-8c9d-d7fa298e7b06/0/howtoinvolvepeoplewithlearningdisabilitiesinchoosingwhosupportsthemopt2.pdf.

Eaton, S. (2000) 'Beyond unloving care: linking human resource management and patient care quality in nursing homes', *International Journal of Human Resource Management*, vol 11, no 3, pp 591-616.

Eborall, C. and Griffiths, D. (2008) *The state of the adult social care workforce in England 2008: The third report for Skills for Care's Skills Research and Intelligence Unit*, Leeds: Skills for Care.

Edmondson, A.C. (2004) 'Learning from failure in health care: frequent opportunities, pervasive barriers', *Quality and Safety in Health Care*, vol 13, no 2, pp ii3-ii9.

Elangovan, A.R. (2001) 'Causal ordering of stress, satisfaction and commitment, and intention to quit: a structural equations analysis', *Leadership & Organization Development Journal*, vol 22, no 4, pp 159-65.

El Enany, N., Currie, G. and Lockett, A. (2013) 'A paradox in healthcare service development: professionalization of service users', *Social Science & Medicine*, Volume 80, pp 24-30.

Eneau, J. (2008) 'From autonomy to reciprocity, or vice versa? French personalism's contribution to a new perspective on self-directed learning', *Adult Education Quarterly*, vol 58, no 3, pp 229-48.

Engelbrecht, L.K. (2006) 'Plumbing the brain drain of South African social workers migrating to the UK: challenges for social service providers', *Social Work/Maatskaplike Werk*, vol 42, no 2, pp 101-21.

Eraut, M. (1985) 'Knowledge creation and knowledge use in professional contexts', *Studies in Higher Education*, vol 10, no 2, pp 117-33.

Evans, D. and Kearney, J. (1996) *Working in social care: A systemic approach*, Aldershot: Arena/Ashgate Publishing.

Evans, S. and Huxley, P. (2009) 'Factors associated with the recruitment and retention of social workers in Wales: employer and employee perspectives', *Health & Social Care in the Community*, vol 17, no 3, pp 254-66.

Evans, S., Huxley, P., Gately, C., Webber, M., Mears, A., Pajak, S., Medina, J., Kendall, T. and Katona, C. (2006) 'Mental health, burnout and job satisfaction among mental health social workers in England and Wales', *British Journal of Psychiatry*, vol 188, no 1, pp 75-80.

Evans, S., Huxley, P., Webber, M., Katona, C., Gately, C., Mears, A., Medina, J., Pajak, S. and Kendall, T. (2005) 'The impact of "statutory duties" on mental health social workers in the UK', *Health & Social Care in the Community*, vol 13, no 2, pp 145-54.

Ezzamel, M. and Willmott, H. (1998) 'Accounting for teamwork: a critical study of group based systems of organizational control', *Administrative Science Quarterly*, vol 43, no 2, pp 358-96.

Fairfield, K.D. and London, M.B. (2003) 'Tuning into the music of groups: A metaphor for team-based learning in management education', *Journal of Management Education*, vol 27, no 6, pp 654-72.

Farson, R. and Keyes, R. (2002) 'The failure-tolerant leader', *Harvard Business Review*, August.

Feinberg, R.A., Kim, I.S., Hokama, L., de Ruyter, K. and Keen, C. (2000) 'Operational determinants of caller satisfaction in the call center', *International Journal of Service Industry Management*, vol 11, no 2, pp 131-41.

Fenton, W. (2011) *The size and structure of the adult social care sector and workforce in England, 2011*, Leeds: Skills for Care.

Ferguson, I. (2007) 'Increasing user choice or privatizing risk? The antinomies of personalization', *British Journal of Social Work*, vol 37, no 3, pp 387-403.

Ferguson, I. (2008) *Reclaiming Social Work; Challenging neo-liberalism and promoting social justice*, London: Sage.

Finn, R. (2008) 'The language of teamwork: reproducing professional divisions in the operating theatre', *Human Relations*, vol 61, no 1, pp 103-30.

Fisher, E.A. (2009) 'Motivation and leadership in social work management: A review of theories and related studies', *Administration in Social Work*, vol 33, no 4, pp 347-67.

Fleming, G. and Taylor, B.J. (2007) 'Battle on the home-care front: perceptions of home-care workers of factors influencing staff retention in Northern Ireland', *Health & Social Care in the Community*, vol 15, no 1, pp 67-76.

Flynn, M. (2012) *Winterbourne View: A serious case review*, Thornbury, South Gloucestershire: South Gloucestershire Safeguarding Adults Board.

Fook, J. and Askeland, G.A. (2007) 'Challenges of critical reflection: "nothing ventured, nothing gained"', *Social Work Education*, vol 26, no 5, pp 520-33.

Ford, J. and Lawler, J. (2007) 'Blending existentialist and constructionist approaches in leadership studies: An exploratory account', *Leadership & Organisational Development Journal*, vol 28, no 5, pp 409-25.

Forsythe, S. and Polzer-Debruyne, A. (2007) 'The organisational benefits of perceived work-life balance support', *Asia Pacific Journal of Human Resources*, vol 45, no 1, pp 113-23.

Foster, J. (1999) 'Women senior managers and conditional power: the case in social services departments', *Women in Management Review*, vol 14, no 8, pp 316-24.

Foucault, M. (1984) *The history of sexuality. Volume 3: The care of the self*, London: Penguin.

Francis, R. (2013) *Report of the Mid Staffordshire NHS Foundation Trust Public Inquiry*, London: The Stationery Office.

Fredrickson, B.L. and Losada, M.F. (2005) 'Positive affect and the complex dynamics of human flourishing', *American Psychologist*, vol 60, no 7, pp 678-86.

French, J.P. and Raven, B.H. (1986) 'The bases of social power', in D. Cartwright and A.F. Zander (eds) *Group dynamics: Research and theory* (3rd edn), New York: Harper & Row, pp 607-623.

French, W. and Bell, C. (1995) *Organization development* (5th edn), Englewood Cliffs, NJ: Prentice Hall International.

Friedman, F. (2005) *A brief history of the 21st century: The world is flat*, New York: Farrar, Strauss & Giroux.

Ferguson, I., (2008) Reclaiming Social Work Challenging neo-liberalism and promoting social justice, London: Sage

Freeman, T. (2002) 'Using performance indicators to improve health care quality in the public sector: a review of the literature', *Health Services Management Research*, 15, pp 126-137.

Gallop, L. and Hafford-Letchfield, T. (2012) *How to be a better manager in social work and social care: Essential skills for managing care*, London: Jessica Kingsley Publishers.

Galpin, D. (2009) 'Who really drives the development of post-qualifying education and what are the implications of this?', *Social Work Education*, vol 28, no 1, pp 65-80.

Garthwaite, T. (2005) *Social work in Wales: A profession to value. The report of the ADSS-led multi-agency group on the recruitment and retention of local authority social workers in Wales* (Garthwaite Report) (www.adsscymru.org.uk/resource/m_e_Social_Work_in_Wales_-_A_Profession_to_Value.pdf).

Germain, C.B. and Gitterman, A. (1996) *The life model of social work practice*, New York: Columbia University Press.

Gherardi, S. (1994) 'The gender we think, the gender we do in our everyday organizational lives', *Human Relations*, vol 47, no 6, pp 591-619.

Gibson, F., McGrath, A. and Reid, N. (1989) 'Occupational stress in social work', *British Journal of Social Work*, vol 19, no 1, pp 1-18.

Gilmore, A. and Moreland, L. (2000) 'Call centres: How can service quality be managed?', *Irish Marketing Review*, vol 13, no 1, pp 3-11.

Glendinning, C. (2003) 'Breaking down barriers: integrating health and care services for older people in England', *Health Policy*, vol 65, no 2, pp 139-51.

Glennerster, H. (1992) *Paying for welfare: The 1990s*, Hemel Hempstead: Harvester Wheatsheaf.

Glisson, C. and Green, P. (2006) 'The effects of organizational culture and climate on the access to mental health care in child welfare and juvenile justice systems', *Administration and Policy in Mental Health and Mental Health Services Research*, vol 33, no 4, pp 433-48.

Glisson, C. and Hemmelgarn, A.L. (1998) 'The effects of organisational climate and inter-organisational coordination on the quality and outcomes of children's service systems', *Child Abuse & Neglect*, vol 22, no 5, pp 401-21.

Glisson, C., Dukes, D. and Green, P. (2006) 'The effects of the ARC organizational intervention on caseworker turnover, climate, and culture in children's service systems', *Child Abuse & Neglect*, vol 30, no 8, pp 855-80.

Godard, J. (2001) 'Beyond the high-performance paradigm? An analysis of variation in Canadian managerial perceptions of reform programme effectiveness', *British Journal of Industrial Relations*, vol 39, no 1, pp 25-52.

Goldman, R. (2013) *Narrative summary of the evidence review on supervision of social workers and social care workers in a range of settings included integrated settings*, London: SCIE

Goldstein, B.P. (2002) 'Catch 22 – Black workers' role in equal opportunities for black service users', *British Journal of Social Work,* vol 32, no 6, pp 765-78.

Gordon, G.G. (1991) 'Industry determinants of organizational culture', *Academy of Management Review*, vol 16, no 2, pp 396-415.

Gordon, J., Cooper, B. and Dumbleton, S. (2009) *How do social workers use evidence in practice?*, Milton Keynes: The Open University.

Gould, N. (1996) 'Using imagery in reflective learning', in N. Gould and I. Taylor (eds) *Reflective learning for social work*, Aldershot: Arena Publishing, pp 63-77.

Gould, N. (2000) 'Becoming a learning organisation: a social work example', *Social Work Education*, vol 19, no 6, pp 585-96.

Grant, S. and Humphries, M. (2006) 'Critical evaluation of appreciative inquiry: Bridging an apparent paradox', *Action Research*, vol 4, no 4, pp 401-18.

Gratton, L., Hope-Hailey, V., Stiles, P. and Truss, C. (1999) 'Linking individual performance to business strategy: the people process model', *Human Resource Management*, vol 38, no 1, pp 17-31.

Gray, I., Parker, J. and Immins, T. (2008) 'Leading communities of practice in social work: Groupwork or management?', *Groupwork*, vol 18, no 2, pp 26-40.

Gray, I., Parker, J., Rutter. L. and Williams, S. (2010) 'Developing communities of practice: A strategy for effective leadership, management and supervision in social work', *Social Work and Social Sciences Review*, vol 14, no 2, pp 55-72.

Greenleaf, R.K. (1996) *On becoming a servant leader*, San Francisco, CA: Jossey-Bass.

Green, F. (2001) 'It's been a hard day's night: The concentration and intensification of work in late twentieth century Britain', *British journal of Industrial Relations*, vol 39, vol 1, pp 53-80.

Gregory, A. and Milner, S. (2009) 'Editorial: Work–life balance: A matter of choice?', *Gender, Work & Organization*, vol 16, no 1, pp 1-13.

Gregory, A. and Milner, S. (2011) 'Fathers and work–life balance in France and the UK: policy and practice', *International Journal of Sociology & Social Policy*, vol 31, no 1/2, pp 34-52.

GSCC (2005) *Specialist standards and requirements for post-qualifying social work, education and training: Leadership and management*, London: GSCC.

GSCC (2007) *Leadership and management specialist standards*, London: GSCC.

GSCC (2008) *Social work degree under spotlight in new research*, London: GSCC.

Guest, D. (2002) 'Human resource management, corporate performance and employee well-being: Building the worker into HRM', *Journal of Industrial Relations*, vol 39, vol 1, pp 53-80.

Guest, D. (2007) 'Human resource management and the worker: Towards a new psychological contract?', in P. Boxall, J. Purcell and P. Wright (eds) *Oxford handbook of human resource management*, Oxford: Oxford University Press, pp 489-508.

Guest, E.D. and Conway, N. (2004) *Employee well-being and the psychological contract: A report for the CIPD*, Research report, London, CIPD publication.

Gutek, B. (1989) 'Sexuality in the workplace: key issues in social research and organisational practice', in J. Hearn, D. Sheppard, P. Tancred-Sheriff and G. Burrel (eds) *The sexuality of organisation*, London: Sage Publications.

Hackman, J.R. and Wageman, R. (2007) 'Asking the right questions about leadership', *American Psychologist*, vol 62, no 1, pp 43-7.

Haddock, J. (1996) 'Towards further clarification of the concept "dignity"', *Journal of Advanced Nursing*, vol 24, no 5, pp 924-31.

Hafford-Letchfield, T. (2007) *Practicing quality: Quality assurance and performance management in social care*, Exeter: Learning Matters.

Hafford-Letchfield, T. (2009) *Management and organisations in social work* (2nd edn), Exeter: Learning Matters.

Hafford-Letchfield, T. (2010) *Social care management: Strategy and business planning*, London: Jessica Kingsley Publishers.

Hafford-Letchfield, T. (2010a) 'The age of opportunity? Revisiting assumptions about the lifelong learning needs of older people using social care services', *British Journal of Social Work*, vol 40, no 2, pp 496-512.

Hafford-Letchfield, T. (2011) 'Sexuality and women in care organisations: Negotiating boundaries within a gendered cultural script', in P. Dunk-West and T. Hafford-Letchfield (eds) *Sexual identities and sexuality in social work: Research and reflections from women in the field*, Aldershot: Ashgate.

Hafford-Letchfield, T. and Bourn, D. (2011a) 'How am I doing?' Advancing management skills through the use of a multi-source feedback tool to enhance work-based learning on a post-qualifying post-graduate leadership and management programme', *Social Work Education*, vol 30, no 5, pp 497-511.

Hafford-Letchfield, T. and Chick, N.F (2006) 'Talking across purposes: The benefits of an inter-agency mentoring scheme for managers working in health and social care settings in the UK', *Work Based Learning in Primary Care*, vol 4,

Hafford-Letchfield, T. and Chick, N.F (2006a) 'Succession planning: developing management potential in a social services department', *Diversity in Health and Social Care*, vol 3, no 3, pp 191-203.

Hafford-Letchfield, T. and Harper, W. (2013) 'State of the arts: Using literary works to explore and learn about theories and models of leadership', *Social Work Education* (https://eprints.mdx.ac.uk/11449/).

Hafford-Letchfield, T. and Lawler, J. (2010) Guest Editorial: 'Reshaping leadership and management: The emperor's new clothes?', *Social Work and Social Sciences Review*, vol 14, no 1, pp 5-8.

Hafford-Letchfield, T., Couchman, W., Webster, M. and Avery, P. (2010) 'A drama project about older people's intimacy and sexuality', *Educational Gerontology*, vol 36, no 7, pp 1-18.

Hafford-Letchfield, T., Leonard, K., Begum, N. and Chick, N. (2008) *Leadership and management in social care*, London: Sage Publications.

Haijtema, D. (2007) 'The boss who breaks all the rules', *Odewire Magazine*, 21 January, (http://odewire.com/53859/the-boss-who-breaks-all-the-rules.html).

Hales, C. (1993) *Managing through organisations*, London: Routledge.

Halford, S and Leonard, P. (2001) *Gender, Power and Organisations*, Palgrave Macmillan.

Hall, J. and Donnell, S.M. (1979) 'Managerial achievement: The personal side of behavioral theory', *Human Relations*, vol 32, no 1, pp 77-101.

Halton, W. (1994) 'Some unconscious aspects of organisational life: Contributions from psychoanalysis', in A. Obholzer and V. Zagier Roberts (eds) *The unconscious at work: Individual and organisational stress in the human services*, London: Routledge, pp 11-18.

Hamama, L. (2012) 'Burnout in social workers treating children as related to demographic characteristics: Work, environment and social support', *Social Work Research*, vol 36, no 2, pp 113-25.

Handy, C.B. (1999) *Understanding organisations* (4th edn), London: Penguin.

Hans Böckler Foundation/European Trade Union Institute (2004) *Workers' participation at board level: Reports on the national systems and practices*, Brussels: European Trade Union Institute.

Harlow, E. (2004) 'Why don't women want to be social workers any more? New managerialism, post-feminism and the shortage of social workers in social services departments in England and Wales', *European Journal of Social Work*, vol 7, no 2, pp 167-79.

Harlow, E. (2008) 'New managerialism, social service departments and social work practice today', *Practice*, vol 15, no 2, pp 29-44.

Harlow, E. (2003) 'Why don't women want to be social workers anymore?: new managerialism, postfeminism and the shortage of social workers in social services departments in England and Wales' *European Journal of Social Work*, 7(2), 4, pp.167-179.

Harper, W. and Hafford-Letchfield, T. (2011) 'Learning to lead: A literary approach', Peer review paper published as proceedings of 1st International Conference on 'Emerging research paradigms in business and social science', Dubai, United Arab Emirates, 25 November.

Harris, J. (2003) *The social work business*, London: Routledge.

Harrison, G. and Turner, R. (2011) 'Being a "culturally competent" social worker: making sense of a murky concept in practice', *British Journal of Social Work*, vol 41, no 2, pp 333-50.

Harter, J.K., Schmidt, F.L. and Hayes, T.L. (2002) 'Business-unit-level relationship between employee satisfaction, employee engagement, and business outcomes: A meta-analysis', *Journal of Applied Psychology*, vol 87, no 2, pp 268-79.

Hartle, F., Snook, P., Apsey, H. and Browton, P. (2009) *Leadership development in the children and young people's workforce*, London: Hay Group.

Hartley, J. (2005) 'Innovation in governance and public services, past and present', *Public Money & Management*, vol 25, no 1, pp 27-34.

Hawkins, P. and Shohet, R. (2000) *Supervision in the helping professions* (2nd edn), Buckingham: Open University Press.

HCPC (Health and Care Professions Council) (2012) *Code of conduct for social workers*, London: HCPC.

Healy, K. and Darlington, Y. (2009) 'Service user participation in diverse child protection contexts: principles for practice', *Child & Family Social Work*, vol 14, no 4, pp 420-30.

Heard, D. and Lake, B. (1997) *The challenge of attachment for caregiving*, London: Routledge.

Hermann, M.G. and Preston, T. (1994) 'Presidents, advisors and foreign policy: The effect of leadership style on executive arrangements', *Political Psychology*, vol 15, no 1, pp 75-96.

Herriot, P. and Pemberton, C. (1995) *New deals: The revolution in managerial careers*, Chichester: Wiley.

Herzenberg, S.A., Alic, J.A. and Wial, H. (1998) *New rules for a new economy: Employment and opportunity in post industrial America*, Ithaca, NY: ILR Press/Cornell University Press.

Hicks, S. (2008) 'Thinking through sexuality', *Journal of Social Work*, vol 8, no 1, pp 65-82.

Higgins, J. (2001) 'The listening blank', *Health Services Journal*, vol 111, no 5772, pp 22-5.

HMG (Her Majesty's Government) (2007) *Putting people first: A shared vision and commitment to the transformation of adult social care*, London: HMG.

HMSO (Her Majesty's Stationery Office) (1970) *Local Authority Social Services Act 1970, Chapter 42, Arrangement of sections* (www.legislation.gov.uk/ukpga/1970/42/pdfs/ukpga_19700042_en.pdf).

HMSO (2010) *Equality Act 2010, Chapter 15* (www.legislation.gov.uk/ukpga/2010/15/pdfs/ukpga_20100015_en.pdf).

Hodson, R. (2001) *Dignity at work*, Cambridge: Cambridge University Press.

Holmes, L., Munro, E.R. and Soper, J. (2010) *Calculating the costs and capacity implications for local authorities implementing the Laming (2009) recommendations. Report to the Local Government Association*, Loughborough: Centre for Child and Family Research, Loughborough University.

Holt, J. and Lawler, J. (2005) 'Children in need teams: Service delivery and organisational climate', *Social Work and Social Sciences Review*, vol 12, no 2, pp 29-47.

Hood, C. (1998) 'Individualized contracts for top civil servants: Copying business, path-dependent political re-engineering – or Trobriand cricket?', *Governance*, vol 11, no 4, pp 443-62.

Hoogendoorn, W.E., Poppel, M.N.M., van Koes, B.W. and Bouter, L.M. (2000) 'Systematic review of psychosocial factors at work and private life as risk factors for back pain', *Spine*, vol 25, no 16, pp 2114-25.

Houston, S. and Knox, S. (2004) 'Exploring workforce retention in child and family social work: critical social theory, social pedagogy and action research', *Social Work and Social Sciences Review*, vol 11, no 2, pp 36-53.

Houtman, I.L.D., Kornitzer, M., de Smet, P., Koyuncu, R., de Backer, G., Pelfrene, E., Romon, M., Boulenguez, C., Ferrario, M., Origgi, G., Sans, S., Perez, I., Wilhelmsen, L., Rosengren, A., Olofisacsson, S. and Östergren, P. (1999) 'Job stress, absenteeism and coronary heart disease European cooperative study' (the JACE-study): design of a multicentre prospective study', *European Journal of Public Health*, vol 9, pp 52-7.

Hudson, B. (2002) 'Interprofessionality in health and social care: the Achilles' heel of partnership?', *Journal of Interprofessional Care*, vol 16, no 1, pp 7-17.

Huffington, C., Armstrong, D., Halton, W., Hoyle, L. and Pooley, J. (2004) *Working below the surface: The emotional life of contemporary organizations*, London: Karnac.

Hugman, R. (2005) *New approaches in ethics for the caring professions*, Basingstoke: Palgrave.

Hugman, R. (2007) 'The place of values in social work education', in M. Lymbery and K. Postle (eds) *Social work: A companion to learning*, London, Sage Publications, pp 20-9.

Hunter, L. (2000) 'What determines job quality in nursing homes?', *Industrial and Labor Relations Review*, vol 53, no 3, pp 463-81.

Hussein, S. (2010) 'Pay in the adult social care in England', *Social Care Workforce Periodical*, issue 6, May, London: Social Care Workforce Research Unit, King's College London.

Hussein, S. (2011) 'Estimating probabilities and numbers of direct care workers paid under the National Minimum Wage in the UK: A Bayesian approach', *Social Care Workforce Periodical*, issue 16, December, London: Social Care Workforce Research Unit, King's College London.

Hussein, S. and Manthorpe, J. (2011) *Longitudinal changes in care worker turnover and vacancy rates and reasons for job leaving in England (2008-2010)*, London: Social Care Workforce Unit, King's College.

Hussein, S., Moriarty, J., Manthorpe, J. and Huxley, P. (2008) 'Diversity and progression among students starting social work qualifying programmes in England between 1995 and 1998: A quantitative study', *British Journal of Social Work*, vol 38, no 8, pp 1588-609.

Huxham, C. and Vangen, S.W. (2000) 'Leadership in shaping and implementation of collaboration agendas: how things happen in a (not quite) joined up world', *Academy of Management Journal*, vol 43, no 6, pp 1159-75.

Huxley, P., Evans, S., Gately, C., Webber, M., Mears, A., Pajak, S., Kendall, T., Medina, J. and Katona, C. (2005) 'Stress and Pressures in Mental Health Social Work: The Worker Speaks', *British Journal of Social Work,* vol 35, no 7, pp 1063-79.

IAS (Institute of Alcohol Studies) (2010) Fact sheet: 'Binge drinking nature, prevalence and causes', London: IAS.

I&DeA (Improvement and Development Agency) (2009) *Evaluation of the national programme for third sector commissioning, Baseline report*, London: I&DeA.

IFSW (International Federation of Social Workers)/IASSW (International Association of Schools of Social Work) (2000) *The definition of social work*, Berne: IFSW.

IFSW (2004) Statement of Ethical Principles, IFSW, 3 March 2012, (http://ifsw. org/policies/statement-of-ethical-principles/).

ILM (Institute of Leadership and Management) (2010) *Leading change in the public sector*, London: ILM.

Ingraham, P.W. (2005) 'Performance: Promises to keep and miles to go', *Public Administration Review*, vol 65, no 4, pp 390-5.

Jacelon, C.S., Connelly, T.W., Brown, R., Proulx, K. and Vo, T. (2004) 'A concept analysis of dignity for older adults', *Journal of Advanced Nursing*, vol 48, no 1, pp 76-83.

Jacobson, N. (2007) 'Dignity and health: a review', *Social Science & Medicine*, vol 2, no 64, pp 292-302.

James, L., Choi, R., Carol, C., Ko, C.-H.E., McNeil, P.K., Minton, M.K., Wright, M.A. and Kwang-il, K. (2007) 'Organizational and psychological climate: A review of theory and research', *European Journal of Work and Organizational Psychology*, vol 17, no 1, pp 5-32.

Johnson, G. (1989) 'Re-thinking incrementalism', in D. Asch and C. Bowman (eds) *Readings in strategic management*, London: Macmillan, pp 37-56.

Johnson, S.C., Cooper, C., Cartwright, I., Taylor, D.P. and Millet, C. (2005) 'The experience of work-related stress across occupations', *Journal of Managerial Psychology*, vol 20, no 2, pp 178-87.

Jones, C. (2001) 'Voices from the front line: state social worker and new labour', *British Journal of Social Work*, vol 31, no 4, pp 547-62.

Jordan, B. (1978) 'A comment on "Theory and practice in social work"', *British Journal of Social Work*, vol 8, no 11, pp 23-5.

Kadushin, A. (1992) *Supervision in social work* (3rd edn), New York: Columbia University Press.

Kadushin, A. and Harkness, D. (2002) *Supervision in social work* (4th edn), New York: Columbia University Press.

Kant, I. (1988) 'Groundwork of the metaphysics of morals', in L.A.W. Beck (ed) *Kant selections*, New York: Macmillan, p 277.

Kaplan, R.M. (1978) 'Is beauty talent? Sex Interaction in the attractiveness halo effect', *Sex Roles*, vol 4, no 2, pp 195-204.

Karasek, R. and Theorell, T. (1990) *Healthy work: Stress, productivity, and the reconstruction of working life*, New York: Basic Books.

Kerr, M.M. (1995) 'Project 2000 student nurses take the stage with interactive drama to facilitate health promotion', *Innovations in Education and Training International*, vol 32, no 2, pp 162-74.

Kim, H. and Lee, S.Y. (2009) 'Supervisory communication, burnout, and turnover intention among social workers in health care settings', *Social Work in Health Care*, vol 48, no 4, pp 364-85.

Kinman, G. and Grant, L. (2010) 'Exploring stress resilience in trainee social workers: The role of emotional and social competencies', *British Journal of Social Work*, vol 41, no 2, pp 261-75.

King's Fund, The (2011) *The future of leadership and management in the NHS. No more heroes. Report from The King's Fund Commission on Leadership and Management in the NHS* (edited by Edwina Rowling), London: The King's Fund.

Kirby, P., Lanyon, C., Cronin, K. and Sinclair, R. (2003) *Building a culture of participation: Involving children and young people in policy, service planning, delivery and evaluation*, Research report, London: Department for Education and Skills.

Kivimäki, M., Leino-Arjas, P., Luukkonen, R., Riihimäi, H., Vahtera, J. and Kirjonen, J. (2002) 'Work stress and risk of cardiovascular mortality: prospective cohort study of industrial employees', *British Medical Journal*, vol 325, no 7369, pp 857-60.

Klein, R., Day, P. and Redmayne, S. (1996) *Managing scarcity: Priority setting and rationing in the National Health Service*, Buckingham: Open University Press.

Knapman, J. and Morrison, T. (1998) *Making the most of supervision in health and social care*, Brighton: Pavilion Press.

Kochan, T.A. (2001) 'Rebuilding the social contract at work', *Perspectives on Work*, vol 4, no 1, pp 1-25.

Kochan, T.A., McKersie, R.B., Eaton, A., Adler, P., Segal, P. and Gerhart, P. (2005) *The Kaiser Permanente Labor Management Partnership: 2002-2004*, Cambridge, MA: MIT, Sloan School of Management, Institute for Work and Employment Research.

Kotter, J.P. (1995) 'Why transformation efforts fail', *Harvard Business Review*, May-June, pp 59-67.

Kotter, J.P. (1996) *Leading change*, Boston, MA: Harvard Business School Press.

Kotter, J.P. and Cohen, D.S. (2002) *The heart of change: Real-life stories of how people change their organisation*, Boston, MA: Harvard Business School Press.

Kubler-Ross, E. (1987) *Aids: The ultimate challenge*, New York: Macmillan.

Kuhn, T. (1970) *The structure of scientific revolutions*, Chicago, IL: Chicago University Press.

Lambley, S. (2011) 'Managers: Are they really to blame for what's happening to social work?', *Social Science and Social Services Review*, vol 14, no 2, pp 6-20.

Lambley, S. and Marrable, T. (2013) *Practice enquiry into supervision in a variety of adult care settings where there are health and social care practitioners working together*, London: Social Care Institute for Excellence.

Laming, H. (2003) *The report of the inquiry into the death of Victoria Climbié*, London: The Stationery Office.

Laming, H. (2009) *The protection of children in England: Action plan*, London: The Stationery Office.

Landy, D. and Sigall, H. (1974) 'Task evaluation as a function of the performer's physical attractiveness', *Journal of Personality and Social Psychology*, vol 29, no 3, pp 299-304.

Langan, M. (2000) 'Social services: Managing the third way', in J. Clarke, S. Gewirtz and E. McLaughlin (eds) *New managerialism, new welfare?*, London: Sage Publications, pp 152-68.

Latham, G.P. and Mann, S. (2006) 'Advances in the science of performance appraisal: Implications for practice', *International Review of Industrial and Organisational Psychology*, vol 21, no 3, pp 295-338.

LAWIG (Local Authority Workforce Intelligence Group) (2005) *Adult, children and young people: Local authority social care workforce survey*, Report No 36, Social Care Workforce Series, London: LAWIG.

Lawler, J. (2005) 'The essence of leadership? Existentialism and leadership', *Leadership*, vol 1, no 2, pp 215-31.

Lawler, J. and Bilson, A. (2010) *Social work management and leadership: Managing complexity with creativity*, Abingdon: Routledge.

Lawless, J. and Moss, C. (2007) 'Exploring the value of dignity in the work-life of nurses', *Contemporary Nurse: Nurse Recruitment & Retention*, vol 24, no 2, pp 225-36.

Lee, I.M., Shiroma, E.J., Lobelo, F., Puska, P., Blair, S.N. and Katzmaryk, P.T. (2012) 'Effects of physical inactivity on major non-communicable diseases worldwide: an analysis of burden of disease and life expectancy', *The Lancet*, vol 380, pp 219-29.

Lee, M.M. (1997) 'The developmental approach: A critical reconsideration', in J. Burgoyne and M. Reynolds (eds) *Management learning*, London: Sage Publications, pp 199-214.

Lee, M.M. (2001) 'A refusal to define HRD', *Human Resource Development International*, vol 4, no 3, pp 327-41.

Lees, A., Meyer, E. and Rafferty, J. (2013) 'From Menzies Lyth to Munro: The problem of managerialism', *British Journal of Social Work*, vol 43, no 3, pp 542-58.

Leonard, K., Hafford-Letchfield, T. and Couchman, W. (2013) '"We're all going Bali" – Utilising Gamelan as an educational resource for leadership and team work in post-qualifying education in health and social care', *British Journal of Social Work*, vol 43, no 1, pp 173-90.

Leonard, M. and Frankel, L. (2012) *How can leaders influence a safety culture?*, London: The Health Foundation.

LGA (London Government Association) (2009) *Respect and protect: Respect, recruitment and retention in children's social work*, London: LGA.

LGA (2013) *Winterbourne View Joint Improvement Programme*, London: LGA.

Liao, H., Joshi, A. and Chuang, A. (2004) 'Sticking out like a sore thumb: Employee dissimilarity and deviance at work', *Personnel Psychology*, vol 57, no 4, pp 969-1000.

Lymbery, M. (2001) 'Social work at the cross roads', *British Journal of Social Work*, vol 31, no 3, pp 369-84.

Lymbery, M. (2010) 'A new vision for adult social care? Continuities and change in the care of older people', *Critical Social Policy*, vol 30, no 1, pp 5-26.

Lymbery, M. and Postle, K. (2010) 'Social work in the context of adult social care in England and the resultant implications for social work education', *British Journal of Social Work*, vol 40, no 8, pp 2502-22.

McAlister, J. (2012) 'Frontline can help rebrand social work', *The Guardian*, 6 November.

McAllister, K. and Luckcock, T. (2009) 'Appreciative inquiry: A fresh approach to continuous improvement in public services', *Housing, Care and Support*, vol 12, no 1, pp 30-3.

McAllan, W. and MacRae, R. (2010) 'Learning to lead: Evaluation of a leadership development programme', *Social Work and Social Sciences Review*, vol 14, no 2, pp 55-72.

McLaughlin, H. (2009) 'What's in a name: "client", "patient", "customer", "consumer", "expert by experience", "service user" – What next?', *British Journal of Social Work*, vol 39, no 6, pp 1101-17.

McLoughlin, J. and Clark, J. (1988) *Technology change at work*, Milton Keynes: Open University Press.

McMullen, J. (2011) 'Balancing the right to manage with dignity at work', *Perspectives: Policy and Practice in Higher Education*, vol 15, no 1, pp 3-6.

Maddock, S. (1999) *Challenging women: Gender, culture and organisation*, London: Sage Publications.

Magill, G. and Prybil, L. (2004) 'Stewardship and integrity in health care: A role for organizational ethics', *Journal of Business Ethics*, vol 50, no 1, pp 225-38.

Maher, B., Appleton, C., Benge, D. and Perham, T. (2003) 'The criticality of induction training to professional social work care and protection practice', Paper presented at the Ninth Australian Conference on Child Abuse and Neglect, Sydney.

Makaros, A. (2011) *Collaboration between business and social work: findings from an Israeli study*. Administration in Social Work, 35(4), pp.349-363.

Marchington, M. and Grugulis, I. (2000) '"Best practice" human resource management: perfect opportunity or dangerous illusion?', *International Journal of Human Resource Management*, vol 11, no 6, pp 1104-24.

Marsh, P. and Triseliotis, J. (1996) *Ready to practise? Social workers and probation officers: Their training and first year in work*, Aldershot: Avebury.

Martell, R.F., Guzzo, R.A. and Willis, C.E. (1995) 'A methodological and substantive note of the performance-cue effect in ratings of work group behaviour', *Journal of Applied Psychology*, vol 80, pp 191-5.

Martin, G.P. (2008) 'Representativeness, legitimacy and power in public involvement in health-care management', *Social Science & Medicine*, vol 67, no 11, pp 1757-65.

Martin, R., (2011) *Fixing the game: Bubbles, Crashes, and What Capitalism Can Learn from the NFL* (Harvard Business Review Press.

Martin, G.P., Currie, G. and Finn, R. (2009) 'Leadership, service reform and public service networks: the case of cancer-genetics pilots in the English NHS', *Journal of Public Administration Research and Theory*, vol 19, no 4, pp 769-94.

Martin, V., Charlesworth, J. and Henderson, E. (2010) *Managing in health and social care*, London: Routledge.

Martinez, J. and Martineau, T. (1998) 'Human resources in healthcare reform: a review of current issues', *Health Policy and Planning*, 13, pp 345–58.

Massó Guijarro, P., Aranaz Andrés, J.M., Mira, J.J., Perdiguero, E. and Aibar, C. (2010) 'Adverse events in hospitals: the patient's point of view', *Quality and Safety in Health Care*, vol 19, no 2, pp 144-7.

Mavin, S. (2009) 'Navigating the labyrinth: senior women managing emotion', *International Journal of Work Organisation and Emotion*, vol 3, no 1, pp 81-7.

Melin Emilsson, U. (2011) 'The role of social work in cross-professional teamwork: Examples from an older people's team in England', *British Journal of Social Work*, vol 43, no 1, pp 116-34.

Mena, K.C. and Bailey, J.D. (2007) 'The effects of the supervisory working alliance on worker outcomes', *Journal of Social Services Research*, vol 34, no 1, pp 55-65.

Menzies-Lyth, I.E.P. (1979) 'Staff support systems: task and anti-task in adolescent institutions', in I.E.P. Menzies-Lyth (ed) *Containing anxiety in institutions: Selected essays*, London: Free Association Books.

Menzies Lyth, I.E.P. (1988) 'The functioning of social systems as a defence against anxiety', in I.E.P. Menzies Lyth (ed) *Containing anxiety in institutions: Selected essays, Volume 1*, London: Free Association Books.

Meyer, J.P. and Allen, N.J. (1997) *Commitment in the workplace: Theory, research, and application*, Thousand Oaks, CA: Sage Publications.

Miles, N. (not dated) *The double-glazed ceiling: Lesbians in the workplace*, London: Stonewall, supported by Lloyds TSB.

Millen, D. (1997) 'Some methodological and epistemological issues raised by doing feminist research on non-feminist women', Sociological Research Online, *Journal of International Women's Studies*, vol 2, no 3 (www.socresonline. org.uk/2/3/3.html).

Milmo, C. (2012) 'The venture capitalists and the scandal-hit children's homes', *The Independent*, 24 May (www.independent.co.uk/life-style/health-and-families/health-news/the-venture-capitalists-and-the-scandalhit-childrens-homes-7782676.html).

Moore, S. and Ryan, A. (2006) 'Learning to play the drum: An experiential exercise for management students', *Innovations in Education and Teaching International*, vol 43, no 4, pp 435-44.

Mor Barak, M.E., Travis, D.J., Pyun, H. and Xie, B. (2009) 'The impact of supervision on worker outcomes in child welfare, social work, and mental health settings: a meta-analysis and state of the art review', *Social Science Review*, vol 81, no 1, pp 3-32.

Morgan, G. (2006) *Images of organisation*, London: Sage Publications.

Moriarty, J., Hussein, S., Manthorpe, J. and Stevens, M. (2011) 'International social workers in England: Factors influencing supply', *International Social Work*, vol 55, no 2, pp 169-84.

Moriarty, J., Manthorpe, J., Stevens, M. and Hussein, S. (2011a) 'Making the transition: Comparing research on newly qualified social workers with other professions', vol 41, no 7, pp 1340-56.

Morris, N. (2009) '"Shocking" sickness rates in social work: Stress blamed for absence rate that is 60% higher than national average', *The Independent*, 16 September (www.independent.co.uk/news/uk/home-news/shocking-sickness-rates-in-social-work-1787970.html).

Morrison, T. (2009) *Supervision guide for social workers*, Leeds: Children's Workforce Development Council.

Morrison, T. and Wonnacott, J. (2010) *Supervision: Now or never. Reclaiming reflective supervision in social work*, Haslemere: In-Trac training and Consultancy Ltd (www.in-trac.co.uk/reclaiming-reflective-supervision.php).

Munro, E. (2005) 'A system's approach to investigating child abuse deaths', *British Journal of Social Work*, vol 35, no 4, pp 531-46.

Munro, E. (2010) 'Learning to reduce risk in child protection', *British Journal of Social Work*, vol 40, no 4, pp 1135-51.

Munro, E. (2010a) *The Munro review of child protection. Part one: A systems analysis*, London: London School of Economics and Political Science.

Munro, E. (2011) *The Munro review of child protection. Final report: A child-centred system*, London: The Stationery Office.

Munro, E. (2011a) *The Munro review of child protection. Interim report: The child's journey*, London: London School of Economics and Political Science.

Munro, E. and Hubbard, A. (2011) 'A systems approach to evaluating organisational change in children's social care', *British Journal of Social Work*, vol 41, no 4, pp 726-43.

Netten, A., Jones, K., Knapp, M., Fernandez, J.L., Challis, D., Glendinning, C., Jacobs, S., Manthorpe, J., Moran, N., Stevens, M. and Wilberforce, M. (2011) 'Personalisation through individual budgets: Does it work and for whom?', *British Journal of Social Work*, vol 42, no 3, pp 461-79.

Ng, T. and Sorensen, K. (2008) 'Towards further understanding of the relationship between perceptions of support and work attitudes', *Group and Organization Management*, vol 33, pp 243-68.

NICE (National Institute of Health and Clinical Excellence) (2009) *Promoting mental wellbeing through productive and health working conditions: Guidance for employers*, London: NICE.

NMC (Nursing and Midwifery Council) (2008) *The code: Standards of conduct performance and ethics for nurses and midwives*, London: NMC.

Northouse, P.G. (2011) *Introduction to leadership concepts and practice* (2nd edn), London: Sage Publications.

NSASC (National Skills Academy for Social Care) (2011) *Outstanding leadership in social care*, London: NSASC.

NSWQB (National Social Work Qualifications Board) (2004) *Induction study: A study of the induction of newly qualified and non-nationally qualified social workers in the health boards*, Dublin: NSWQB.

Obholzer, A. (1994) 'Social anxieties in public sector organisations', in A. Obholzer and V. Zagier Roberts (eds) *The unconscious at work: Individual and organisational stress in the human services*, London: Routledge, pp 169-78.

Obholzer, A. and Zagier Roberts, V. (1994) *The unconscious at work: Individual and organisational stress in the human services*, London: Routledge.

Ofsted (2010) *Learning lessons from serious case reviews 2009-2010* (www.ofsted. gov.uk/resources/learning-lessons-serious-case-reviews-2009-2010).

Ofsted (2012) *Serious case review evaluations: April 2007 onwards* (www.ofsted.gov. uk/resources/serious-case-review-evaluations-april-2007-onwards).

Oldham, C. (2003) 'Deceiving, theorizing and self-justification: A critique of independent living', *Critical Social Policy*, vol 23, no 1, pp 44-62.

O'Reilly, D. and Reed, M. (2010) '"Leaderism": An evolution of managerialism in UK public service reform', *Public Administration*, vol 88, no 4, pp 903-1145.

Orme, J. (2009) 'Managing the workload', in R. Adams, L. Dominelli and M. Payne (eds) *Practising social work in a complex world*, Basingstoke: Palgrave, pp 158-66.

Parton, N. and O'Byrne, P. (2000) *Constructive social work*, Basingstoke: Macmillan.

Patmore, C. (2003) *Understanding home care providers: Live issues about management, quality and relationships with social services purchasers*, York: Social Policy Research Unit, University of York.

Payne, M. (2005) *Modern social work theory*, Basingstoke: Macmillan.

Payne, M. (2009) 'Management and managerialism', in R. Adams, L. Dominelli and M. Payne (eds) *Practising social work in a complex world*, Basingstoke: Palgrave, pp 143-57.

Pearson, C., Watson, N., Stalker, K., Lerpiniere, J., Paterson, K. and Ferrie, J. (2011) 'Don't get involved: an examination of how public sector organisations in England are involving disabled people in the Disability Equality Duty', *Disability & Society*, vol 26, no 3, pp 255-68.

Penhale, B. and Parker, J. (2008) *Working with vulnerable adults*, London: Routledge.

Peters, T.J. and Waterman, R.H. (1982) *In Search of Excellence – Lessons from America's Best-Run Companies*, London, HarperCollins Publishers.

Petrie, S. (2010) 'The commodification of "children in need" in welfare markets', *Social Work and Social Sciences Review*, vol 14, no 1, pp 9-26.

Phillipson, J. (2009) 'Supervision and being supervised', in R. Adams, L. Dominelli and M. Payne (eds) *Practising social work in a complex world* (2nd edn), Basingstoke: Palgrave, pp 188-95.

Policy Research Institute on Ageing and Ethnicity/Help the Aged (2001) *Dignity on the ward: Towards dignity: Acting on the lessons from hospital experiences of black and minority ethnic older people. A report from Policy Research Institute on Ageing and Ethnicity for the Dignity on the Ward Campaign*, London: Help the Aged.

Pollitt, C. (1990) *Managerialism and the public service: The Anglo-American experience*, Cambridge, MA: Basil Blackwell.

Postle, K. (2007) 'Value conflicts in practice', in M. Lymbery and K. Postle (eds) *Social work: A companion to learning*, London: Sage Publications, pp 251-60.

Prokop, J., Bundred, K. and Green, J. (2010) 'Background paper on London serious case reviews completed April 2006–September' (www.londonscb.gov.uk/resources_for_lscbs/)

Pullen-Sansfaçon, A., Spolander, G. and Engelbrecht, L. (2011) 'Migration of professional social workers: Reflections on challenges and strategies for education', *Social Work Education*, vol 31, no 8, pp 1032-45.

Purcell, J., Kinnie, N., Hutchinson, S., Rayton, B. and Swart, J. (2003) *Under-standing the People and Performance Link: unlocking the Black Box*, London, CIPD.

Raelin, J. (2004) 'Don't bother putting leadership into people'. *Academy of Management Executive,* vol 18, no 3, pp 131-135

Ranson, S. and Stewart, J. (1994) *Management for the public domain: Enabling the learning society*, London: Macmillan.

Reason, J.T. (1997) *Managing the risks of organisational accidents*, Aldershot: Ashgate Publishing.

Reason, J.T. (1998) 'Achieving a safe culture: theory and practice', *Work and Stress*, vol 12, no 3, pp 293-306.

Renner, L.M., Porter, R.L. and Preister, S. (2009) 'Improving the retention of child welfare workers by strengthening skills and increasing support for supervisors', *Child Welfare*, vol 88, no 5, pp 109-27.

Richardson, R.F. (2010) '360-degree feedback: Integrating business know-how with social work values', *Administration in Social Work*, vol 34, no 3, pp. 259-74.

Rittel, H.W.J. and Webber, M.M. (1973) 'Dilemmas in a general theory of planning', *Policy Sciences*, vol 4, no 2, pp 155-69.

Robinson, S.R. and Morrison, E.W. (2000) 'The development of psychological contract breach and violation: A longitudinal study', *Journal of Organizational Behavior*, vol 21, no 5, pp 525-46.

Roebuck, C. (2011) *Developing effective leadership in the NHS. A short report for The King's Fund*, London: The King's Fund.

Rosenfeld, P. (2007) 'Workplace practices for retaining older hospital nurses: Implications from a study of nurses with eldercare responsibilities', *Policy, Politics, & Nursing Practice*, vol 8, no 2, pp 120-9.

Rossiter, A. (2011) 'Unsettled social work: The challenge of Levinas's ethics', *British Journal of Social Work*, vol 41, no 5, pp 980-95.

Rousseau, D. M. (2001) 'Schema, promise and mutuality: the building blocks of the psychological contract', *Journal of Occupational and Organizational Psychology*, 74, pp 511–541.

Rousseau, D. M. (2003) 'Extending the psychology of the psychological contract', *Journal of Management Inquiry*, 12, pp 229-38.

Rousseau, V. and Aube, C. (2010) 'Social support at work and affective commitment to the organization: The moderating effect of job resource adequacy and ambient conditions', *Journal of Social Psychology*, vol 150, no 4, pp 321-40.

Ruch, G. (2009) 'Identifying the "critical" in a relationship-based model of reflection', *European Journal of Social Work*, vol 12, no 3, pp 349-62.

Ruch, G. (2011) 'Where have the feelings gone? Developing reflective and relationship-based management in child care social work', *British Journal of Social Work*, vol 42, no 7, pp 1315-32.

Rutgers University Center for International Social Work (2008) *Social work education and the practice environment in Europe and Eurasia* (www.usaid.gov/locations/europe_eurasia/dem_gov/docs/best_practice_in_social_work_final_121008.pdf).

Rutter, D., Manley, C., Weaver, T., Crawford, M.J. and Fulop, N. (2004) 'Patients or partners? Case studies of user involvement in the planning and delivery of adult mental health services in London', *Social Science & Medicine*, vol 58, no 10, pp 1973-84.

Sayer, A. (2007) 'Dignity at work: Broadening the agenda', *Organization*, vol 14, no 4, pp 565-81.

Schein, E.H. (1997) *Organizational culture and leadership*, San Francisco, CA: John Wiley & Sons.

Schneider, B. (1990) 'The climate for service: An application of the climate construct', in B. Schneider (ed) *Organizational climate and culture*, San Francisco, CA: Jossey-Bass, pp 383-412.

Schorr, L. (1997) *Common purpose: Strengthening families and neighbourhoods to rebuild America*, New York: Doubleday/Anchor Books.

SCIE (Social Care Institute for Excellence) (2010) *Dignity in care*, SCIE Guide 15, London: SCIE.

SCIE (2012) *Dignity in care: Meaning and practice*, London: SCIE.

Scott, T., Mannion, R., Davies, H.T.O. and Marshall, M.N. (2003) 'Implementing culture change in health care: theory and practice', *International Journal for Quality in Health Care*, vol 15, no 2, pp 111-18.

Scott, T., Mannion, R., Marshall, M.N. and Davies, H.T.O. (2003a) 'Does organisational culture influence health care performance? A review of the evidence', *Journal of Health Services Research & Policy*, vol 8, no 2, pp 105-17.

Scottish Executive (2006) *Changing lives: Report of the 21st century social work review*, Edinburgh: Scottish Executive.

Scourfield, P. (2010) 'Going for brokerage: A task of "independent support" or social work?', *British Journal of Social Work*, vol 40, no 3, pp 858-77.

Scourfield, P. (2011) 'Caretelization revised and the lessons of Southern Cross', *Critical Social Policy*, vol 32, no 1, pp 137-48.

Sedan, J. and Reynolds, J. (eds) (2003) *Managing care in practice*, London: Routledge.

Seddon, J. (2008) *Systems thinking in the public sector*, Axminster: Triarchy Press.

Seebohm, F. (1968) *Report of the Committee on Local Authority and Allied Personal Social Services*, Cm. 3703, London, HMSO.

Senge, P.M. (1990) *The fifth discipline: The art and practice of the learning organization*, New York: Doubleday Currency.

Sewell, G. (1998) 'The discipline of teams: the control of team-based industrial work through electronic and peer surveillance', *Administrative Science Quarterly*, vol 42, no 2, pp 397-428.

Shardlow, S. (2009) 'Values, ethics and social work', in R. Adams, L. Dominelli and M. Payne (eds) *Social work: Themes, issues and critical debates* (3rd edn), Basingstoke: Palgrave, pp 30-40.

Sidebotham, P. (2011) 'What do serious case reviews achieve?', *Archives of Disease in Childhood*, vol 97, no 3, pp 189-92.

Sidebotham, P., Brandon, M., Powell, C., Solebo, C., Koistinen, J. and Ellis, C. (2010) *Learning from serious case reviews: Report of a research study on the methods of learning lessons nationally from serious case reviews*, London: Department for Education.

Simmons, H. and Hicks, J. (2006) 'Opening doors: using the creative arts in learning and teaching', *Arts and Humanities in Higher Education*, vol 5, no 1, pp 77-90.

Simmons, R. (2009) 'Understanding the "differentiated consumer" in public services', in R. Simmons, M. Powell, and I. Greener (eds) *The consumer in public services: Choice, values and difference*, Bristol: Policy Press.

Simmonds, J. (2010) 'Relating and relationships in supervision: Supportive and companionable or dominant and submissive?', in G. Ruch, D. Turney and A. Ward (eds) *Relationship-based social work: Getting to the heart of practice*, London: Jessica Kingsley Publishers.

Sinclair, I. (2008) 'Inspection: a quality-control perspective', in M. Davies, *The Blackwell companion to social work* (3rd edn), Oxford: Blackwell.

Skills for Care (2007) *nmds-sc briefing* (www.nmds-sc-online.org.uk/Get.aspx?id=285944).

Skills for Care (2008) *Mapping of leadership and management standards for health and social care, Leadership and Management Product 3* (2nd edn), London: Skills for Care.

Skills for Care (2008a) *What leaders and managers in adult social care do*, Leeds: Skills for Care.

Skills for Care (2010) *Common induction standards*, Leeds: Skills for Care.

Skills for Care (2011) *Social work*, Leeds: Skills for Care.

Skills for Care (2011a) *Capable, confident, skilled. A workforce development strategy for people working, supporting and caring in adult social care*, Leeds: Skills for Care.

Skills for Care (2012) *Assessed and Supported Year in Employment (ASYE)*, Leeds: Skills for Care.

Skinner, D., Saunders, M.N.K. and Beresford, R. (2004) 'Towards a shared understanding of skill shortages: differing perceptions of training and developing needs', *Education and Training*, vol 46, no 4, pp 182-93.

Slettebo, T. (2013) 'Partnership with parents of children in care: A study of collective user participation in child protection services', *British Journal of Social Work*, vol 43, no 3, pp 579-95.

Smith, P. (1995) "On the unintended consequences of publishing performance data in the public sector", *International Journal of Public Administration*, 18, pp 277-310.

Smith, P.B. (1984) 'Social service teams and their managers', *British Journal of Social Work*, vol 14, no 1, pp 601-13.

Social Care Institute for Excellence (SCIE) (2013, p 2)

Snell, S.A. (1996) 'Human resource management, manufacturing strategy, and firm performance', *Academy of Management Journal*, Special Issue, 39(4): 836-66.

Social Work Taskforce (2009) *Building a safe, confident future*, London: Department for Education.

Sparr, J. and Sonnentag, S. (2008) 'Feedback environment and well-being at work: The mediating role of personal control and feelings of helplessness', *European Journal of Work and Organisational Psychology*, vol 17, no 3, pp 388-412.

Spell, C. and Arnold, T. (2007) 'A multi-level analysis of organisational justice climate, structure, and employee mental health', *Journal of Management*, vol 33, no 5, pp 724-51.

Spolander, G., Martin, L., Cleaver, P. and Daly, G. (2010) *Scoping a social work career framework: Pilot project undertaken with five local authorities in the West Midlands*, Coventry: Coventry University.

Spool, M.D. (1978) 'Training programs of observers of behaviour: A review', *Personnel Psychology*, vol 31, pp 853-85.

Sronce, R. and Arendt, L.A. (2009) 'Demonstrating the interplay of leaders and followers: An experiential exercise', *Management Education*, vol 33, no 6, pp 699-724.

Stanley, N. and Manthorpe, J, (2004) *The age of the inquiry: Learning and blaming in health and social care*, London: Routledge.

Steele, J. and Hampton, K. (2005) *Unlocking creativity in public services*, London: Office for Public Management.

Stellnberger, M. (2010) 'Evaluation of appreciative inquiry interventions', Unpublished thesis in partial fulfilment of the requirements of the Degree of Master of Management Studies, Victoria, University of Wellington.

Stinglhamber, F. and Vandenberghe, C. (2003) 'Organizations and supervisors as sources of support and targets of commitment: A longitudinal study', *Journal of Organizational Behavior*, vol 24, no 3, pp 251-70.

Stokes, J. (1994) 'The unconscious at work in groups and teams: Contributions form the work of Wilfred Bion', in A. Obholzer and V. Zagier Roberts (eds) *The unconscious at work: Individual and organisational stress in the human services*, London: Routledge, pp 19-27.

Stone, A.G., Russell, R.F. and Patterson, K. (2003) 'Transformational Versus Servant Leadership – A Difference in Leader Focus', Paper from the Servant Leadership Roundtable, October http://www.regent.edu/acad/cls/2003ServantLeadershi pRoundtable/Stone.pdf

Sullivan, H. and Skelcher, C. (2002) *Working across boundaries: Collaboration in public services*, Basingstoke: Palgrave.

Tadd, W., Hillman, A., Calnan, S., Calnan, M., Bayer, T. and Read, S. (2011) 'Right place, wrong person: dignity in the acute care of older people', *Quality in Ageing and Older Adults*, vol 12, no 1, pp 33-43.

Tafvelin, S., Hyvönen, U. and Westerberg, K. (2012) 'Transformational leadership in the social work context: The importance of leader continuity and co-worker support', *British Journal of Social Work* (http://bjsw.oxfordjournals.org/content/early/2012/11/19/bjsw.bcs174.abstract).

Tanner, D. (2007) 'Starting with lives: supporting older people's strategies and ways of coping', *Journal of Social Work*, vol 7, no 1, pp 7-30.

Tanner, D. (2009) 'Modernisation and the delivery of user-centred services', in J. Harris and V. White (eds) *Modernising social work critical considerations,* Bristol: The Policy Press.

Taplin, I.M. and Winterton, J. (2007) 'The importance of management style in labour relations', *International Journal of Sociology and Social Policy*, vol 27, no 1/2, pp 5-18.

TCSW (The College of Social Work) (2010) *Purpose and functions of The College of Social Work: Consultation paper*, London: TCSW (www.collegeofsocialwork.org/files/purposeandfunction.pdf).

Tehrani, N., Humpage, S., Willmott, B. and Haslam, I. (2007) *What's happening with wellbeing at work?*, London: Chartered Institute of Personnel and Development.

Tepper, B. (2007) 'Abusive supervision in work organisations: Review, synthesis and research agenda', *Journal of Management*, vol 33, no 3, pp 261-89.

Thorndike, E.L. (1920) 'A constant error on psychological rating', *Journal of Applied Psychology*, vol 4, no 1, pp 25-9.

Tourish, D. and Pinnington, A. (2010) 'Learning from current trends in leadership development in Scotland', in Z. van Zwanenberg (ed) *Leadership in social care*, London: Jessica Kingsley Publishers, pp 198-216.

Treptow, R. (2010) 'Global governance in social work', in S.K. Amos (ed) *International educational governance*, International Perspectives on Education and Society Series, vol 12, no 1, pp 217-39.

Triggle, N. (2013) 'Poor NHS care "like a cancer", says Stafford inquiry QC', BBC News, 10 May.

Tsui, M. (2005) *Social work supervision contexts and concepts*, London: Sage Publications.

Tsui, M.-S. and Cheung, F.C.G. (2004) 'Gone with the wind: the impacts of managerialism on human services', *British Journal of Social Work*, vol 34, no 3, pp 437-42.

Tsui, M.-S. and Ho, W.S. (1998) 'In search of a comprehensive model of social work supervision', *The Clinical Supervisor*, vol 16, no 2, pp 181–205, DOI: 10.1300/J001v16n02_12.

Turnball James, K. (2011) *Leadership in context: Lessons from new leadership theory and current leadership development practice*, London: The King's Fund.

Turner, M. and Beresford, P. (2005) *Contributing on equal terms: Service user involvement and the benefits system*, Adult Services Report 8, London: Social Care Institute for Excellence.

Ulrich, D. (1997) *Human Resource Champions: The next agenda for adding value and delivering results*, Boston, MA, Harvard Business Review Press.

Unison (2004) *The way forward for Scotland's social work* (www.unison-scotland. org.uk/socialwork/wayforward.html).

Unison (2008) 'Progress report on safeguarding', Unison memorandum to Lord Laming (www.unison.org.uk/acrobat/B4364a.pdf).

Utting, W. (1997) *People like us: The report of the review of the safeguards for children living away from home*, London: The Stationery Office.

Vakola, M. and Nikolaou, I. (2005) 'Attitudes towards organizational change: What is the role of employees' stress and commitment?', *Employee Relations*, vol 27, no 2, pp 160-74.

van Berkel, R., van der Aa, P. and van Gestel, N. (2012) 'Professionals without a profession? Redesigning case management in Dutch local welfare agencies', *European Journal of Social Work*, vol 13, no 4, pp 447-63.

van de Luitgaarden, G.M.J. (2009) 'Evidence-based practice in social work: Lessons from judgment and decision-making theory', *British Journal of Social Work*, vol 39, no 2, pp 243-60.

van Dooren, W., Bouckaert, G. and Halligan, J. (2010) *Performance management in the public sector*, London and New York: Routledge.

van Hees, G. (2007) *Introduction to the launching of the network supervision in the Bachelor and Master of Social Work in Europe*, Maastricht: CESRT, Hogeschool Zuyd.

van Heugten, K. (2010) 'Bullying of social workers: Outcomes of a grounded study into impacts and interventions', *British Journal of Social Work*, vol 40, no 2, pp 638-55.

van Zwanenburg, Z. (2010) 'Leadership for the 21st century', in Z. van Zwanenberg (ed) *Leadership in social care*, London: Jessica Kingsley Publishers, pp 13-26.

van Zwanenberg, Z. (2010a) *Leadership in social care*, London: Jessica Kingsley Publishers.

Walker, A. and Walker, C. (2011) 'From the politics and policy of the cuts to an outline of an oppositional strategy', in N. Yeates, T. Haux, R. Jawad and M. Kilkey (eds) *In defence of welfare: The impacts of the spending review*, Social Policy Association.

Walsh, T., Wilson, G. and O'Connor, E. (2010) 'Local, European and global: an exploration of migration patterns of social workers into Ireland', *British Journal of Social Work*, vol 40, no 6, pp 1978-95.

Walton, M. (2004) '"No blame" culture: Creating a "no blame" culture: have we got the balance right?', *Quality and Safety in Health Care*, vol 13, no 3, pp 163-4.

Walton, R.E. (1985) 'Toward a strategy of eliciting employee commitment based on policies of mutuality', in R.E. Walton and P.R. Lawrence (eds) *Human resource management: Trends and challenges*, Boston, MA: Harvard Business School Press, pp 35-65.

Warne, T. and McAndrew, S. (eds) (2010) *Creative approaches to health and social care education*, Basingstoke: Palgrave Macmillan.

Waterhouse, R. (2000) *Lost in care: Report of the Tribunal of Inquiry into the abuse of children in care in the former county council areas of Gwynedd and Clwyd since 1974*, London: The Stationery Office.

Watson, J.E.R. (2008) '"The times they are a changing" – post-qualifying training needs of social work managers', *Social Work Education*, vol 27, no 3, pp 318-33.

Webb, C.M. and Carpenter, J. (2011) 'What can be done to promote the retention of social workers? A systematic review of interventions', *British Journal of Social Work*, vol 42, no 7, pp 1235-55.

Webster, M. and Tofi, H.J. (2007) 'Postgraduate social work management education in Aotearoa New Zealand: A unique framework for the study of management', *Aotearoa/New Zealand Social Work Review*, Spring, pp 48-57.

Weick, K.E., Sutcliffe, K.M. and Obstfeld, D. (1999) 'Organizing for high reliability: processes of collective mindfulness', *Research in Organizational Behavior*, vol 21, pp 81-123.

Welsh Government (2011) *Protecting children in Wales: Arrangements for multi-agency child practice reviews: Draft guidance* (http://wales.gov.uk/docs/dhss/consultation/120109draften.pdf).

Whitaker, B.G., Dahling, J.J. and Levy, P. (2007) 'The development of a feedback environment and role clarity model of job', *Journal of Management*, vol 33, no 4, pp 570-91.

White, V. (2006) *The state of feminist social work*, London: Routledge.

White, V. and Harris, J. (2007) 'Management', in M. Lymbery and K. Postle (eds) *Social work: A companion to learning*, London: Sage Publications, pp 240-50.

Whitener, E. (2001) 'Do "high commitment" human resource practices affect employee commitment? A cross-level analysis using hierarchical linear modeling', *Journal of Management*, vol 27, no 5, pp 515-35.

WHR World Health Report (2006) *Working Together for Health*, Geneva, World Health Organisation.

Williams, P. and Sullivan, H. (2011) 'Lessons in leadership for learning and knowledge management in multi-organisational settings', *International Journal of Leadership in Public Services*, vol 7, no 1, pp 6-20.

Wilson, D.C. and Rosenfield, R.H (1990) *Managing organisations*, New York: McGraw Hill.

Wilson, K., Ruch, G., Lymbery, M. and Cooper, A. (2008) *Social Work: An introduction to contemporary practice*, London: Pearson Longman, p 7.

Wilson, S. (2007) 'Leading practice improvement in front line child protection', *British Journal of Social Work* (2007), 1 of 17 doi:10.1093/bjsw/bcm093

Wimpfheimer, S. (2004) 'Leadership and management competencies defined by practicing social work managers', *Administration in Social Work*, vol 28, no 1, pp 45-56.

Yoder, J.D. (2001) 'Making leadership work more effectively for women', *Journal of Social Issues*, vol 57, no 4, pp 815-28.

Zacharatos, A., Barling, J. and Iverson, R. (2005) 'High-performance work systems and occupational safety', *Journal of Applied Psychology*, vol 90, no 1, pp 77-93.

Index